ALEXANDER STEWART

ALEXANDER STEWART

A TRANSFORMED LIFE AND MINISTRY

James Sievewright

THE BANNER OF TRUTH TRUST

THE BANNER OF TRUTH TRUST

Head Office
3 Murrayfield Road,
Edinburgh, EH12 6EL
UK

North America Office
610 Alexander Spring Road
Carlisle, PA 17015
USA

banneroftruth.org

First published 1822

*

ISBN
Print: 978 1 80040 446 5
Epub: 978 1 80040 447 2

*

Typeset in 11/14 Adobe Garamond Pro
at The Banner of Truth Trust, Edinburgh

Printed in the USA by
Versa Press Inc.,
East Peoria, IL.

N.B. Footnotes placed in square brackets in this edition have been added by the publisher.

CONTENTS

FOREWORD

Introducing Alexander Stewart

Some very distinguished ministers of the Scottish church began their ministry in spiritual darkness. Alexander Henderson was one. Thomas Chalmers a second. A third was an older contemporary of Chalmers, Alexander Stewart, successively minister in Moulin, Dingwall, and Edinburgh. It is Stewart's story that is told in this biography.

Alexander Stewart became parish minister of Moulin near Pitlochry, Perthshire, in 1786. He was twenty-two years old. He would later destroy all the sermons preached in the first years of his ministry, one small manuscript volume alone being spared. It dates from 1788 and was preserved 'as a monument of his former ignorance.' An inscription, added in 1817, and translated by his son from the original Latin, reads as follows:

Youthful Trifles,
produced in the season of ignorance and darkness,
possessing nothing of the savour of the gospel,
abounding in errors,
fit only to be pitied,
fit only to be destroyed;
to be pardoned solely by the clemency of a merciful God,
through the grace of his only-begotten Son.

'I was,' he confesses, 'in a great measure ignorant of the peculiar doctrines of Christianity, the corruption of the human will, the fullness and freeness of the redemption which is in Christ, justification by faith, and the necessity of the Holy Spirit's agency on the human soul; and what I knew not myself I could not declare to others.'

The change came slowly. Two men in particular were instrumental. The first was his friend David Black, then minister in the Perthshire village of St Madoes; later of Lady Yester's Church in Edinburgh. In *The Pastor of Kilsyth*, the memoir by Islay Burns of his father William Hamilton Burns, he is referred to as 'the saintly and tenderly plaintive David Black – the M'Cheyne of those days.' He had begun his ministry in St Madoes only a year before Stewart settled in Moulin and there was only a small difference in age. Long afterwards Stewart would write, 'The dear name (of Mr Black) is always associated with my first perceptions of divine truth and redeeming love.' They were talking together in the garden of the St Madoes manse and David Black was telling him about a sister of his who had died in great faith and spiritual comfort. It made an indelible impression on Stewart. His own beliefs, he knew, could not account for such a death.

It seems to have been sometime in 1791 that this visit was made. Later that year the two friends began a correspondence which only ended with David Black's death in 1806. Many of the letters are preserved in Stewart's biography. They chart the progress in Stewart's understanding of the gospel and the beginnings of a change in his preaching. A personal narrative, drawn up years afterwards, does the same.

Through this exchange of letters with David Black and the reading of books by men like John Newton and Thomas Scott, the enlightenment grew. Then came the climax in 1796 with the visit to Moulin of Charles Simeon of Cambridge. David Black, by this time in Edinburgh, had given Simeon a letter of introduction to Stewart. It was, he says, by 'a random thought that occurred to me, I cannot tell why or how.' Equally unplanned was Simeon's stay in Moulin over a Communion Sunday. In his diary, Simeon records how he preached twice, judging himself to have been 'barren and dull'. But then in the evening Stewart came up to his room 'and we had much and useful conversation about the ministry. He complained much of unprofitableness, and was much affected during the conversation. We prayed together and parted very affectionately.'

From a letter to David Black we learn what an impact Simeon's preaching and conversation had on him. Stewart dismisses the idea that what he had experienced was a mere revival. 'It was no *revival.* I never was alive till then. I think, however, I was in a state of preparation. I was gradually acquiring a knowledge of divine truth. It was given me to *see* that such truths were contained in the Scriptures, but I did not *feel* them: Indeed, I yet feel them very imperfectly. I know nothing to which I can so fitly compare myself as to Ezekiel's dry bones, when they were covered with flesh and skin, but were without life or sensation. It was reserved for Mr Simeon to be the man who should be appointed to prophesy to the wind, and say, "Come from the four winds, O breath, and breathe upon this dead body, that it may live."'

From that time on Stewart began to preach Christ with what he describes as 'some degree of knowledge and confidence.' The effect on his congregation was immediate. 'The novelty of the matter,' he says, 'and some change in the manner of preaching, excited attention. People began to think more, and sometimes to talk together, of religious subjects and of the sermons they heard.' At the time of his settlement in Moulin most were as ignorant of the gospel as he was. As he puts it himself, 'The opinion of their own works recommending them to the favour of God, and procuring a reward from his bounty, was almost universal.' Now they began to think as differently about such things as their minister did.

Lives, too, began to be changed. And in growing numbers. From March to July 1799, for example, Stewart preached a series of sermons on Regeneration. 'These were attended,' he records, 'with a more general awakening than had yet appeared among us. Seldom a week passed in which we did not see or hear of one, two, or three persons, brought under deep concern about their souls, accompanied with strong convictions of sin, and earnest inquiry after a Saviour.' Coming to see things for himself in August 1800 David Black could write in his diary, 'My visit to Moulin was peculiarly gratifying. Such a revival I never witnessed before – it is truly the doing of the Lord, and marvellous in our eyes.'

Stewart knew of about seventy in his congregation whom he could reckon 'truly enlightened with the saving knowledge of Christ'. Among them were two teenagers, James Duff and Jean Rattray, who were later to marry. Their son, Alexander Duff, the great missionary to India, said of his father, 'the spark of light and life then enkindled in his soul, far from becoming dim … continued ever since to shine more and more with increasing intensity and vividness.' Another convert – also named Alexander Stewart – went on eventually to do pioneer missionary work in Canada.

The rest of Stewart's story may be briefly told. In 1805 he became parish minister of Dingwall in the north-east of Scotland. Though his ministry there was faithful from beginning to end he did not see the revival and conversions he had seen in Moulin. He was to serve in Dingwall for fifteen years until ill-health necessitated a move to Edinburgh. There he became co-pastor with Walter Buchanan of the Canongate Kirk but his ministry lasted less than a year. He died on the 27th of May 1821 at the age of fifty-seven. Brief as his Edinburgh ministry was it was greatly valued. His biographer says, 'those hearers who had previously known the grace of the Saviour enjoyed a rich repast, and confessed there was a savour of divine things diffused over his discourses, that was most refreshing to their souls, and mightily animated them in their way to heaven.'

Alexander Stewart was married twice. Two of his sons became ministers also. One of them, Charles Calder Stewart, was minister of a number of Perthshire congregations. Charles' better known brother, another Alexander, was minister for more than twenty years in the north-east fishing village of Cromarty. Hugh Miller, geologist, stone-mason, and editor of the hugely influential evangelical newspaper, the *Witness*, regarded Alexander Stewart of Cromarty as one of the two men who had most influenced his thinking (the other being Thomas Chalmers).

Introducing the biography

A biography of Alexander Stewart was published in 1822, the year after his death. The original title is as follows: *Sermons by the late Rev. Alexander Stewart, D.D., one of the Ministers of Canongate, Edinburgh. To which is prefixed a Memoir of his Life including Letters*. The wording suggests that the sermons predominate and that the memoir is proportionately short. Actually the reverse is the case. The memoir, including the preface, extends to three hundred and seventy-nine pages and is followed by a mere half dozen sermons.

In this new edition, the text of the memoir has been reproduced without alteration. The original preface, however, along with some of the footnotes and a few paragraphs introducing the sermons have been omitted. So too the sermons themselves. According to his biographer, Alexander Stewart was a far more effective preacher in Gaelic than in English. 'They who understood both languages,' he says, 'counted the English exercise tame and unequal to the other.' Furthermore, he admits that besides being in English, the six sermons printed 'are by no means proposed as favourable specimens of Dr Stewart's happiest style of address. For they are deficient in those apt illustrations, and beautifully striking similitudes, which he often introduced with great ingenuity, and powerful effect. These, however, came with spontaneous readiness in the act of delivery, and had no place in his written preparations; and hence, those sermons are unequal to his spoken discourses in point of liveliness and force.' For these reasons the sermons have not been included in this new edition. Additional footnotes, enclosed in square brackets, have been supplied by the editor and publishers. For ease of reading the memoir has also been divided into chapters. Since it was originally written as one continuous narrative the transition from chapter to chapter is sometimes rather abrupt.

Introducing the author

James Sievewright was born in Drumdelgie, a village in Aberdeenshire, in 1783. After finishing his studies at Marischal College in Aberdeen he worked for a while as a tutor to Alexander Stewart's family when Stewart was a minister in Dingwall. In 1815 he was ordained by the Presbytery of Edinburgh as minister of the Church of Scotland congregation in Gateshead-on-Tyne. After three years' ministry there he became minister of the Church of Scotland congregation in Markinch in Fife. One historian refers to how 'the pulpit of the parish church was filled very efficiently' in Sievewright's time and to his 'able and evangelical preaching.' He remained in Markinch till his death in 1852, first as parish minister and then, after the Disruption in 1843, as minister of the Free Church congregation.

He was Moderator of the Free Church General Assembly in 1847. It was during its sittings that Dr Thomas Chalmers died. At Chalmers' funeral Dr Sievewright, 'walking a little apart, and alone, with feeble and tottering steps, was an observed figure. His bloodless and thoughtful features, his keen eye, his jet-black wig, and his moderator's dress, suggested an old-world cut of a seventeenth century divine. He looked as if he had stepped out of a picture-frame to join the sable gathering.' Besides his biography of Alexander Stewart, Sievewright wrote on sanctification and published a volume of sermons. *Memorials of a Ministry*, containing extracts from his unpublished writings and a brief sketch of his life, was published in 1856.

DAVID CAMPBELL
Preston, Lancashire
February 2024

Map of Scotland.

CHAPTER I

A NEW MINISTER FOR MOULIN

ALEXANDER STEWART, D.D. was born at the manse of Blair in Athole, on the 29th of January 1764. Of this parish, his great grandfather, a younger son of the Laird of Invernahiel, in Argyleshire, had been minister some time during the temporary establishment of Episcopacy in Scotland; but on the Episcopal form giving place to a more approved order of ecclesiastical polity, Mr Stewart, not choosing to conform, was either ejected, or voluntarily resigned his ministerial charge. Little more is known of him, than that, having married the grand-daughter and heiress of the Bishop of Argyle, he purchased several estates in the counties of Argyle and Perth. Strathgarry, one of these estates, about three miles from Blair, and of no great extent, descended to a younger son, who followed no profession, and left the paternal inheritance to his eldest surviving son, who was also minister of Blair. He married a Miss Isabella Robertson, a lady of gentle and rather reserved manners, but of fervent piety; and of their five children, Alexander, the subject of this memoir, was the youngest.[1]

His mother was well advanced in life, at the period of his birth; and having had no child for nine years preceding, she no doubt regarded him with peculiar fondness. But whatever indulgence he met with in early life, it certainly produced no injurious effects on his natural temper, which was singularly good. His excellent mother survived the birth of Alexander about three years. His father, who was much respected for his piety and worth, was particularly distinguished for eloquence in Gaelic, a language in which the principal part of public worship in that neighbourhood is still conducted, and in which his son afterwards attained uncommon skill. He was a popular preacher, and appears to have held evangelical principles. He died in 1780. For some months previous to his decease, he is said to have felt

[1] The rest of the family were as follows:

DUNCAN, who became minister of Balquhidder, and died 1804.

CECILIA, married to Gilbert Stewart, Esq. of Foncastle, also deceased.

JANE, married to the Rev. A. Small, successively minister of Kirkmichael, Newtyle, and Kilconquhar. Mrs Small still survives.

MARGARET, who died in 1819, unmarried, having lived mostly with her brother at Moulin, previous to his translation to Dingwall.

a presentiment that the time of putting off his earthly tabernacle was at hand, in the expectation of which he put his house in order, and expressed an earnest desire to administer the Lord's supper to his people, as for the last time. He lived till the stated season of that solemnity, preached from Psalm 43:3. 'O send forth thy light and thy truth; let them lead me, let them bring me unto thy holy hill, and to thy tabernacles. Then will I go unto the altar of God,—unto God my exceeding joy!' In his exhortation at the communion service, he was observed to be singularly warm and pathetic, repeating, with much feeling, these words: 'Some of us shall drink no more of the fruit of the vine, until we drink it new in our Father's kingdom.' The remaining part of the week was passed in his usual health and pursuits; but on the Saturday evening, after due preparation had been made for the expected public services of the following day, he began to feel himself unwell, and having slept two hours, awoke only to breathe for a few moments, and then quietly sunk into everlasting rest.

Descended of such parents, Alexander entered life in circumstances highly advantageous; and perhaps, were an enlightened mind calmly to survey the various conditions in which human beings may be placed, on their first entrance into life; and were then to select the most favourable for improving the intellectual powers, and for acquiring habits of virtue and religion, the house of such a minister would be preferred, where literary taste is encouraged in its development, and directed in its tendencies; where there is not only a vigilant guardianship exercised, to prevent the deterioration of native character, but likewise the constant exhibition of a higher standard, in the objects on which the affections habitually repose, and which are the most likely to engage the imitative faculty, while the best methods are at the same time sedulously employed, to lead the soul to the true knowledge of its origin, its interests, and its end. And though it be seen, in the instance of Alexander Stewart, that no training of man, however skilful, avails to make the plant of corruption grow up into a right tree, whose fruit is good; yet he, doubtless, had much reason for thankfulness to the Providence that placed him under the care of parents so well qualified to be guardians of his unthinking days.

The lines had indeed fallen to him in pleasant places. The scene of his nativity possesses localities of beauty and grandeur seldom surpassed. The pass of Killiecranky, which a distinguished modern traveller compares to the far-famed Vale of Tempe,[1] lies in the vicinity of Blair Manse; and besides that enchanting ground, several objects not less striking to a youthful mind surrounded his home, and would have some influence in expanding his imagination, and fostering a taste for the sublime and beautiful in nature and in art.

[1] [A gorge in the Thessaly region of northern Greece.]

Of his early studies there is no account; only it is known that he was never entered at a public school. His father, it seems, was one of those,

> ——Who, busy as they are,
> Yet make their progeny their dearest care,
> A father blessed with an ingenuous son,
> Father, and friend, and tutor all in one.[1]

And perhaps the beautiful simplicity of character, by which his son was distinguished through life, was not a little owing to the domestic culture he enjoyed, and the unreserved freedom of social intercourse with persons who were too wise to practise artifice, or to initiate him into habits of insincerity, in order to fit him for the world. And in this respect, private education has one singular advantage over public,—for if a greater emulation to excel be excited by the comparison and the competition of a numerous school, and if a superior address and knowledge of character be there more promptly acquired, it is often at the expense of qualities ornamental in youth, and elementary of future worth.

Several years previous to his father's death, he had been placed with his brother-in-law, Mr Small, at that time the minister of a neighbouring parish, and a scholar of no secondary rate. Under such skilful direction, he

[1] [From the poem, 'Tirocinium; or, A Review of Schools,' by the English poet William Cowper (1731–1800).]

appears to have advanced rapidly in classical learning. That he made early proficiency is certain, for, at the age of thirteen, he was fully qualified to commence studies at St Andrews, a university once the most celebrated seat of learning in Scotland. There his industry must have been unremitted, and successfully applied, for he obtained the highest honours his college could bestow; and though among his contemporaries were several scholars of note, in the competition for prizes he was generally successful, and sometimes carried away the first.

What his motives for the exertions he then made to acquire eminence in literature were, we cannot now ascertain; probably they terminated in something he himself would, in more enlightened days, disallow and condemn. But, in the meantime, that God, who knows all his works from the beginning, and who designed him for a path in which sanctified literature was essential to his usefulness, thus gave his mind a determination to aspire after the highest intellectual attainments; and favoured his exertions to excel.

There were three departments of study in which he appears to have prosecuted his researches with great diligence and success— grammar, mathematics, and metaphysics, for which he had a mind peculiarly adapted. He possessed a certain intuitive clearness of perception, which readily seized and wielded abstract ideas, and delighted in tracing their analogies and relations. His mind had an intellectual vigour, capable of pursuing its inquiries long and far, without the consciousness of fatigue; and though classical literature was not neglected by him, the abstract sciences seem to have been regarded with partiality, and prosecuted with uncommon ardour.

At the age of eighteen, he entered on the study of divinity, with a view to qualify himself for the ministry; about which time he went to reside in the family of Mr Graham of Greigston, as private tutor to his sons. There is reason to believe his residence in this family was highly agreeable to himself; and as their country house was only five miles from St Andrews, in which the family were accustomed to spend their winters, he had every facility for prosecuting his own studies, while directing those of his pupils.

Mrs Graham was a woman of good understanding and cultivated taste, having paid more attention to classical learning and ethical studies, than ladies usually think necessary, and was therefore capable of appreciating the qualities of Mr Stewart. In this family he lived four years, and the kindly intercourse that was maintained for many years after, was a proof of the esteem in which he was held, and the fidelity with which he had discharged his trust.

That he was useful to the souls of any in that family, it cannot be said; for hitherto, though generally beloved for his amiableness, and honoured for his genius and accomplishments, he knew not the things of his own peace, and could not guide others by a way he had not known.

From the opportunities he possessed from his earliest years to hear religious truths, and see them exemplified, it might be thought he could hardly grow up ignorant of religion. If religion mean nothing more than an acquaintance with the principles of revelation, and the formal observances of external duties, he was religious betimes. But if religion be the result of a divine influence acting on the mind, to turn it to God, communicating light, and working with power, to produce an abiding spirituality of character in the knowledge of Christ; to this he was then, and long after, greatly a stranger. From his letters, however, it appears, that during the period of his attendance at the Divinity Hall, some serious impressions of a religious character were made on his mind.

But whatever means were employed to cherish those new impressions, they seem to have quickly died away; and he appears to have left the Divinity Hall with little knowledge of spiritual things, or at least with little experience of their abiding power.

But whatever else he brought from college, he certainly carried away a mind rich in literary acquirements of the first order; and when he came to be proposed as a candidate for license, he was able to produce the most flattering testimonials from the professors under whom he had passed through his academical course.

About this time, 1785, the parish of Moulin, adjoining to his father's scene of ministerial labour, becoming vacant, his friends employed their influence to procure from the Duke of Athole a presentation to the charge. On this occasion, his college furnished him with honourable recommendations; and many individuals being zealous to promote his nomination (among whom the late Principal Hill deserves to be particularized for his activity), after some delay, his appointment to Moulin took place.

Of his state of mind at the time, a judgment may be formed from the following letter, describing his first visit to Moulin, to preach before the people, previous to the moderation of a call.

'I have had a most agreeable excursion to the Highlands. The object of my journey, the friendly reception I met with wherever I came, good spirits, choice weather, and agreeable company, all conspired to heighten the enjoyment. I thought I had never seen Athole to such advantage before. Every wood, every hill and stream, looked jocund. I felt my heart warmed when I approached the village of Moulin, with an affection somewhat similar, I suppose, to what one feels for his new-born offspring. I preached on the 28th ult.[1] in

[1] [ult. = *ultimo*: in or of the month preceding the present one.]

English and Gaelic. The church was very full. I am told I gave satisfaction. My call, as for as can be judged, was unanimous. The people showed great earnestness in my favour. This, you can believe, was highly pleasing to me, and I indulged the pleasure without scruple, because I thought myself in no hazard of gratifying my vanity by that indulgence; for I have been little in that country since I was a child, and therefore am little known or liked on my own account. The people's attachment to me proceeds from a cause vastly more grateful than the highest compliments they could pay to my own merits, that is, the respect they retain for my father's memory. I was happy in thinking that I could attribute their attachment wholly to that cause.

'The living of Moulin is, upon the whole, good; the society good; the manse not so good as I could wish, but I have seen many worse. I was not, when I saw it, nor am I yet, in a humour to find fault. The situation, the prospect, is in summer the most delectable. A piece of the most delightful birch wood, in the neighbourhood, afforded me one of the most delightful strolls I ever enjoyed. It seems made to invite the early contemplator to pursue

> The wildly devious morning walk.[1]

[1] [From the poem, 'The Seasons,' by the Scottish poet James Thomson (1700–48).]

'The country in general abounds in birch, a harmless kind of wood that excites neither the dread nor the detestation of the beholder, as in a neighbouring country; but, on the contrary, possesses every beauty, except perhaps the beauty of utility; but even that is not wanting, for it is much used on the roofs of cottages.

'One day I rode out of my way on purpose to see the pass of Killiecranky, a deep, narrow gully, of about a mile long. The Garry runs below, black and deep, but not rapid, unless when swollen with rain. The banks are very steep, heathy, and covered with wood, and rise to a very considerable height. The public road is cut out of the face of the bank, but broad and well-finished. Here I had often seen the torrent boil along the rocks, and heard

> The angry spirit of the waters shriek.[1]

'At this time it was calm and silent, but its very silence was grim. I recollected the many tales I had heard of goblins and demons being seen or heard to yell in this den. I began to think the vulgar faith in such apparitions not so unnatural as I used to account it. Such is the influence of local scenery over the imagination, and the power of the imagination over the understanding.

'I spent a night at the Manse of Blair, in which I first drew breath. The glebe is pretty large, and has some

[1] [From *Flowers of Literature for 1806*, edited by English journalist and author Francis William Blagdon (1777–1818)].

oak and birch on it. I walked out alone in the morning, to make my orisons in the wood where I had often strayed. I found in every tree, and in every spring, an old acquaintance:

> Dear lovely bowers of innocence and ease,
> Seats of my youth, where every spot could please,[1]

said I, as I traversed the ground. I stood on a hillock and looked around me.—The view was worth a thousand homilies! The days of other years rushed on my mind; "the memory of joys that are past, pleasant and mournful to the soul." The sensations and emotions which this visit awakened in my breast, were such as no beauties of nature or art could have raised. They were such as Dr Beattie ascribes to the power of national music, in his essay on that subject. The passage is so singularly beautiful, that I cannot forbear transcribing the whole.

""That man must have a hard heart, or a dull imagination, in whom, though endowed with musical sensibility, no sweet emotions would arise on hearing, in his riper years, or in a foreign land, those strains which were the delight of his childhood. What though they be inferior to the Italian? What though they be even irregular and rude? It is not their merit which, in the

[1] [From the poem, 'The Deserted Village,' by the Anglo-Irish poet and novelist Oliver Goldsmith (1728–74)].

case supposed, would interest a native, but the charming ideas they would recall to his mind; ideas of innocence, simplicity, and leisure, of romantic enterprise, and enthusiastic attachment; and of scenes which, on recollection, we are inclined to think that a brighter sun illuminated, a fresher verdure crowned, and purer skies, and happier climes, conspired to beautify, than are to be seen in the dreary paths of care and disappointment."

'I hope I have profited both in mind and body by this jaunt. During twelve days absence, I rode, or walked, or both, every day, except two, from seven to twenty-four miles. The change of scene, and company, kept my mind in a state of cheerfulness, and the exercise kept the animal spirits in play. I frequently read on the road, walking with my bridle in my hand.'

In this extract, there is much feeling and much taste displayed; but the feeling is not spiritual, nor the taste sanctified. Imagination wanders over the romantic field, but never comes in contact with a religious reality; the 'morning orisons' he poured forth 'in the wood,' no doubt flowed from a heart full of tenderness and emotion; and it is not for us to determine the measure of acceptance with which such sincere, though ill-informed effusions, may come up before the Hearer of prayer. As yet, however, he knew not his own character in the judgment of God, and could hardly be humble; he knew not the character of the Being he addressed, and could not be rationally devout; neither had he any proper discernment of spiritual objects, and could not ask, in faith, for blessings untasted and undesired. In youth, when the mind of sensibility looks abroad on the scenes that call up the powers of a warm imagination, there is often a vague aspiration of the soul heavenwards; there is a movement of nature towards something grand and vast, and some undefined idea of deity breaking in upon the soul; the language of adoration flows; and this fervent oratory passes for prayer. But when the high-wrought feeling subsides, it appears like the bubble formed on the agitated water, which breaks and leaves the stream to flow on;—so these transient and superficial acts of devotion pass away with their exciting causes, and produce no alteration on the general tenor of life and character. A Rousseau[1] thinks himself devout, and pours the language of adoration from a full heart, when he is only sacrificing to the idol of his own imagination, and disclaims the true God whom the Scriptures reveal. The fallacy of youthful fervour is sometimes never detected, until a painful consciousness of guilt brings the soul to cry simply for mercy; and then the presumption of its high-toned orisons is recollected with shame.

[1] [Jean-Jacques Rousseau (1712–78) was a Genevan philosopher, writer, and composer. His political philosophy influenced the progress of the Age of Reason throughout Europe, as well as aspects of the French Revolution and the development of modern political, economic, and educational thought.]

In his first visit to the scene of his intended labours, there appears nothing of serious reflection on the probable consequences of his assuming so important a charge. To guide souls to eternity is no trivial office; and he who feels his own responsibility, and is aware how much his own eternal state, and theirs also, may depend on the relation he is about to form with a congregation, can hardly survey the countenances of his listening audience for the first time, without an overwhelming sense of the magnitude and the difficulty of the ministerial profession. 'Who is sufficient for these things?' an apostle asks trembling. 'Who is not sufficient for these things?' the carelessness and the incompetency of many self-sufficient candidates for the charge of souls, seem to demand.

The people of Moulin, it appears, received their new minister with abundance of respect and cordiality. They had been accustomed to venerate the father, and were disposed to entertain a hereditary regard for the son. His first appearances were, no doubt, able and prepossessing in their own style; and of anything beyond correct moral sentiment, and easy elocution, they were ill qualified to judge. Indeed, the ignorance that prevails in many places, as to the truths of religion, is often not sufficiently regarded. Even where the gospel has been preached, we may sometimes meet with instances of surprising ignorance, respecting the first principles of Christian doctrine, and the common elements of

Christian experience. And if this occur even among the stated hearers of evangelical truth, what is to be expected from those to whom the peculiar doctrines of the gospel are seldom or never delivered?

Yet experience proves, that people who remain in a very unenlightened state themselves, commonly give a preference to an evangelical ministry; but that the judgment of those people, in such preference, is not founded on any just discernment of its nature, appears from this,—that if a preacher discourse fluently, and seem much interested himself, though very sparing in the production of evangelical sentiment, they will give him credit for being an able minister of the New Testament.

And perhaps the chief reason why so many people, not personally religious, hang upon the lips of an evangelical clergyman, is the earnestness of his manner, and the seriousness of his appeals (necessarily arising from his deep concern for their salvation), appeals, which, though the hearers remain unimpressed with the spirit of his doctrine, give a sort of natural interest to attendance on ordinances, which dies away under the languid and the lifeless ministrations of a man too moderate to break in upon the repose of feelings he thinks it impious to awaken on sacred ground.

That the people to whom Mr Stewart was sent, were very incompetent judges of his qualifications, will appear from the authentic account he himself has given in a narrative he published in his more enlightened days. 'The inhabitants of the Highlands,' says he, 'have, as you know, the Scriptures in Gaelic, their native tongue. The New Testament, the Book of Psalms, and the Assembly's Shorter Catechism, have long been read in the schools. By these means, the people in this part of the country had some knowledge of the principal events in the history of the creation and fall of man, and of our Saviour's life, death, resurrection, and ascension. They knew also some of the great outlines of Christian doctrine; but in general, their knowledge of the principles of Christianity was superficial and confused, and their religious opinions were in many important points erroneous. Very few, indeed, knew the way in which the gospel informs us a sinner may be reconciled to God. The opinion of their own works recommending them to the favour of God, and procuring a reward from his bounty, was almost universal. It discovered itself in their ordinary speech, in their common remarks on more solemn occasions, and in almost every religious sentiment that was uttered. Their apprehensions of the demerit and consequences of sin, were exceedingly defective. I have heard many on a sick-bed, after acknowledging in common form that they were sinners, deny that they ever did any ill. And in the view of death, they have derived their hopes of future happiness from the reflection, that they never had wronged any person. Very few seemed to annex any meaning to their words, when they said they expected pardon for Christ's sake. Being without the true knowledge of God, of Christ, of the gospel, of their own character and state, they lived, as might be expected, to themselves and to the world. They were not, indeed, addicted to open vice, if we except lying and swearing. They were rather distinguished for sobriety, industry, and peaceable behaviour; but they were destitute of religious principle. Men may love and adore an unseen God, but they cannot love or serve an unknown God. They may dread pain, or death, or eternal misery, but that is not to fear God. Our people were alike strangers to the true fear and true love of God. They had evidently little concern about the present, or the future state of their souls. They attended church, and partook of the sacraments, and rested from their work on the Sabbath. But these outward observances were almost the only appearances of religion. There was little reading of the Scriptures at home; little religious instructing of children; hardly any family worship; no religious conversation; no *labouring* in any manner for the meat which endureth unto everlasting life. Even on the Lord's day, most of the time was spent in loitering, visiting, and worldly talk; and on other days, religion was scarcely thought of.'

Such was the state of the people among whom Mr Stewart was appointed to labour.

Let us next hear, from the same authentic report, what his own feelings were on coming among them.

'I was settled,' says he, 'minister of this parish in 1786, at the age of twenty-two. Although I was not a "despiser" of what was sacred, yet I felt nothing of the power of religion on my soul. I had no relish for its exercises, nor any enjoyment in the duties of my office, public or private. A regard to character, and the desire of being acceptable to my people, if not the only motives, were certainly the principal motives that prompted me to any measure of diligence or exertion. I was quite well pleased when a diet of catechising was ill attended, because my work was the sooner over; and I was always satisfied with the reflection, that if people were not able, or did not choose to attend on these occasions, that was no fault of mine. I well remember, that I often hurried over that exercise with a good deal of impatience, that I might get home to join a dancing party, or read a sentimental novel. My public addresses and prayers were, for the most part, cold and formal. They were little regarded by the hearers at the time, and as little recollected afterwards. I preached against particular vices, and inculcated particular virtues. But I had no notion of the necessity of a radical change of principle; for I had not learned to know the import of those assertions of Scripture, that "the carnal mind is enmity against God"; that "if any man be in Christ, he is a new creature"; and that, "except a man be born of water and of the Spirit, he cannot enter into the kingdom of God." I spoke of making the fruit good; but I was not aware that the tree was corrupt, and must first be itself made good, before it could bear good fruit. The people, however, were satisfied with what they heard, and neither they nor I looked farther. Almost the only remark made by any on the discourse, after leaving church, was, "What a good sermon we got today!" to which another would coldly assent, adding, "Many good advices do we get, if we did but follow them." Such a heartless compliment was all the improvement made of the discourse and I believe all the fruit of my preaching. The hearers readily gave me credit for a desire to do my duty; and they as readily took credit to themselves for a willingness to be taught their duty. But whether any improvement was actually going forward, whether there was any increase of the fruits of righteousness, was a point which gave neither minister nor people much concern.

'If there were any persons in the parish at the time, who lived a life of faith, under the influence of pure evangelical principles, I did not know them, nor was I qualified to discern and understand what spirit they were of. I have since had reason to believe that there were a very few spiritually-minded persons; but their life was hid, and they had left this world, all but one or two, before they could acknowledge me as a brother. I was in a great measure ignorant of the peculiar doctrines of Christianity, the corruption of the human will, the fulness and freeness of the redemption which is in Christ, justification by faith, and the necessity of the

Holy Spirit's agency on the human soul; and what I knew not myself could not declare to others. I never thought of praying for divine direction in my search after divine truth. I believe I had read the Confession of Faith of our church[1] before I declared my belief of its contents; but I had taken little pains to compare it with the Scriptures. I certainly did not distinctly understand, nor was I at all persuaded of the truth of many propositions contained in it. Yet I do not remember that I had any scruples about subscribing it as the confession of my faith, or about declaring my assent to it solemnly, in the presence of that congregation whereof I was about to take the pastoral charge.'

From such a ministry, operating on such a population, what result was to be expected? A ministry which takes human nature as it finds it, and, without enforcing the necessity of regeneration, labours to smooth and polish it into character by precepts of morality, and dissuasives from vice;—a ministry, which, overlooking the momentous fact of man's enmity to God, neglects to preach reconciliation through the blood of the cross, and leaves sinners unbesought to reconciliation, and the abandonment of disaffection towards their Maker;—a ministry, which proposes salvation to men, not on the grant of a Saviour held forth as the object of immediate trust, but on some uncertain terms of sincere

[1] [The Westminster Confession of Faith.]

obedience, and dispensing grace, the extent of which no man pretends to define;—a ministry, that has not for its object the calling of sinners to repentance towards God, and faith towards our Lord Jesus Christ, that they may be saved freely by grace, and enjoy the comfort of hope, as well as of holiness, in the present time;—such a ministry cannot be effectual, because it falls not in with the method of saving sinners which God has revealed in the New Testament dispensation. He who works according to this method, may not always succeed; but to succeed in working against it, is impossible.

That Mr Stewart's early ministrations were exceedingly defective in point of doctrine, there is sufficient evidence extant, in a small manuscript volume of sermons which were preached in that period; and which he kept back from the flames, to which the rest of them were heartily consigned, as a monument of his former ignorance, with the following judgment inscribed:—

Juveniles ineptiae,
temporibus ignorantiae caecitatisque editae,
odore Evangelii nullo imbutae,
multis scatentes erroribus,
miserandae, abjiciendae;
tantum dementia Dei misericordis,
Filii sui unigeniti gratia,
ignoscendae.
1817.[1]

[1] Thus translated by his son, Mr D. S. medical student.

The volume is dated 1788, the above character was inscribed in 1817. The first discourse has for its motto, 'Be ye stedfast and immoveable, always abounding in the work of the Lord, forasmuch as ye know that your labour is not in vain in the Lord.' And the following extract from the first page will show what his doctrinal views at that time were.—

'In a world abounding with iniquity, the exhortation which a preacher of the gospel has oftenest occasion to repeat to his hearers, is, to forsake their sins, to turn from their evil ways, to cease to do evil, to learn to do well. We hope that this exhortation is not repeated so often in vain. We hope there are persons who may have been addicted to evil habits, on whom the Spirit of God may have wrought, by the preaching of the word, or the administration of ordinances, with such power as to make them forsake their evil practices. Such a hope we must be allowed to indulge, for it is one of our chief encouragements in the prosecution of our labour. But, my friends, after you have attained thus much; after you have once purified your hearts, and reformed your lives;

Youthful Trifles,
produced in the season of ignorance and darkness,
possessing nothing of the savour of the gospel,
abounding in errors,
fit only to be pitied, fit only to be destroyed;
to be pardoned solely by the clemency of a merciful God,
through the grace of his only-begotten Son.

neither your labour nor ours is yet at an end. A resolution once formed is of no use unless it be kept. Purposes of amendment and improvement are good for the time in which they are made; but if they be afterwards broken, what profit do they bring? Therefore it is still our part to urge the exhortation in my text, and it is your part to lay it to heart,—not to think it enough that you have once attained a certain degree of holiness, or imagine that your business is then done, but to exert all your powers to continue stedfast, immoveable; to go on improving and abounding more and more in the work of the Lord.'

Here, in referring to what he taught, and what they had received, (and we have quoted all the doctrine the sermon contains), there is no mention of the name which is above every name; and it is remarkable that the Saviour is passed by, as a person with whom neither the preacher nor his hearers had anything to do. How different is this from the spirit of him who 'determined to know nothing save Jesus Christ, and him crucified.' How could souls be won to Christ, when his name, glory, and work, were concealed? What stedfastness could they realize, but stability in self-righteousness, who were not rooted, and grounded, and built up in Christ? Such a ministry might succeed in all its aims, and yet not save a single soul; for it is possible to be all Mr Stewart commends, and yet want that faith, without which it is impossible to please God.

In their minister, the people of Moulin had an example of conduct morally correct and honourable; they had a guide amiable in society, respectable for his talents and literature, and by no means inattentive to official duties, either in public or in private; and they were mutually pleased.

Perhaps not a few parishes in Britain, who rise no higher in point of religious character than they, labour under greater disadvantages, as to means of instruction. Such means, however, proved ineffectual there, and must in every place alike fail; because they are not the means appointed by God for reconciling the world unto himself, that they may be saved.

In the first years of his ministry, Mr Stewart seems to have prosecuted his favourite studies in metaphysics and philology. The Gaelic language, in particular, became an object of favourite research; and though he had few helps, and at the time of his ordination was but barely competent to preach in it with freedom, he soon became critically versed in its unwritten idioms and syntax. 'When I come to speak of my Gaelic studies,' says he, in a letter written during his attendance at the Divinity Hall, 'I am somewhat at a loss what to say in vindication of myself. I find I am not able to give a regular account of my plan of study, or of my progress. All I can say is, that I have been reading the Gaelic Testament, and the small treatise I have from you; but with what profit I cannot well determine. When I meet with a word or phrase that I do not understand, I have neither master, dictionary, nor grammar to apply to, which much retards my progress in learning the language. When you consider, then, my unfavourable situation in this respect, I hope you will think I am not wholly without excuse, if my knowledge does not increase fast. I am not a little chagrined at being disappointed of Mr John S.'s Gaelic grammar, on which I had depended so much. The Hebrew goes on better. I am provided with a good Bible, grammar, and dictionary, besides an analysis of the Book of Genesis. I go on analysing passages of Scripture with some facility. I thank you with all my heart for your exhortation to go on with my studies. You pathetically lament your own inability to accomplish the wish of your heart, and do justice to the languages; and while you exclaim,

O mihi praeteritos referat si Jupiter annos,[1]

you call upon those that are young to take up the task. Whatever else is in your power, I am confident of one thing that has not left you, and that is, the power of rousing the ardour of the young,—of some of them at least. I never read your letter over, without being animated with the keenest desire of becoming acquainted with the language, manners, and history of my honest progenitors; and then, transporting myself some generations backwards, I converse with the hardy sons of

[1] ['Oh, if only Jupiter would bring back the neglected years!' (Ovid).]

the hills. I admire and imbibe your generous spirit and enthusiastic patriotism, which indeed has characterized my country.'

This patience of study was crowned with success; for both in Gaelic and in Hebrew he acquired such skill, as to be eminently useful to the church in his own time, while he has left fruits of his proficiency to benefit future ages.

Of his metaphysical acumen, he gave a specimen on the publication of Dr Gregory's literary and philosophical essays, in which it was proposed to demonstrate the moral liberty of man on mathematical principles. Mr Stewart wrote him a letter of many folio pages on these essays; controverting his positions, and pointing out what appeared to him inconclusive in the celebrated physician's reasonings. These animadversions passed through the hands of the greatest metaphysician of his time, Professor Dugald Stewart;[1] and Dr Gregory deemed them worthy of a long and elaborate reply. This correspondence might gratify a philosophical reader, but we must hasten to circumstances in Mr Stewart's life more generally interesting, and to himself of far greater importance.

[1] [Dugald Stewart (1753–1828) was a Scottish philosopher and mathematician. Regarded as one of the most important figures of the later Scottish Enlightenment, he was renowned as a popularizer of the work of Irish philosopher Francis Hutcheson (1694–1746) and of Scottish economist and philosopher Adam Smith (c. 1723–90).]

CHAPTER 2

THE DAWNING OF SPIRITUAL CONCERN

FOR some years after his settlement at Moulin, Alexander Stewart's mind seems to have been left unimpressed with any serious concern either about his own spiritual state, or that of others. The set time to favour him, however, was approaching; and among the means employed to interest his heart in divine things, his connection with Mr Black, then minister of St Madoes, occupies a prominent place. Mr Black was nearly of the same age with himself; but having been called to an early knowledge of the truth, he was in spiritual life greatly his elder; for while the one walked uncertainly, and with doubtful perceptions of the truth, in the twilight of grace, the other, with open face and assured steps, enjoying the Sun of righteousness as he went, proceeded from strength to strength in the everlasting way.

Directed by an invisible power, Mr Stewart had been led to pay a visit to Mr Black at St Madoes. Instead of repelling his advances, and looking down with a mixture of pity and disdain on the unequal attainments of his guest, Mr Black received him with great frankness, and without bringing forward his own peculiar views, left what he had, as it were, incidentally seen and heard, to operate with silent influence on his heart. 'Wisdom is justified of her children,' and this unobtrusive conduct of Mr Black produced the happiest effects. Mr Stewart always referred to a conversation with his friend at St Madoes, as connected with the commencement of his spiritual life. Mr Black, as they sat together in an arbour in the garden, took occasion to describe the triumphant dying scene of a deceased sister. Such a fact was not to be accounted for on Mr Stewart's principles; and the event made an impression on his mind never afterwards wholly effaced. Many years after this incident, he writes, 'The dear name (of Mr Black) is always associated with my first perceptions of divine truth and redeeming love. My thoughts took a long flight backwards, and the parlour and the garden at St Madoes, appeared to me like an upper chamber in Jerusalem, and like the garden of Gethsemane.' Happy is it when Christians so improve such apparently casual interviews, that the savour of them is grateful to the mind after many days.

There was something now at work in Mr Stewart's heart, that would not let him rest from inquiries after truth; and though several years revolved before any decided manifestation of change appeared, yet, from that hour, his midnight darkness had passed, and he was hastening gradually and imperceptibly to the day of greater things.

In 1791, he entered into a correspondence with Mr Black, which was continued with great regularity and the utmost freedom of communication on either side, until the period of Mr Black's lamented death. From these letters, which of themselves would make an interesting volume, we shall select a few, which will exhibit the progressive state of Mr Stewart's mind in the knowledge of religious truth, better than any other method of representation we could adopt. These letters are perfectly artless; and of an active minister's letters, it may be remarked in general, that a want of leisure, and the tedium of composition derived from the quantity of written preparation needful for the pulpit, seldom allow them to be anything more than the unstudied and hasty expression of present feeling and present duty.

The first letter addressed to Mr B. is dated Moulin, October 3, 1791, and is as follows:—

'Dear Sir, I cannot but regret that I missed the pleasure of seeing you when you called a fortnight ago at Moulin, though sister told me your stay was but short. I must make it up to myself by staying the longer next time I go to St Madoes. Mr —— too, favoured me with a call. As soon as I heard of it, it struck me that it was a favour I was not entitled to. He is a man for whom I have a regard, though I have as yet little acquaintance with him, but that is really my own fault, for he has been kind enough to make advances toward an acquaintance, though I have been so negligent as not to return them. I will certainly wait on him the next time I go to Perth, but I have need of the good offices of a friend to introduce me, and bespeak his good opinion.

'I thank you sincerely for your present of Scott's *Narrative*.[1] I had taken the liberty to carry it to one or two places, and show it to some of my friends, who were much gratified with the perusal of it. The writer is a striking example of the efficacy of the *ordinary* appointed means of divine grace in enlightening the understanding and reforming the heart; and in that view, I think, his example affords strong encouragement for using these means, studying the Scriptures, and prayer. In this, I apprehend, chiefly consists the difference between his case and that of eminent saints, from St Paul downwards, who have been converted by *extraordinary* means. One feels a curiosity to see his letters to Mr Newton[2] at the

[1] [*The Force of Truth*, by Thomas Scott (1747–1821).]

[2] [John Newton (1725–1807), whose friendship and counsel contributed significantly to Scott's conversion.]

time he began a correspondence with him on subjects of controversy; however, it is probable nothing more would be learned from them, than from the account he himself gives of their spirit and intention.

'Sister and I have lately been reading a volume of sermons by Mr Haweis,[1] the same, I think, to whom Mr Newton addressed the letters, containing an account of his life before his conversion. These sermons contain a compendium of Christian doctrine, arranged in a systematic form; and are executed in a masterly manner. From many hints and recommendations in Newton's letters, and from this memoir of Scott's, I long to try to preach a course of such sermons in Gaelic to my people (English is out of the question); but I have a diffidence of my qualification for it, and a shyness, I believe I may properly call it, of discussing or inculcating subjects which they have not been much accustomed to hear, which has hitherto prevented me from doing more than touching on these subjects occasionally. I dare say I have just the same dread of being charged with filling my people's heads with uncharitable notions and speculative whims, instead of teaching social duties, as Mr Scott had of being termed a Methodist. Yet it is as clear as daylight, that one may just as well think to gather grapes of thorns, as to make virtues grow on the wild stock of man's natural heart. The operation of

[1] [Thomas Haweis (1734–1820), an evangelical Anglican minister. He was a key figure in the eighteenth-century evangelical revival.

engrafting must surely be first performed, or Apollos, or Paul himself, may water for ages without effect. I hope you received a note I sent several weeks ago, with some kind of explanation of those names of places you had mentioned to me. I am just now employed in collecting a few more articles of information for Sir J. Sinclair,[1] which I hope will finish my work in that way.

'May I expect a letter from you at your leisure? The avocations of the summer and autumn are nearly over. As the evenings lengthen, I wish to settle myself down to the enjoyments and pursuits of the fireside. I have had in my time one hobby-horse after another. One while mathematics, another while grammar, another while statistics. I tired of them all. My mind has not that spring in it which will carry it keenly forward through any pursuit for a length of time without some spur. I wish to fix my attention at last on some more interesting objects, and, like Scott, study my Bible. In this and other objects connected with it, I shall wish to ask sometimes your help or encouragement. I know, however, that I shall often feel the same diffidence and reluctance in writing you on such subjects, as I do in playing the fiddle before a connoisseur, but I shall get over it.'

[1] [Colonel Sir John Sinclair (1754–1835), 1st Baronet, was a Scottish politician, military officer, planter, and writer who was one of the first people to use the word 'statistics' in the English language in his pioneering work, *Statistical Accounts of Scotland*, which was published in 21 volumes.]

The above letter is very characteristic of that openness of heart, and freedom in disclosing his sentiments, for which the writer was distinguished through life. On this occasion, his correspondent acted a wiser part than to check the communications of his friend, by premature animadversions; and, by a compliance with that rule, —'him that is weak in the faith receive ye, but not to doubtful disputation,' proved the efficacy of its lenient spirit. That he regarded the proposed correspondence in a providential light, appears from the following extract from his diary in reference to it:

'*Oct.* 10, 1791.—Received a letter lately from Mr Stewart of Moulin, in which he expresses a wish to be taught the way of God more perfectly. Scott's *Force of Truth* seems to have been blessed to him. I answered his letter last week.'

In answering his letter, without receding from his own ground, he spake kindly to his friend, and, as if the distance was small between them, encouraged him to come on. 'I was favoured,' says he in reply, 'with yours of the 2d curt.[1] which gave me sincere pleasure. The confidence you are pleased to place in me, merits a suitable return, and however unqualified I feel myself to give the least advice to one from whom I should be most willing

[1] [The second day of the current month, i.e. October 2nd. The reference is to the letter just quoted (dated, however, October 3rd).]

to receive instruction; I am exceedingly ready to enter into a friendly correspondence on the important topics you have suggested, which may prove mutually pleasing and profitable. From the frankness with which you have communicated your thoughts to me, I confess I feel an interest in what relates to you, and a sincere desire to enter into closer and more intimate habits. It gives me pleasure to find you have read Scott's Narrative with so much satisfaction. His case, though remarkable, is not altogether singular. There have been several instances of persons entering into the office of the ministry, totally devoid of real religion, who have afterwards been brought to a happy change in their sentiments and conduct. Mr Walker of Truro[1] (whose works, if you are not already acquainted with them, are well worthy of your perusal) is as striking an instance of it as Mr Scott. The means employed were of the *ordinary* kind too. If I recollect right, it was by means of a conversation with a pious friend, that Mr Walker received his first serious impressions of the truth. The effects produced were great. From being a dry useless preacher to a careless unconcerned congregation, he became a zealous and faithful minister of the gospel, and was the honoured instrument of the conversion of many souls. I have

[1] [Samuel Walker of Truro (1714–61), an evangelical Anglican minister. For a short biography of his life see J. C. Ryle, *Christian Leaders of the Eighteenth Century* (Edinburgh: Banner of Truth Trust, 2017, 287-307.]

likewise by me a short account of Mr Sherriff,[1] the first minister of Lady Glenorchy's Chapel, in Edinburgh, who experienced a like happy change, a considerable time after he was a preacher. He died a young man, in the midst of his years and usefulness, but not before he had given a very full and comfortable testimony to the truth of those doctrines, which are derided by the world under the name of *Methodism* and *Enthusiasm*.

'I heartily approve of your design of preaching to your people a set of sermons on the great and leading doctrines of the gospel. A general neglect of that kind of preaching, is, I am persuaded, the chief reason why so many ministers do so little good in their parishes. Till men are thoroughly convinced of their lost and undone state by nature, and brought to a simple reliance on the blood and spirit of Christ, as the only appointment of God for the salvation of sinners, all attempts to reform the life and manners are vain and fruitless. Outward restraints may have a temporary effect, but the heart will remain unchanged, and the power of sin unsubdued, till the grace of God in the gospel is understood, felt, and believed. A skilful physician will probe the wound before he attempts to administer the healing balm, and a faithful minister must plainly lay before his people their sin and danger, if he would hope to be successful in promoting their reformation.'

[1] [Francis Sherriff (c. 1750–78).]

In his next letter, Mr Stewart gives an account of the state of religion in his parish, which shows, that even then he was diligent and conscientious, and much interested to have his people embrace all he himself knew of divine truth.

'They are in general far from being ignorant. As few of them read Gaelic, and scarcely one of them can read English with any profit, their knowledge and opinions on religious subjects are almost entirely derived from their teachers. I find them sufficiently ripe on the doctrine of the atonement of Christ, but they seem to have less apprehension of that of imputed righteousness. I have found it requisite to insist a good deal on this point in my preaching, and at my diets of examination a stranger would be ready sometimes to mistake me for an Antinomian. I hope, however, there is little hazard of such an error gaining ground here, for they have very convincing ideas of the obligations of morality. On examining the schools through my parish, of which there are several, taught by persons who undertake the business of their own accord, I find, that though the children learn to read tolerably, and to repeat questions, etc. yet they learn very little of Christian knowledge. I have therefore proposed to some of my heritors to get a Sunday's school erected in this village, where the children may be taught the catechism in Gaelic, and be made to understand and attend to what they repeat. The gentlemen approve of it, and I hope I shall soon get it established. My English discourses are of so little use, that it is with reluctance I sit down to compose one. I am frequently for weeks, perhaps months, without writing any English. This season, as Christmas and New Year's day both fell on Sunday, I thought I could not well avoid writing a sermon for each of them. My texts were, Luke 2:13, 14 and Job 14:14.

'You may be a little surprised, perhaps, at my writing always about myself, and my doings. This was my intention from the time that I solicited the favour of your correspondence, that I might have the benefit of your remarks and corrections. Thus far I have told only what could give myself pleasure in the telling. By and bye, if I am encouraged, my confessions must come in their turn. That is indeed a less pleasant task, but I hope it may turn out a profitable one.'

Mr Black's letter in answer to this, is well worth inserting.

'I received your letter in due course, and with much satisfaction. I acknowledge myself to blame for not answering it sooner. There is no subject can be more agreeable or interesting to me, than what relates to yourself. I shall use the like freedom in my turn, and by a candid communication of my undisguised sentiments, endeavour to repay the confidence with which you are pleased to honour me. I believe, from the strain of your letters, that our sentiments in material points pretty much coincide. The doctrine of imputed righteousness which you mention having insisted on so much of late, appears to me the grand and important article which marks the difference between the preachers of free grace, and those of the legal or Arminian cast. If this doctrine be well understood, and firmly believed, it will pave the way for the reception of all the other doctrines of grace. And upon no other scheme, I think, can the glory of the Redeemer, and the hope of poor sinners, be firmly established. I would not violently contend for any term or mode of expression, that is not evidently scriptural; but, till a better can be found, why should we give up the term *imputed* righteousness, since the idea expressed by it is abundantly plain and simple, and we think clearly founded in Scripture. When a sinner is truly convinced of sin, and perceives the dreadful danger to which he is exposed by his wilful and numberless transgressions of the law of God, the most important question to him in the world is, How shall I escape the wrath of God? How shall I obtain the favour of my Maker? The gospel, in this case, points to the atonement of Christ, and discovers to the anxious sinner's mind, in his all perfect sacrifice, a full security against the day of wrath. But the gospel does more. It speaks of eternal life as the hope of believers. Upon what foundation does this hope rest? Upon my own imperfect doings, or my Saviour's finished obedience? It makes little difference to say, that the works of believers are wrought by the Spirit of Christ, and in this view may in some degree be meritorious. Still they are imperfect works, and the hope that is built on them must be a fluctuating hope: To entitle me to entertain the well-grounded hope of eternal life, I must be able to plead, at the tribunal of God, a righteousness broad as the commandments of God, and free from the least mixture of sin. And such a righteousness the gospel reveals for the salvation of every guilty sinner, who sees and feels his need of it, and is willing to be saved in this humbling, self-abasing manner. This I take to be the plain meaning of imputed righteousness; and here is the spring of all true holiness. The belief of this precious, peace-inspiring truth, gives a vigour and energy to the mind unknown before. The love of Christ constrains to obedience. But I cannot now enter on the practical influence of this blessed doctrine. I hope you know something of it in experience. A good life is the best refutation of the objections of adversaries.

'*P. S.* If you had an opportunity, I should be glad to be favoured with a reading of some of your late compositions for the pulpit, partly, on the peculiar doctrines of the gospel.'

The request in the postscript drew from Mr Stewart the following:—

'Your favour of the 13th January reached me in course. I wish to get rid, as soon as may be, of the formalities of apologies; however, I must mention as the chief cause of my long silence, a visit I made to Fife, to see my friends in St Andrews, and at Kilconquhar, the name of Mr Small's new parish. This not only occupied some weeks of my time, but likewise put it out of my power to comply, so soon as I wished, with your kind request of sending you some of my compositions for the pulpit, for I wished to carry some of my late productions with me to read to Mr Small, before I should send them out of my custody. Since my return, I have been occupied one week with a fair which is held annually in this village, and which breaks in much on my time, and another with a visit from my brother. I now comply with pleasure with your request, and send you two sermons by way of specimen, composed, the one for Christmas last, the other for New Year's Day, but not delivered till the 8th of January. It would be a childish kind of shyness to refuse to submit these to your judgment, because I hope to profit by your remarks, whether you approve or censure. They are free from one blemish, that is, an elaborate and polished style. However sensible I am to the beauties of style, yet I cannot help considering a high degree of polish and ornament as out of place, and improper in compositions for the pulpit. In the discourse upon Luke 2:13, 14, I have stated some of the leading doctrines of Christianity in a way which I believe to be agreeable to reason.

You can judge how far my sentiments are conformable to the Calvinistic scheme, of which (so far as I know it from what Calvinistic writers say of it in their writings, for I have not read Calvin's works), I profess myself a sincere votary. The sermon from Job 14:14 is my first attempt to arrange and put into writing my thoughts on a subject of some obscurity and difficulty. I have endeavoured to follow scripture closely as my guide; and I have attained to a decided opinion on the subject. I am by no means sure that I have been successful in stating my opinion distinctly; and still less, that I have supported it properly. On this head I must request your judgment and remarks; for you will allow me to observe, that by asking a reading of these discourses on the footing of friendship and intimacy, you have come under a kind of tacit obligation to say how far they please you. This I shall look for at your leisure and conveniency. I lately received, though I know not by whom transmitted, a copy of the resolutions of the members of your presbytery friendly to the abolition of the slave-trade, and of the abridgement of the evidence before the House of Commons, drawn up at their desire. I believe I shall find use for this pamphlet, in handing it about among some of my neighbours. I have circulated, also, some copies of an address on the propriety of abstaining from sugar and rum, and not altogether without effect; at least, the effect of this short spirited address on myself and household has been steady, for we have not tasted a particle of sugar for some weeks past. People may say that it is presuming, or assuming, or interfering, or meddling too much, for the clergy to come forward with petitions to Parliament; but none can tell me that I do anything inconsistent with my duty, when I sacrifice my taste to my feelings, and to my indignant sense of wrong, so far as to abstain from this abhorred luxury, till the rearing of it is put upon a different footing from the present. I am impatient to see what will be done in Parliament this session.'

Perhaps some may judge Mr Stewart's abstinence from colonial produce, on the ground of the inhumanities that accompany the manufacture of it, a needless scruple. And probably, among all who at that time raised an indignant voice against the atrocities of the slave-trade, not many had sufficient resolution to deny their taste for the sake of principle. His determination, at least, showed a decision of mind, which, though in a little thing, little minds will never imitate. A single conquest of this kind does much to promote the ascendancy of mind; and it is by inuring the senses to the control of an enlightened judgment, that men proceed in the formation of high and independent character.

When he consented to submit his pulpit compositions to Mr Black's review, it doubtless sprung from some distrust of his own sentiments, and a desire to obtain the opinion of one whom he considered well qualified to say whether his views were correct; and as he was willing to learn, so his friend was not reluctant to give the judgment he sought. His letter affords an example of *faithfulness* without censure, and commendation without compromising truth; and as it may give some insight into the strain of Mr Stewart's preaching at that time, it may not be improperly inserted at length.

'I wrote you, about two months ago, a hasty scrawl, in which I promised to give you my sentiments at large, on the sermons you were kind enough to send me, and which I now return with many thanks. I have read them, upon the whole, with pleasure, but shall take the liberty now to make some remarks, where I think they are liable to exception.

'The first discourse on Ananias pleases me much. In the second discourse on the same subject, you speak of "adherence to truth improving into complete righteousness, and obtaining eternal life from the God of salvation." This appears to me an unscriptural mode of speaking. I know, "that without holiness no man shall see the Lord"; and that all pretensions to faith, which are not justified by a life of sincere obedience to the will of God, are vain and delusive; but I read, at the same time, that eternal life is the gift of God, and that the complete righteousness, on account of which we are accepted in the sight of God, is not a righteousness wrought in us, or done by us, but imputed for our justification, and received by faith. The passage alluded to in the 24th Psalm, I suppose, applies to Christ.

'The two discourses on Christian steadfastness, contain many excellent practical instructions, but I cannot help thinking they might have been written in a more evangelical strain; the exhortations to duty might have been interwoven more closely with the peculiar doctrines of the gospel. I would not say "that God hath promised his grace on condition of our exerting our own endeavours," because this supposes that these endeavours give some claim to the divine assistance; but I would say, that the promise of divine assistance does not supersede the necessity of our own exertions, but affords the highest encouragement to perseverance in them. So I think the matter is clearly stated, Phil. 2:12, 13. The promise of divine assistance is proposed as the motive to labour and diligence. The paragraph beginning—"Your Creator," etc. in my humble apprehension, is liable to much greater exception. I do not believe that man, in his natural state, has in him "the principles of virtue." He has reason and conscience, it is true, but these are so depraved and corrupted by sin, that till the soul is renewed by the Spirit of God, he is incapable of doing anything that is truly good, or acceptable in the sight of God. The way of proposing religion as a task, which, with the assistance of divine grace, must be done in order to obtain the promised reward, is, I conceive, unsafe, because it leads men to entertain ideas of their own powers, and of their own merit, which appear to me to have no foundation in the word of God. Men must be dealt with as sinners, who are saved wholly by grace; and duty should be pressed not as a task, giving some sort of claim to future reward, but as a service of love and gratitude, flowing from new evangelical principles, and producing a meetness for the glorious inheritance of the saints in light.

'The sermon "on the death of Stephen," is beautifully written. —"The faithful servant of God *forced* to swallow the draught." Does not this suppose a reluctance inconsistent with resignation? "Favours of *fortune*,"—I would rather say *providence*. I am best of all pleased with the following discourses on affliction in youth. They discover considerable acquaintance with human nature, and human life, and I hope I have read them with profit. "Piety springing up naturally in the soul,"—not very consistent with what the scripture says,—"The imagination of men's hearts are evil, only evil, from their youth."

'Thus, my dear friend, I have given you my sentiments with the utmost freedom. I hope you will excuse the long delay, and gratify me with a letter soon. What do you think of the present state of things in the country? I shall be glad to hear you are well. May the Lord abundantly bless your ministry, and spare you long for usefulness.'

Mr Stewart's next letter enters still more fully into his own state of mind, and will be perused with interest.

'*Moulin, January* 27, 1793.

'I have put off writing to you from week to week, till I should get your observations on my discourses, which I received two days ago. I should be sorry, by any further delay, to give you room to suspect that your criticisms could fail of being highly acceptable. I think I am sincere, and I hope you will believe me to be so, when I say that I perfectly approve and concur in your censures. I think I told you when I sent them, that I now discovered many things in them myself, which I could by no means sustain as just and orthodox. I allowed these passages, however, to remain, and to pass under your review, purposely, that you might have something which you might censure with freedom and confidence, in hopes that you might then venture to point out other errors or faults, which might more easily have escaped myself, or which perhaps I might not be so ready to acknowledge. You will readily observe from this acknowledgement, that my sentiments on some important points of doctrine have altered a good deal in the course of a few years, and even since I entered on the office of the ministry. Whatever erroneous opinions I formerly entertained, I cannot say that my persuasion of their truth was firm, or that my mind was fully made up on them. Indeed, I seem to myself to have been an indolent inquirer, and to have taken up my religious opinions at hazard, from such books as happened to come in my way, and which I heard well spoken of. I have learnt, however, that many of these were unscriptural and erroneous. I have been much indebted on this occasion to the writings of Doddridge,[1] Baxter,[2] Newton, etc. I have often consulted with great satisfaction Mr Scott's book which you gave me, and for which I hope I have thanked you before now. After attending carefully to my own mind, I think I do give a firm and hearty assent to the doctrines which these writers maintain, and which appear to be expressly asserted in the scriptures. How happens it, can you tell me, that this persuasion, or this belief (if I may venture to call it so), makes so very little impression on my heart, and is accompanied with so little emotion or desire? I feel wonderfully little of those ardours of gratitude and love, of fear, or of desire, which are always described as the effects of a firm belief of the gospel. But indeed I need not ask you a question which I can too well answer myself. But it is no matter; I will read with pleasure any answer with which you may favour me. I send along with this, two volumes of Cowper's poems, which I think you once told me you had not seen. I am sure you will be pleased with them. I suspect I promised you a perusal of them; if I did, I have been too late in sending them.

[1] [Philip Doddridge (1702–51), English Nonconformist minister.]
[2] [Richard Baxter (1615–91), English Puritan minister.]

'You ask me my opinion on the state of public affairs. I could say a great deal, I think, on this subject. A more critical period, and more fraught with important and even alarming consequences, has seldom occurred. Last night's post brought us the intelligence of the execution of the unfortunate King of France.[1] Wretched king of a more wretched state! What a spectacle is that people become to the world! The judgment of Ephraim seems to have been pronounced against them, "Let them alone." It is a most awful object for a spectator to observe from a distance. Hurricanes and earthquakes are nothing to it. "Happy the man," says Cowper, "who sees a God employed in all the good and ill that chequer life." It is the only consideration that can inspire composure, that the Lord reigns over all, that he himself rides in the whirlwind, "and directs the storm." This kingdom, too, has received a gentle but serious warning. I am hopeful that the Almighty has directed our legislators to such measures as may be the means of preserving quietness at home, and perhaps of warding off danger from abroad. I do not think there is yet any reason to apprehend commotions, or an attempt at revolutions in this country. But if we are to guess at the fate that awaits us from the progress of irreligion and licentiousness among us,

[1] [Ultimately unwilling to cede his royal power to the Revolutionary government, Louis XVI was found guilty of treason and condemned to death. He was executed by the guillotine on January 21, 1793.]

what have we not to apprehend? And if we do not take warning by the fate of France, and amend at least some of our ways, who knows how soon our turn may come to be torn asunder by civil tumults?—for licentiousness, turbulence, violence, and anarchy, seem to be but the natural consequences of that wealth and prosperity in which we at present glory so much. At this day, when we say, with no little self-applause and exultation, "that we are rich, and increased in goods," how little do we reflect that we are, in the most important respects, "wretched, and miserable, and poor, and blind, and naked!" If I were a politician, I would ask, where is the necessity for such mighty preparations for war with France? It is enough for me, however, to believe that Providence has some wise end or other to serve by that measure, and that his people are secure under his protection, whatever disturbances happen around them.

'I long to ask a favour of you,—will you tell me how soon I may do it? It is to get a reading of some of your discourses. If I shall read them with partiality, which must be the case, it shall be with so much the more profit.'

From Mr Black in answer.

'*St Madoes, 18th March,* 1793.

'Dear Sir,

'I thank you sincerely for your last letter. Your taking in so good part the few plain remarks I made on your discourses, was nothing more than I expected; yet it cannot fail to heighten the regard I formerly entertained for you. I am persuaded the change which has taken place in your sentiments within these few years, is not only comfortable to your own mind, but likewise highly beneficial to your people. There is but one way of preaching, as our friend Mr Newton observes, which God in every age has been pleased to own and bless. By the wise men of the world, this way is accounted foolishness, and those who adopt it are deemed weak hot-brained enthusiasts; but it is found in experience to be the power of God, and the wisdom of God. It is my earnest wish and prayer that you may be more and more confirmed in the belief of those precious truths, that, feeling the comfort of them in your own soul, you may boldly, faithfully, and successfully preach them to others.

'The question proposed in your letter, How happens it, that the persuasion or belief of the doctrines of the gospel makes so little impression, and is accompanied with so little emotion or desire? is a question that has often occurred to myself, in respect to which I have equal, if not greater cause, to make the same complaint that you do. I wish you had added some resolution of the question. In my own case, I have attributed the want of those lively feelings you speak of, very much to the weakness of faith; and I think there is little doubt, were our faith of divine truth stronger, more like what the apostle calls "the substance of things hoped for, and the evidence of things not seen," the impressions upon our minds would be more powerful, and the emotions of love, gratitude desire, etc. proportionally greater. In some happy moments, when the objects of faith appear with the brightest evidence to our minds, the devout affections of the soul are most powerfully awakened. But I do not suppose that we are to judge of the strength of our faith, altogether by the warmth of our affections. It cannot be expected, in the present state of human nature, that this warmth of affection can be always alike. It is partly excited by novelty and other circumstances, and must of course abate when these circumstances cease to operate. You love a friend whom you have found worthy of esteem, with a warm and steady affection. But the first transports of affection quickly subside, and your friendship gradually ripens into a calm and settled regard. You cannot always be thinking of your friend, for the mind continually bent upon one object loses its tone; but supposing your friend in distress or in danger, or supposing you meet him after a long absence, your affections are immediately stirred, and you find the principle of friendship, though less sensible in its operations, greatly confirmed or increased by length of time. I leave the application to yourself, only observing, that as the certain fruit of faith is love, so the best evidence of love is obedience, and that practical habits of self-denial, and a readiness to take up the cross, when worldly interest and duty come in competition, is a surer mark of love to Christ, and of a firm belief of the gospel, than the greatest ardours of affection when these are wanting.

'The authors' names you mention as having been useful to you, are men whose writings I highly esteem. I would recommend another of the same stamp, a man of great genius, as well as piety, from whom I have received much profit, as well as delight; I mean Dr Watts.[1] His sermons, and other prose works, if you have not read them, are well worth your perusal. Dr Watts was a real poet, and his style possesses all the fire and animation of poetry. I thank you kindly for sending me Cowper's poems; they are truly excellent, and this is a kind of reading in which, with you, I find great pleasure. I hope you will allow me to keep them a little while, and I promise you they shall be returned carefully. I agree perfectly with you in your judgment of public affairs. It is an eventful period, but we know who is at the helm, and that it shall be well with the righteous, happen what may. I look upon the French as under the most awful infatuation, and hope the measures adopted by government will give a timely check to their wild ambition.'

How far Mr Stewart acquiesced in his friend's observations, will appear from what he wrote in reply.

[1] [Isaac Watts (1674–1748), English Congregational minister and hymn-writer.]

'*Moulin Manse*, 17*th May*, 1793.

'Your answer to my complaints of insensibility to divine truths, and the illustration you give, seem perfectly just. Steady resolute obedience, or the conformity of the will to the will of God, is no doubt the most unequivocal, and therefore the most satisfactory evidence of faith and of love. But still we are told, that "with the *heart* man believeth." This expression has always struck me strongly, as marking the difference between *speculative belief*, and *operative* (to apply a new epithet) *faith*, that faith which *worketh*, whether by love, or by any other passion which it awakens and puts in motion. Giving an assent to the truth of facts or of declaration, is what I would call *belief*; feeling one's own interest in the truth of those facts or declarations, is what I would generally understand by *faith*. I remember Mr Robert Walker,[1] in one of his sermons, maintains, that the reason why men are so little impressed with the important truths of the gospel, is that they do not seriously believe them. This seems to imply, that belief is necessarily accompanied with corresponding emotions, desires, resolutions, endeavours, and action. For my own part, I should think that a man may be thoroughly convinced, may fully believe certain truths, and yet may have no perceptible emotions or desires corresponding

[1] [The reference, in all likelihood, is to Robert Walker (1755–1808), a minister of the Canongate Kirk, Edinburgh.]

to the belief. Indeed, I cannot help considering myself as an instance in point. I think I believe, as confidently as I believe my senses, many scriptural doctrines, even those that seem at first sight most repugnant to reason, and which once I thought inadmissible; and yet it is wonderful to myself how little I am affected by them. Perhaps, however, this same interval of insensibility may have its use. When those emotions and desires of which I now find the want, come to be felt, I may be the more strongly convinced, that however belief might be supposed to be a natural act of the understanding, yet faith, in its full extent, must be confessed to be the immediate gift of God.'

If Mr Stewart's distinction between *faith* and *belief* be admitted, there is a great propriety in pressing on a multitude of believers the apostle's question, 'Have ye received the Holy Ghost since ye believed?' When 'the spirit of wisdom and revelation in the knowledge of Christ' is given, and when 'the light shineth out of darkness, to give the light of the knowledge of the glory of God, in the face of Jesus Christ,' faith is no more a cold, lifeless, heartless thing. The glory of its object rouses attention, and awakens love, and the believer walks in the comfort of the Holy Ghost, as Mr Stewart afterwards happily knew by experience. Agreeably to his request, Mr Black sent him a parcel of his sermons for perusal, requesting at the same time, his judgment on their structure and contents. Without giving the whole of his criticisms, we shall only insert his animadversions on 'a single point, which,' says he, 'I am not prepared to disprove, but to which I do not fully assent. It is stated, that "a man may be perfectly orthodox in his creed, and yet remain a stranger to purity of heart," etc. I have been accustomed to think, that there are doctrines revealed in Scripture, to which "the natural man" cannot even give a rational assent, that is, believe to be true in the common sense of the expression. In other words, is it not as impossible for a man to believe certain doctrines of revelation, without having his mind enlightened by the Holy Spirit, as it is to obey the precepts of the gospel, without having his heart renewed by the Holy Spirit? Is not this opinion supported by Matt. 16:17; 1 Cor. 12:3; John 5:1, 4, 5; Eph. 1:18; and especially 1 Cor. 2:14?'

Mr Black wrote the following, in answer to the criticism of his friend:—

'*St Madoes, 23d September*, 1793.

'I cannot soon repay what I owe you for your last long and affectionate letter. The critique you have been so good as send along with the discourses, I highly value. It is favourable indeed, much beyond the merit of the discourses, but as I know my friend is far above flattery, so I can make some allowance for the favourable eye with which the most candid and impartial must always peruse the performance of one whom they love and esteem. But I assure you, my dear friend, your approbation, and the coincidence of sentiment which this approbation necessarily supposes, are on many accounts to me highly gratifying. It is a small matter to be judged of man's judgment, nor does our faith stand in the wisdom or opinion of men, but in the power of God; at the same time there is something truly delightful in finding, that others who are seeking after the knowledge of divine truth, entertain the same sentiments with yourself on the great and leading articles of the Christian faith. I am happy to find I have expressed myself on these fundamental points in such a manner as to meet in general your full assent and approbation.

'The remark you make on the expression, "a man may be perfectly orthodox in his creed, and yet a stranger to purity of heart and life," has frequently occurred to myself; nor am I quite certain but you are in the right. On the one hand, it is clear that there are certain doctrines which appear to the natural mind as foolishness: and which no man can receive, but by the Holy Ghost. On the other hand, it is equally evident from the word of God, that there is such a thing as a dead faith, and that a man may talk and write learnedly on the peculiar doctrines of the gospel, who is far from feeling their influence, or living under their power. I do not say that such a one truly understands or believes the gospel, but at least he thinks he does so; he has a connected system in his head, and can reason and argue on the most important points of scripture doctrines, with as much clearness and precision as the most established believers. Perhaps some error lies at the bottom, which only the great Searcher of hearts can discover. Faith is the gift of God, nor can all the reading and reasoning in the world impart it without divine influence. It is the light of the gospel shining into the mind. Read 1 Cor. 13:1, 2, and, if you please, give me your opinion.'

This letter also contained Mr Black's congratulations on his friend's marriage, which had taken place a few weeks prior to his writing. Miss Louisa M'Pherson, the object of his choice, was a young lady, who, he informs his correspondent, 'besides the more common qualifications of good dispositions, economical skill, etc., possesses the more uncommon recommendation of a heart deeply impressed with a genuine sense of religion. Mutual esteem, approbation of friends, and reasonable, though moderate prospects with regard to worldly fortune, all concur to brighten the prospect of our expected union. In these circumstances I feel a pleasure in communicating my happiness to my kind sympathising friends, and "rejoice with me" is the only language in which I am disposed at present to address them.'

But whatever accession to happiness his marriage had afforded, and whatever he had gained in point of correct principle in his researches after truth, his heart still remained in a very unsatisfied state, as the following plaintive letter to Mr Black will tell.

'*Moulin*, *27th April*, 1794.

'I remember I said in one of my letters a considerable while ago, that in writing to so intimate a friend as I wished to reckon you, I might probably speak sometimes of my own tenderest concerns, and perhaps use the language of complaint. I had this strongly in my mind when I solicited your correspondence. I have different times wished to do it, to communicate to you my apprehensions and regrets, and reasons for being dissatisfied with myself, and I have as often been hindered by a shyness, natural enough perhaps, but which has deprived me of many advantages. For some weeks past, in particular, I have attempted repeatedly to unburden myself, and request your friendly counsel.

'You can hardly imagine what a severe rebuke, though you did not mean it as such, was conveyed in a passage of your last letter, where you say, that "when you observe my growing acquaintance with divine truth, you wish to be provoked to a holy emulation in the same glorious path." A wretched pattern indeed should I be to anyone that wished to make progress in that path! Yet, if I have made any attainment at all in religion, I believe it is in knowledge, which I hope is more correct than it once was, in what respects the distinguishing and essential truths of Christianity. I was more interested than you might suppose in the question I once proposed to you, Whether a firm belief of religious truths was not to be reckoned the work of the Holy Spirit, as well as the faithful performance of religious duties? I was anxious to have this question answered in the affirmative, for it seemed to be the only evidence I could bring of my being at all under the guidance of the divine Spirit. Yet I was afraid, and am so still, that this evidence is not conclusive. I had read in Scripture of a *dead faith*; you stated the same thing in your discourses, and I had undeniable experience in myself of its reality; for if ever *faith* could be called *dead*, mine deserved that name. As to any fruits of the Spirit, either in the desires of my heart, or in active exertions in my divine Master's service, I was as barren as the fig tree in the parable, which only cumbered the ground. One of the most melancholy circumstances in my case, and the most unequivocal mark of my being in a state of spiritual decay, is, that the spirit of prayer, if ever I possessed it, has quite left me. I cannot rouse myself to offer any petition with earnestness, and indeed I hardly know what I ought to pray for. A listlessness and indolence hang about me, and withstand every attempt at exertion of any kind. I find my books a great snare to me. I would seek no other employment, the whole day long, than poring over some classical, or philosophical, or historical, or statistical composition. I generally find the perusal of a religious book, unless it contain something metaphysical or critical, insipid and tiresome. If it is of a pathetic and impressive kind, I find it extremely irksome, for I am perfectly sensible how I ought to be affected by what I read, but at the same time conscious that I am not affected in that manner, and this makes me uneasy.

'Though I am convinced that my case is a dangerous one, I cannot say that it gives me much real alarm; but I believe the cause of that is the very languor and insensibility which constitute my disease. I am in hopes that I may yet be delivered from it myself, but I lament its continuance on account of my people, for I think that in my present frame, my ministrations can be of little service to them. Many pathetic addresses do I meet with in Doddridge's writings, which I dare not use in my own discourses. They are so remote from what my own dull feelings in their present state would suggest, that I cannot adopt nor utter them.

'I have not occasion to go far to seek a remedy for my complaints. I have the Holy Scriptures at hand, which contain the words of eternal life, and which testify of the Lord Jesus. Nor am I without the assistance of pious and judicious writers. But the difficulty is, to bring myself to quit my ordinary reading, and apply to these with earnestness and diligence. I must prescribe to myself a fixed regimen in reading, for I find that intemperance in that respect is at present the most dangerous to me of any. Let me, however, request of you, my dear friend, to give me your advice and assistance as soon as you conveniently can, and let me especially have your prayers, that the Dresser of the vineyard may be pleased to dress about this fig tree, that it may yet bear some fruit, to the praise of his skill and his goodness.'

As all solicitude about eternal things is by some thought to proceed from a weak understanding, declining health, or disappointed hopes, it may be here observed, that Mr Stewart's heaviness of spirit could be accounted for on no such grounds; for, instead of disappointment, he had abundance of respect from all who knew him, with as large a portion of domestic happiness as usually falls to the lot of man. As to health, he was at this time in the prime of a solid and unbroken constitution, and he was so far from having any constitutional tendency to what is called lowness of spirits, that his cheerfulness tended to an extreme; and when he was a much older man, he complained of it as a defect in his character, that he possessed too little gravity;—and not only had he a vigorous mind, but he kept it in vigorous exercise, for, besides the utmost diligence in parochial duties, he was then engaged in perfecting himself in the Gaelic, into which he had rendered Watts' 'Preservative from sin and folly,' for the benefit of his flock. This was his first essay in translating into Gaelic, though a little before this he had surprised Dr D. Smith, one of the first Gaelic scholars of his time, with an elaborate theory of the Gaelic noun. 'I am forced,' said that veteran scholar, 'to admire your scheme of it, though it be different from my own, which will as soon as possible be submitted to your inspection, along with a draught of the Gaelic verb.' Such deference shown to a young man in his first essay in a language long cultivated by Dr Smith, gives a high idea of Mr Stewart's active researches and proficiency.

In such studies, diversified with the best social endearments, and relieved occasionally with music (in the theory and practice of which he was no mean proficient), with the esteem of many friends, and every expectation he could have reasonably indulged with respect to this world, fully realized, Mr Stewart found himself not happy. On the principles of the world, his infelicity is inexplicable, but easily accounted for on religious views. His God had begun a good work in him, and as it advanced, a dissatisfaction with objects of an opposite character, and a distaste for things congenial to the natural mind, was the necessary result. It is the property of grace, that it works to the mortification of what is contrary; and the least true influence of it in the heart, though perhaps not in force to subjugate the whole soul, will render a man incapable of enjoyment in the pursuit of vanity. There may be resistance or flight, but the heart carries along with it the seed of life, which, as it expands, chokes the weeds of corruption, and at length spreads its own heavenly savour through the soul. Mr Stewart was already under a process of spiritual renovation, which, if we may use the figure, issued in *death* to the world. He had of the Spirit enough to make him disrelish things earthly, but not enough to furnish him with prevailing peace and joy.

In the above letter, we notice an instance of Mr Stewart's honesty in not appearing more skilful in the word than he really was; where he mentions his not delivering to his people the pathetic addresses of other divines, because they were remote from his own actual feelings. It was a question with that profound thinker Cecil,[1] how far a minister should go beyond his own experience in preaching the gospel to others. For ministers may be regarded in the light of witnesses; and as one remarks, 'those are very improperly called witnesses of the truth of anything, who only declare they are very much of opinion that such a thing is true. Those only are proper witnesses, who can, and do testify, that they have seen the truth of the thing they assert.' 'We speak that we do know, and testify that we have seen, not merely what others have known, and what others have seen.' And any testimony we bear beyond actual experience, in representing the internal workings

[1] [Richard Cecil (1748–1810) was a leading Evangelical Anglican minister. In 1783 he was a founder member of the influential Eclectic Society, whose early members included men such as John Newton, John Venn, Thomas Scott, and Henry Foster.]

of true religion, though it may be a testimony for truth, is not a testimony for known truth.

It may be said, were every minister to tell no more than he has himself proved on experience, our pulpit discourses would become tame, and wonderfully limited in range of topic, and in point of interest. It may be so; but if our poverty is positive, and our apparent riches nothing but the parade of borrowed affluence, it were at least more beneficial to ourselves to appear what we are, than to obtain credit for what we are not, a credit too, the facility of which prevents industry, and is commonly ruinous to proficiency in the end.

That an honest testimony to what we know and feel, would have a better influence on our own minds, than to outrun experience, and venture on some things beyond conviction, seems unquestionable; and it may be illustrated in the cases of Mr Stewart and a friend of his in the ministry, who not long after wrote him, 'There are a thousand warm and affectionately pious expressions which I have used in the pulpit to my people, which yet I am well aware I have never felt the full power and force of on my own heart, but I consider it my duty to use them, and more, I use them with pleasure.'

Now, here are two ministers officially guiding souls to eternity, the one fears the least deviation from the line of experience, the other expatiates at large on untried ground, and fears nothing. Which of them acts the wiser part? Let the result determine. Mr Stewart soon gained great progress, while there is no evidence to show that the other did not remain stationary.

One may be eloquent and full of fine imaginations in displaying the facts, illustrating the evidences, or in enforcing the duties of Christianity. But when it comes to the experimental part, the power of faith, the workings of the Spirit, the joys of salvation, and the gracious frame of a sanctified heart, let him beware of testifying what he hath not seen nor felt, otherwise he will expose himself to just censure, when he descends from the pulpit quite another character than he personated in it, a miserable inconsistency too often exhibited! And though he may excuse himself on the ground that it is more edifying to his advanced hearers, not to keep back truths that lie beyond his own experience, but may only be equal to the measure of theirs, yet it can hardly profit his people to deal insincerely with the word; and if he lack experience, let him, like the subject of this memoir, be sensible of his want, and not rest from the faithful use of means, until it be abundantly supplied. Unproved armour, however shining, is not profitable in the conflict we wage; and thus accoutred, we shall not be formidable to the enemy.

How diligently Mr Stewart used accessible means, and how conscientiously he adjusted the strain of his preaching to the discoveries he made in the knowledge of the truth, neither going before light, nor declining to follow its progress, will appear from the following statement of his own narrative;—which, however, refers to a period of his ministry prior to the date of the last inserted letters.

'The writings of pious men, which were put into my hands by one or another Christian friend, were made the means of bringing me acquainted with the truths of the gospel. Among these I may mention the works of the Rev. John Newton and Thomas Scott, as eminently useful to me. I was slow in receiving and embracing the doctrines maintained by these writers. By degrees, however, I was persuaded they were agreeable to Scripture, and that no doubt they must be admitted as true. I therefore durst not preach anything which I conceived to be directly contrary to these doctrines, but I brought them forward rarely, incorrectly, and with awkward hesitation. The trumpet was sounded, but it gave an "uncertain sound." My preaching now consisted of a mixed kind of doctrine. I taught that human nature is corrupt, and requires to be purified,—that righteousness cannot come by the law,—that we cannot be justified in the sight of God by our own works,—that we can be justified only by the righteousness of Christ, imputed to us, and received by faith. But in explaining the nature of saving faith, I conceived it as including many of its effects; not only a cordial acceptance of the plan of redemption by a Mediator, but also ardent gratitude to God our Saviour, on account of that redemption, devotedness to his service, good-will to our brethren of mankind; in a word, every pious and benevolent disposition of heart. I thought and taught, that on our possessing *this* faith, we should, in consideration of it, have an interest in the redemption purchased by Christ, and consequently be accepted by God, and rewarded as righteous persons. Thus, by a short circuit, I arrived at the same point from which I had set out, still resting a sinner's acceptance with God, on the conformity of his will to the divine law, or, in other words, on the merit of his good dispositions, and thus endeavouring to establish a human righteousness under the name of faith in Jesus Christ. It was plain, indeed, that this conformity of the will to the divine law, could be but imperfect in this life; yet, imperfect as it was, it must, in my apprehension, be the ground of our justification and acceptance with God. Here I stumbled on that stumbling-stone of *sincere obedience*, in substance, at least, if not in so many words, imagining, like many in whose writings I have since met with that opinion, that the great favour procured to men by Christ's sufferings and mediation, was a relaxation of the divine law, and that an imperfect obedience, dignified with the name of sincere, was all that was now required. This was "another gospel," which never could be owned by God as the gospel of his Son, nor accompanied by that sanctifying power which belongs exclusively to the truth. If it set any of my people on thinking, it only bewildered and misled them. They remained, as before, unenlightened and unchanged.'

Mr Black was not unmindful of the case so feelingly described in the letter last inserted.

'*St Madoes*, 10*th June*, 1794.

'My dear Sir,

'Had I not been particularly engaged at the time when I received your last letter, I should not have allowed it to remain so long unanswered. It called forth my sincerest sympathy, and demanded an early acknowledgement. The case described in it has been so often my own case, that I confess to you I felt some kind of satisfaction in hearing the same complaints made by a Christian friend, which, alas! I have had but too, too much occasion to make myself. Indolence, especially in the concerns of religion, I think my constitutional sin. I have seldom been able to maintain liveliness in devotion for any length of time; and though I could never lay aside secret prayer, but have always been kept to it from a sense of duty, yet, alas! God knows what poor, fruitless, formal services have often been presented at his footstool. This uncomfortable frame of mind I have experienced particularly in the season of worldly prosperity, when outward circumstances were going well with me, which makes me almost afraid of those successes which are naturally so flattering to our wishes, and so eagerly desired by many.

'I mention these things relating to myself, not with any view to soothe or satisfy your mind in its present declining state (for it is the office of Christian friendship rather to *provoke* unto love and to good works), but merely to show, what I know the great enemy of souls will be ready to deny, that your case, however melancholy, is not singular, nor incompatible with former experience of the grace of God. You are dissatisfied with yourself. You bemoan your present circumstances, not perhaps with all the feeling you think the case requires, for the want of proper feeling is the very distemper under which you groan, and the removal of that insensibility would prove your cure; but at least you must allow it is matter of *sincere* regret, nor could any worldly object inspire you with such joy as the returning light of God's countenance. Now, my dear Sir, let me ask you, who or what has taught you the difference between the presence and absence of God in the duties of devotion? Was there not a time, when, if you prayed at all, your conscience was satisfied with the mere outward performance of duty, without looking farther, and when the language of Christians respecting their frames, and fears, and backslidings, and declensions, sounded somewhat strange in your ears? Bless God if it is otherwise now. Guard against desponding; continue to wait on God, praying as the Psalmist does, Psa. 142:7.[1]

[1] ['Bring my soul out of prison, that I may praise thy name: the righteous shall compass me about; for thou shalt deal bountifully with me.']

'In the close of your letter, you suggest very suitable means for recovery from your present uncomfortable situation. Doubtless, faith and prayer are the natural and proper remedies. One thing allow me to hint, which I have found useful to myself; I mean, to set apart some time extraordinary for devotion, more or less, as your circumstances will allow. You may possibly feel considerable reluctance to this proposal. The indisposition to prayer you complain of, may appear an invincible objection. But do try,—persevere in humble importunity, and with a believing dependence on the intercession of our great high priest, and it shall not be in vain. You seem to think that your present languid frame will lessen your usefulness among your people. I am of a different opinion. I believe, in the issue, it will greatly increase it. It is necessary, my dear Sir, that we should know experimentally the bitter as well as the sweets of religion, that we may be able to speak a word in season to the weary soul; and when the Lord is pleased to return your former comforts, you will have cause to bless him for all the way by which he hath led you.'

The general strain of this letter is truly excellent, conveying both sympathy and direction; and Mr Stewart needed both; though, perhaps, there was less need of arguments to reconcile him to his situation, than of exhortation to look for a higher dispensation of the Spirit, and to press towards it in faithful hope.

That dispensation, however, was at hand. His mind, for a while, had been like an Arctic day, at that period when the sun approaches the horizon, without surmounting it. He enjoyed a partial light with little warmth, and without any enlivening discoveries of the author and finisher of faith; but it was not long until he could say, 'mine eyes have seen thy salvation.'

CHAPTER 3

THE FULL LIGHT OF DAY

VARIOUS secondary causes had co-operated, through the disposition of the Spirit, to form his mind into deeper seriousness and concern; and among these causes, his own narrative enumerates the following.

'The biographical sketches in the *Evangelical Magazine*,[1] were principal means of impressing my heart, of opening my eyes to perceive the truth, of exciting a love to godliness, and a desire after usefulness. The power of divine grace appeared illustrious in the composure, the joy, the triumph, with which many pious Christians left the world. I saw their triumphant

[1] [*The Evangelical Magazine* was a monthly magazine which ran from 1793 till 1904. It had a strong missionary emphasis.]

hope supported, not by a complacent reflection on a well-spent life, but by a confidence in the unmerited love of Christ, and in his power and willingness to save even the chief of sinners. I was particularly struck with the account of ministers who had laboured with much diligence and success, and had died at an early period of life, full of good fruits; while I, who had already lived longer, and been longer in the ministry than they, could not say that I had taken any pains with my people, nor that I had been the means of reclaiming one sinner from the error of his way, or of saving one soul from death. The conversation and example of some persons of a truly spiritual mind, to whose acquaintance I was admitted, and who exhibited to my view what I found only described in written memoirs, conduced much to impress on my mind the truths with which I was gradually becoming more acquainted. I cannot omit mentioning, in this connection, the blessing I enjoyed in the preaching, the prayers, and the conversation of that much favoured servant of Christ, the Rev. Charles Simeon,[1] of King's College, Cambridge. He was a man sent from God to me, was my guest for two days in June 1796, preached in my church, and left a savour of the things of God, which has remained with us ever since.'

[1] [Charles Simeon (1759–1836) was minister of Holy Trinity Church, Cambridge, from 1783 till the end of his life.]

Indeed, from the latter circumstance, Mr Stewart always dated his own entrance into the fulness and freedom of a state of grace in Christ Jesus; and a visit apparently casual and undesigned on the part of Mr Simeon, constituted the most important era in Mr Stewart's mortal life.

That Mr Simeon's visit was connected with an actual change in Mr Stewart, his subsequent life, compared with the preceding part of it, furnished the most unequivocal evidence. But if it be inquired, What was the amount of the change? it belongs not to us to form an estimate. It is sufficient to observe, that from this time his heart *was enlarged*, as well as his understanding enlightened; and that he spoke the language *of faith*, and did *the works* that necessarily spring from it. That he was without the Spirit until then, we dare not affirm; but that an extraordinary influence then rested on him, both of light and power, it were against the clearest testimonies to deny. For *henceforth* his faith grew exceedingly, his knowledge in divine things made him a master in Israel. He was conscious of a *newness of life*, with its spiritual concomitants of *feeling and desire*,—and whereas before, he spake of Christ doubtingly, and preached him with hesitation or unconcern, he now found, that to him to live was Christ; and that to fulfil his ministry was to preach Christ, and him crucified,—as 'the wisdom of God, and the power of God unto salvation.' To attempt to account for Mr Stewart's altered character,—altered, too, at a given time and place,—an alteration that showed itself to be permanent and uniform as life itself,—to explain this phenomenon in the moral world, without having recourse to the communication of a supernatural principle, operating with power to the conversion of the heart, and formation of the new character, were to resort to the unphilosophical method of accounting for changes without assigning a *sufficient cause*. For without divine influence, there is nothing attending Mr Simeon's visit that will account for the circumstances connected with it.

The following letter was written by Mr Simeon on his return home, and may afford, to those who have never seen that eminently useful servant of Christ, some idea of the singular spirit of grace dwelling in him, with which every feature seems animated, and every movement and action evidently characterized.

'My very, very dear Friend,

'Among the many rich mercies which God vouchsafed to me, in my late excursion, I cannot but consider the sweet interview which I enjoyed with you as one of the greatest. There is an unaccountable union of heart with, or, if I may so express myself, an outgoing of the soul towards some persons, which we feel instantaneously, and we know not why. There is something that irresistibly impresses the mind with affection, and disposes one to communicate one's ideas with freedom and familiarity; such I felt almost the first instant I saw my dear friend at Moulin. I hope it is an earnest of that everlasting union which our souls shall enjoy in the regions of light and love. Often have I reflected on the peculiar circumstances which, contrary to my own intention, brought me to stop under your hospitable roof. It had been Mr H.'s[1] purpose and my own to have been with you on Friday to tea, and either have stopped with you that night, or gone to Blair, as might appear expedient. Our horses were actually saddled and brought to the door, and we were going to mount. But I felt a very unusual languor and fatigue, by means of the long walk we had taken at Dunkeld; and on my proposing to abide there that night, Mr H. readily acquiesced. Even then we had no idea of spending the Sabbath at Moulin. Our great object was to get to Glasgow by a certain day; and though this was far from being our reason for accepting your invitation to return from Blair, yet the circumstance of our being somewhat advanced in our journey weighed a little in the scale, perhaps as much as one part in twenty. The circumstance of your having the sacrament, of our being able to enjoy the company of your other visitors, of there being no service at Blair, and of our having a longer intercourse with yourself, were our principal inducements to return to you. But

[1] [James Haldane (1768–1851), Scottish Independent minister and evangelist.]

had not so many circumstances concurred, it is more than probable we should have abode at Blair. It has often brought to my mind that expression of the Evangelist, "he *must needs* go through Samaria." Why so? It lay in his way, you will say, from Judea to Galilee; true, but how often had he taken a circuit, going through the towns and villages round about. But the Samaritan woman was there, and for her God designed an especial blessing. What thanks can we ever render to God for those turns in his providence, which at the time appear insignificant, but afterwards are found to have been big with the most important consequences! It is our privilege to expect those invisible interpositions, if we commit our way to him; and every instance that comes to our notice should encourage us to acknowledge him in all our ways. I am exceedingly comforted, my dear brother, with the account which you give of your soul. O how desirable is it for all, but especially for ministers, to have their souls deeply and devoutly impressed! What is religion without this? What are duties without this? Alas! a dry, insipid, unsatisfying, unproductive form. I pray God that what you now experience may only be as the drop before the shower. Surely this is happiness, to taste the love of God, to find delight in his service, and to see that we are in a measure instrumental to the imparting of this happiness to others,—this, I say, is a felicity which nothing but heaven can exceed. Often have I implored this blessing upon yourself and upon your sister (with whose unaffected piety my soul was much refreshed), and upon your whole family; and I hope, that to my dying hour, my prayers and thanksgivings upon your account shall yet ascend up before God. I hope, too, that you will bear my unworthy name upon your heart, whenever you get within the veil.

'The account you give me of the dear poor woman rejoices my heart. How often does God magnify the exceeding riches of his grace towards objects whom the world looks upon with contempt; and angels esteem it an honour to minister to those who have hardly the necessaries of life! I admire this! I adore God for it; it is to me a delightful proof of his goodness, and of his all-sufficiency to make us happy. Pray give my fervent love to her. If I could, I should very cheerfully send her something more substantial. I bless God for Mrs S.'s recovery, and, with Christian respects to her and your sister, remain yours,' etc.

Immediately on his going away, Mr Stewart thus addressed his correspondent[1] in Edinburgh.

'What thanks do I not owe you for having directed my two late visitors to call at my cottage, as I have thus had the honour and blessing of "entertaining angels unexpectedly"; messengers of grace I must reckon them,

[1] [His friend, David Black, who had moved from St Madoes in 1794 to be the minister of Lady Yester's Church, Edinburgh.]

as their visit has been thus far blessed to me, more than any outward dispensation of Providence that I have met with. They were so kind as put up with such accommodation as we could afford them, though our house was a good deal out of order, on account of Mrs Stewart's illness, and spent two nights with us. Mr Simeon gave us his friendly assistance, on occasion of dispensing the Lord's supper, and frankly preached two discourses on the Sabbath, besides serving a table in English. This was the whole of the English service for that day. His sermons, and the conversation and prayers, I have no doubt, of both gentlemen, have indeed been eminently blessed to me. Since I first entered on my sacred office, I have not felt such a lively season as the last week has been. I had some private conversation, too, with my kind friend Mr H. which proved not a little edifying to me. I shall not fail to return his visit when I go next to Edinburgh. When I have such friends as him and you to see, with the prospect of being introduced, perhaps, to Dr Buchanan,[1] possibly to Dr Davidson,[2] etc. I think it will be incumbent on me to make my visits to Edinburgh more frequent than they have been hitherto. And I am sure I shall have vastly more enjoyment in collecting spiritual knowledge, and deriving vigour

[1] [Walter Buchanan (1755–1832), a minister of the Canongate Kirk, Edinburgh.]

[2] [Thomas Randall Davidson (1747–1827), a minister of the Tolbooth Church, Edinburgh.]

and animation from the fountain of life, through the conversation and counsel of the servants of the Lord, than ever I found, or can find, in the conversation of all the Literati or Metaphysicians that your university contains. That I shall ever see Mr Simeon again in the flesh, is hardly probable. I hope, however, he will not entirely forget me. It will be an encouragement to him to offer up a petition sometimes, in behalf of me and my people, to be assured that his prayers have already been in part answered. In some duties to which I have been called these few days,—in conversing with two or three persons in my neighbourhood about their spiritual state,—in exhorting the surviving friends of those who have died of fevers,—and in private prayer, I have found a degree of freedom, ease, and alacrity, to which I was before a stranger. I mention these things that you may inform Mr Simeon of them, for his satisfaction, and that you may both join me in blessing the Lord, the giver of every good and perfect gift, for having visited me in mercy, and pray that I may receive yet more abundant supplies of his grace.

'I go today to visit a young man, whom his friends report to me as deranged. He used to be diligent in reading his Bible. It seems he was strongly affected in time of sermon, on our last sacrament day, and since that time he seeks retirement, reads much, sings Psalms, and sometimes bursts into tears, all which makes his family think him crazed. I long to see him, and examine into these promising symptoms. Perhaps a blessing may follow them to himself, and to some of his relatives. His mother is a serious woman, and used to take pains in instructing her children. A sister of this young man was awakened two or three years ago, and continued some time in great trouble, and under distressing temptations, but was relieved, and continues a watchful and devout Christian. Single instances of this kind are striking and worthy of remark, especially in a dry and barren land, where we have few such. But perhaps, through the free and powerful grace of God, when we are dug about and dunged, we may yet flourish.'

On comparing this letter with the one to Mr Black last inserted, he who can perceive no difference of mind and spirit in the writer, must be blind indeed. The one was full of complaint, and expressive of the most desponding frame, the other only talks of giving thanks, and blessing the Giver of every good and perfect gift, for having visited him in mercy. Before this period, he seemed careless about fellowship with the brethren; but now his heart flowed out in love to them all, and he cannot but indulge himself in the prospect of seeing Dr B. or Dr D. and others in Edinburgh, of whose Christian character he had doubtless often heard, but never until now expressed a wish for nearer intercourse. The learned, whom he had so much admired, he could contentedly give up for the Christians he loved.

It was the remark of one of his friends, many years after this date, that 'his affections were wonderfully improved on his change'; and it is very easy to account for the alteration; for the *love* of God shed abroad in the heart by the Holy Ghost, does not only correct and sanctify the natural tempers, and reduce their selfishness, but is in itself *a new affection*,—an affection, the property of which is, to unite in the bond of love all in whom it dwells.

It cannot escape observation, that Mr Stewart was no sooner set free from bondage, than he goes forth to seek the enlargement of other captives. In none of his former letters to Mr Black, is there any mention of being conversant with the distressed in mind; but, being converted, he strengthens the brethren, and breathes the compassion of his divine Master, who wills not mourners in Zion to sit comfortless.

The next letter to Mr Black, together with his answer, are interesting.

'I have little other news to tell, or subject that I care to write about, except of the Lord's goodness to me, and how he has been multiplying his favours. Ever since the blessed period of Mr Simeon's visit, my thoughts have continued more steadily fixed on divine things, and my communion with God has been more lively by many degrees, than I remember to have experienced before.

'The state of my mind has not indeed been uniformly

the same during this period. A ride I took to Perth threw me a good deal into vain company for two days, and brought on a considerable languor and deadness, but my kind Physician soon recovered me. At other times, I felt myself dull and stupid for nearly a whole day, and been revived in the evening in a few minutes, while engaged in secret prayer. My views of the Lord's goodness and mercy in the work of redemption are clearer, at least they are much more impressive, than they used to be. Indeed, they quite confound and overpower me at times; and yet these attributes must appear still more glorious, when I shall get a distinct sight of what I have not yet discovered, but very imperfectly, that is, my own unworthiness and guilt. Indeed, I have no more doubt of my own total unworthiness and depravity, than I have of God's holiness; but I am sure I shall one day be much more sensible of it than I am at present.

'I have enjoyed not a little of my divine Master's countenance and aid in my public duties of late, particularly while assisting at dispensing the sacrament at B—— and at K——. At the latter place, I met with one or two young communicants, whose state of mind, in respect of knowledge and apprehensions, seemed very promising. I conversed with one of them several times, found he understood and read English well. I gave him some of the Cheap Repository pamphlets, which he read to some of his neighbours with much pleasure. At B——, and afterwards at K——, I made an experiment which I never tried before, which was, to preach English from short notes or outlines, without having composed or written it out beforehand. I was anxious to try this, partly from a persuasion that even an English discourse might find some hearers who would understand and attend to it, if it were fitted to draw their attention; and partly from an emulation of Mr Simeon's energetic manner, in which I saw strikingly exemplified the superior effect of *preaching* above that of reading, or even repeating, a written discourse. I did succeed far beyond my expectation, for I found my thoughts and language flow with more freedom and energy than in the Gaelic, to which I had long been accustomed. I consider this talent of preaching in English, even in such measure as I seem already to possess it, as a mere gift newly bestowed on me, for I never had the least practice in speaking either in clubs or in church courts.

'I have just got from Edinburgh, Edwards on *Religious Affections*; a book from which I hope to reap considerable benefit. Do, my dear friend, pray with me, and for me, that I may be fed and nourished with the sincere milk of the word, that I may grow thereby in grace, and in the knowledge of our common Lord.'

From Mr Black.

'I cannot express the heartfelt joy which I have received from your two last letters. I desire to join with you in giving all the praise to him, to whom alone it is due, who hath showed you the power of his works, and what great things he can and will do for those that hope in his mercy.

'Indeed, the more I think upon the means of your present revival, the more I am filled with astonishment at the methods of the Lord's dealing with his people. Mr Simeon's visit to Scotland was altogether unexpected. He has told me, that till he saw Dr Buchanan, he had no more idea of coming to Scotland, than of going to the East or West Indies. His calling at Moulin was equally unlooked for. The letter which introduced him, was quite a random thought that occurred to me, I cannot tell why or how. Upon what trivial circumstances do many of the most important events of our lives turn! Two strangers from a distance must be sent to Moulin at a season of peculiar solemnity, to become the instruments of good to your soul, and through you to the souls of many.

'O my dear Sir, "magnify the Lord with me, and let us exalt his name together." He "is excellent in counsel, and wonderful in working"; and your experience is now added to that of thousands, who can declare, that verily there is a God that heareth prayer.

'I rejoice to learn that this lively comfortable frame of mind still remains, and that it is attended with renewed alacrity in your public work. Long may it continue so, for your own comfort, and the benefit of your people!

But changes, inward as well as outward, you must expect to meet,—with many a dark and rugged step. But, O! what a privilege is it to know where relief is to be found; to know experimentally the power and grace of our Almighty Physician, and under a daily, deep conviction of our guilt and helplessness, to be committing our souls, our families, our flocks, our every concern, into *his* faithful hands, who careth for us. I have great cause to lament a prevailing deadness and languor of spirit in secret devotion, and cannot say but I was considerably moved, when I read of the happy change which had taken place with you in this respect. O pray for me, my dear friend, that I may be visited as you have been, with the quickening influence of divine grace, that my views of the glory of God, displayed in the work of redemption, may be more enlarged, and my impressions of divine truth more deep, lively, and abiding.'

How much Mr Black rejoiced in the happiness of his friend, appears also from his diary, under the date of Oct. 9, 1796.

'*Oct.* 9, 1796.—'Greatly comforted of late with accounts from my friend and fellow-labourer Mr Stewart of Moulin, whose soul has been wonderfully quickened, and much refreshed by a visit from Mr Simeon of Cambridge, whom I was led in a very providential manner to introduce to Mr Stewart's acquaintance. It has proved like the beginning of a new life to him, and I trust the blessed effects of it will be experienced by his people as well as by himself. Indeed, this seems in some measure to be already the case. Blessed be God for this token of his goodness, this fresh evidence of the power of his grace.'

Whatever might be the opinion of others with respect to the reality and the nature of the change he had experienced, he himself was at no loss as to its character, as appears from an extract from his next letter to Mr Black.

'The sentiments I have felt since Mr Simeon's visit, you, and I believe Mrs Black, have been pleased to call a *revival.* I am not sure but an expression of my sister's, or of my own, might have suggested the word. The word, however, does not strictly apply: It was no *revival.* I never was alive till then. I think, however, I was in a state of preparation. I was gradually acquiring a knowledge of divine truth. It was given me to *see* that such truths were contained in the scriptures, but I did not *feel* them. Indeed, I yet feel them but very imperfectly. I know nothing to which I can so fitly compare myself as to Ezekiel's dry bones, when they were covered with flesh and skin, but were without life or sensation. It was reserved for Mr Simeon to be the man who should be appointed to prophesy to the wind, and say, "Come from the four winds, O breath, and breathe upon this dead body, that it may live."'

We have already stated, that no sooner was Mr Stewart converted, than he essayed to join himself to the brethren; while, towards his former associates, and early friends, he seems to have experienced much of that feeling, in which the apostle of the Gentiles made this protestation of his concern for the conversion of his countrymen the Jews,—'I say the truth in Christ, I lie not, my conscience also bearing me witness in the Holy Ghost, that I have great heaviness and continual sorrow in my heart. For I could wish that myself were accursed from Christ for my brethren, my kinsmen according to the flesh' (Rom. 9:1-3), and, 'Brethren, my heart's desire and prayer to God for Israel is, that they might be saved' (Rom. 10:1).

Under the influence of this spirit, he first addressed himself to a clergyman of taste, talents, and literary acquirements similar to his own, with whom he had been long in habits of close intimacy and correspondence, and whom he now wished to introduce to the knowledge of evangelical truth. His friend in reply stated, with great good humour,—That he had never in his life been a reprobate;—that he had been able to behave with moral decency and propriety, in many trying situations, where many would have yielded and fallen, without the good principles he had imbibed from the early affectionate lessons of a worthy father, attributing his good behaviour to the principles of morality and piety he had imbibed in his early youth, at the same time confessing he had gained little in the way of that true believing love, which makes everything delightful;—that though he never had felt any remarkable enthusiasm in the cause of piety and religion, he had never been a deserter or betrayer of that cause;—and that, though he was not reckoned one of the godly, yet he never could join with many even of his brethren, whom he had seen ridiculing and laughing at the over-righteous, as they termed them, having always had too poor an opinion of himself, or rather that doubt of himself, that he could respect another's sentiments, though very different from his own, because he never was such a complete believer, as to think himself in possession of the only truth.

Mr Stewart renewed his benevolent efforts to impress the mind of his friend, and wrote the following in reply, in which he attempts what is in general so difficult,—to bring the unenlightened mind to a sense of its ignorance, and a conviction that there is something in religion it has not yet learned.

'*Moulin, May* 30, 1797.

'Your letter found me, t'other day, at D. where I preached by appointment of presbytery. You may not readily give me credit, though I tell you, how much I was gratified with the perusal of it. You reckoned it but "poor confused stuff." I easily distinguished all that would have that appearance to you; but I distinguished also some bright luminous rays, not of genius, not of fancy, but of something which our puritanical forefathers would probably have called grace; in short, some sentiments, of which, if I am not mistaken, it may be affirmed, that "flesh and blood have not revealed them to you, but our Father who is in heaven." Why, you must know that, among other new acquisitions, I seem to have got a new way of judging of people's minds. I have learnt this, or rather have begun to learn it, by reading the history of others, but more by attending to the progress of my own sentiments. I hardly remember that ever I was, any more than you, a determined opposer of any doctrines which *I knew* to be contained in Scripture; but I am now perfectly sensible that I was really *ignorant* of some of the most essential and peculiar doctrines of Christianity, and this not only when I was a student, but many years after I had become a teacher of others. The discovery of my ignorance was just the first step towards having it corrected. Now, I am strongly of opinion that you, my dear friend, are in the same way of making the same discovery concerning yourself. I am aware that you may reckon this, at first, rather an odd assertion; and indeed, my dear friend, it is perhaps but the first of several assertions, by which your candour and forbearance with me may be put to the proof. As to the imputation of ignorance, one in your situation may be supposed to reply, "Ignorant of the gospel! pardon me, my dear Sir; I have not been so long conversant with the best writers, and ablest divines, and read and thought to so little purpose, as that I should now be unacquainted with the truths of Christianity. As I know these things, happy were I if I did them. Here, I acknowledge, I fail; but if my practice corresponds with my knowledge, all would be well." I am sure this is precisely what I should have said myself, a few years ago. Allow me to state, as a counterpart to this, a case which has often occurred to my thoughts. Suppose that, in the last year of our Lord's ministration, some old acquaintance should have inquired at one of the disciples, Philip for instance, "I wonder what sort of a person this Jesus of Nazareth is; pray, Philip, do you know him?" Philip would of course answer, "To be sure I do know him, no person knows him better; I have not been two days together out of his company these three years. Many a wonderful work have I seen him do, many a charming discourse have I heard from his mouth. O! neighbour, if you but knew him as well as I do!" Yet this was actually the man to whom our Lord found occasion to say, "Have I been so long time with you, and yet hast thou not known me, Philip?" Query,—May not the same words perhaps be applicable to one disciple which were applied to another, now as well as then?

'In general, all who have had an ordinary religious education, seem to be satisfied that they possess a sufficient knowledge of the doctrines of our religion, and never think of calling their knowledge in question. By attending to one or two pointed declarations of Scripture, I dare say you will agree with me in thinking, that a just and correct knowledge of divine truth, is neither so generally possessed, nor so faintly and equivocally marked in people's conduct and language, as is generally supposed. Our Saviour in interceding for his disciples, prays, "Sanctify them through thy truth: thy word is truth" (John 17:17); intimating, that the truths revealed and asserted in scripture, when known and received, are the means of producing an universal holiness of disposition and life. "This is life eternal, that they should *know* thee, the only true God, and Jesus Christ, whom thou hast sent" (John 17:3). "Yea, doubtless, I count all things but loss, for the excellency of the *knowledge* of Christ Jesus my Lord" (Phil. 3:8). Such was the judgment of one who knew what it was to want, and also to possess this knowledge. "If thou *knewest* the gift of God, and who it is that saith to thee, Give me to drink, thou wouldest have asked of him, and he would have given thee living water" (John 4:10). This implies that divine truth, particularly what relates to the person, character, and offices of Christ, when clearly understood and known, has an instantaneous effect on the heart; it excites a spiritual appetite, and leads to its highest gratification. Whoever knows the gift of God to sinners, its necessity and its worth, will earnestly ask, and will infallibly receive, the highest spiritual blessings. When such effects are ascribed to the knowledge of the gospel, and when these effects are so rarely to be seen, it is but a logical inference, that, even in this Christian land, and among us divines, the true knowledge of scripture-truth is but rare also.

'I will adduce another test of a man's possessing true knowledge. Now, prepare yourself here for some of my oddities; for, depend on it, you will find oddities in me as I advance. The gospel has been called *good tidings*, *good tidings of great joy*; and the appellation well suits its nature. One would think it would also prove *welcome tidings* to everyone that hears it. Accordingly, while an evangelist merely proclaims that the way to heaven is open, I believe his tidings are welcome enough; but, along with his proclamation of peace on earth and good-will to men, there are other facts announced, connected with a sinner's salvation, which are not so readily admitted. There are truths relative to man's condition as a sinner, and to the way of salvation provided for him, which we cannot positively know till they are told us; and which, when told, we can hardly believe, or allow to be true. St Paul found this to be the case, and asserts it in very explicit terms. "The natural man receiveth not the things of the Spirit of God: for they are foolishness to him" (1 Cor. 2:14). Our Saviour's declarations concerning himself, were received in the same manner, even by many of those who had welcomed him as the Messiah.

They said, "This is a hard saying, who can hear it? And many went back, and walked no more with him" (John 6:60, 66). You find in Nicodemus, a man of rank and education, the same difficulty of admitting or assenting to what Christ had affirmed. Even after our Lord had stated to him, that his words were to be understood figuratively, and that he spoke of a spiritual renovation, still the difficulty remained, and "how can these things be?" are the last words of Nicodemus which we find recorded in the conversation (John 3:1-21).

'Now, my dear Sir, if, in the course of your examination or learning of religious truths, you have met with nothing but what was plain and intelligible,—if you have met with nothing that has puzzled your understanding, that startled your belief, that made you recoil at the sense the words seemed manifestly to convey,—in short, that forced you to exclaim with Nicodemus, though more than half shocked at your own distrust of the word of God, "How can these things be so?" it is more than probable that there are doctrines in the scriptures, and necessarily connected with our reception of the rest, which you have not yet known. Marvel not, my friend, at my strong language, but ponder it, and then judge.

'Now, I am sure that I have at last put your candour to the proof, and have exposed myself to as hard thoughts of me, as ever you entertained of a gloomy enthusiast. I am sure you cannot be equally well satisfied with this letter as with the former ones. I must stop to bear my testimony to the character which you so justly give yourself. I remember well, that, from the first of our acquaintance, you showed a steady attachment to principles, both moral and religious, far beyond what *I* felt; you showed your abhorrence of various indecencies and profanities, with which I was little affected. If to this natural force of mind, there was added an ardent love to a Redeemer, and lively affection to his people, with a cordial zeal for extending his kingdom, and saving the souls of men, what a great character, what a valuable member of a Christian community, would it form! But, to form this character, "the truth as it is in Jesus," must be known and felt.'

Many subsequent letters passed, with seriousness on the one side, and candour on the other, but no approximation of sentiments took place.

Mr Stewart's next attempt to communicate his own views of religion, was made to a lady of great respectability, with whom he had lived on the most friendly terms for several years; and in what manner his benevolent design was interpreted, an extract from her reply will show.

'*Sept.* 9, 1797.

'Since you no longer find pleasure in dances, dinners, and suppers, it is natural for you to decline them; at the same time, there is a degree of civility due to those that pay you civility, that I should have thought might have carried you an hour or two to that said ball you mention, without in the least degrading you in any shape. But that is *my ignorance.*

'When you feel in your heart an ardent desire to see your friends in ——, they will be happy to see you. But I acknowledge myself one to whom your visit will afford no sort of satisfaction, if you are to view it as a sacrifice, a murdering of your time, a paying of a debt, or coming as if to pay the interest of money borrowed. No, no, my friend, the pleasure of friendly intercourse must be mutual, or not at all. I entertained no hope of seeing you this season, so what you say on that subject does not the least surprise. Such *sinners* as we, would perfectly pollute you.

'Strange, indeed, to suppose that I would not read, or would read with negligence, any paper you should send me! Into what is your mind about to contract? I read the letter over, and over, and over again, with all the attention I am capable of, and there is nothing in it to which I make the smallest objection; at the same time, I cannot help observing, that the writer of it has an opinion, both of his own divine inspiration, and that of his friends, that suits not at all with my faith. Warmly to pursue the study of the gospel, is highly proper and meritorious in all, more especially, clergymen. But it appears strange to me, that studying the gospel of peace should sour you at the whole world, and make you think that all who are not exactly up to your way of thinking, are no longer worthy of your regard or attention. I really believe that you even refuse us the hope of being saved.'

The benevolence of Mr Stewart was not repressed by this letter, without making another calm appeal to the judgment and the heart. He therefore again writes:—

'*Moulin, Oct.* 6, 1797.

'I am sorry to find that you are so much hurt by what you call my Puritanical principles. I am the more surprised at it, as I do not recollect that in any of my letters for the last twelvemonth, I formally stated any principles at all. I suspect either that you must have heard of them at second hand only, or rather that you have conjectured or inferred them from the style of my letters, but without knowing precisely what were the principles which I avowed. In fact, I was in no haste to declare them. For, however much satisfaction it would give me to find the friends I love best, agree with me in sentiment, yet I do not think myself entitled to impose my creed on anyone. All I would seek to do in this matter is to induce others to examine closely their own principles, and likewise those inculcated in scripture,—to compare the two sets together, and see whether they coincide. This indeed I consider as a work of the highest importance. From being led, no matter how, to make this inquiry into my own case, I found that the scriptures plainly and positively asserted facts of which I had hardly any notion,—that some of the religious principles which I had maintained, disagreed with the scriptures. I saw the fullest reason to be satisfied that the Bible must be right, and that I must have been wrong. I knew, at the same time, that my principles agreed in the main with those of many of my friends, with whose sentiments on religious subjects I had sufficient opportunity to be acquainted. I saw at once that I had been in an error, so must they also. I have been officious enough to tell them so, for I have more than one correspondence of the kind on my hand. Indeed, I consider it as the highest service I can do them. Can you wonder, then, my dear parental friend, if I should be particularly anxious to do it to you, to whom I am under so many obligations, and to whom I have so many reasons to be grateful? With this view, I sent you the copy of a letter (which by the way was written a few months ago by myself to an old college intimate), the purpose of which was to persuade my correspondent, from scriptural declarations, and scriptural examples, that he might positively be in a state of ignorance, and consequently of error, with regard to some of the truths which essentially concerned his eternal welfare. This is precisely the point I would at present urge with you. I do not seek to state of my own accord what those truths are, for then I might be told that I was laying down my own opinions, arrogating to myself inspiration, infallibility, and I know not what. I wish rather that you should discover them, in consequence of your own inquiry; at the same time, it would give me singular pleasure to accompany and assist you in the search, and when we should have made the discovery, we should rejoice together much more than ever Pythagoras or Archimedes did at the discovery of a mathematical truth. But this might be a work of time.

'In one thing I think you will agree with me, that if the discovery of truth be really our object, it would be needless to stop or go out of our way to examine the claims, or the dogmas of the sectarists. We must first know the truth ourselves, before we can pretend to judge who among our forefathers, or our countrymen, may have found it, or who may have missed it. Let Protestants or Papists, Puritans or Methodists, Churchmen or Dissenters, *Reliefers*[1] or Seceders,[2] be in the right or in the wrong, that can be no rule to us; if fools or villains, if fanatics or persecutors, if a Pizarro[3] or a Philip the

[1] [Members of the Scottish Relief Church. It was founded in 1761 by three ministers, Thomas Gillespie, Thomas Boston (Jnr), and Thomas Colier, 'for the relief of Christians oppressed in their Christian privileges'; in particular those Christians who suffered under the imposition of unwanted ministers on Church of Scotland congregations.]

[2] [Members of the various branches of the Scottish Secession Church. It dates from 1733 when four Church of Scotland ministers, Ebenezer Erskine, William Wilson, Alexander Moncrieff, and James Fisher, seceded from the Church of Scotland in protest against the doctrines and practices of the majority party.]

[3] [Francisco Pizarro (c. 1475–1541), Spanish conqueror of the Inca empire and founder of the city of Lima, Peru.]

Second,[1] profess to believe the gospel, and call themselves Christians, that cannot have changed the nature of the truth itself, nor be any reason why we should disbelieve or disregard it. We are not obliged to follow the creed of Calvin, or of Luther, any more than that of Oliver Cromwell, or of Thomas Paine.[2] Our business is with the doctrines of Christ and his apostles,—with those scriptures which were given by inspiration of God, and which alone can make us wise unto salvation. For the same reason, it is unnecessary to spend time in defending myself or my expressions from the charges of illiberality, want of charity, etc. which you have hinted at in your last letter. As for that, *transeat cum ceteris.*[3] The great point which claims the attention of each of us, is, not what is the opinion of such a favourite author, or such an esteemed friend? Is it liberal, or charitable, or the contrary? But, what says the divine oracle? What has the Lord, our Creator, our Sovereign, our Judge, been pleased to tell us? Whatever information he has thought fit to communicate, it surely behoves us to attend to it most seriously, to receive it with submissive docility, and to apply it directly and diligently to our own use.

'Many an hour have we spent together in studying languages, metaphysics, etc. Now that a vastly more

[1] [Philip II (1527–98), King of Spain from 1556 till his death.]

[2] [Thomas Paine (1737–1809), author of *The Age of Reason* and a bitter opponent of Christianity.]

[3] ['Let it pass with the rest.']

interesting object, the acquiring of saving knowledge, has presented itself, you may believe me, that I would gladly join with you in the pursuit of that object with more relish and eagerness than ever I engaged in a philosophical discussion. Could you give me the prospect, by reading or conversation, to lead you to the knowledge of some of those important spiritual truths, of which we both were certainly ignorant a short while ago, then I would fly to visit you with a more "ardent desire" than ever, and I would even postpone some employments, which I would not suspend on any considerations of mere compliment or civility. But if, on the contrary, I should find that my visit had served no such useful purpose, then, indeed, I must confess that I would account it nothing else than what you call it,—a sacrifice,—an unprofitable sacrifice.

'I have no doubt that you will be ready to tell me, that you have often read the Bible with attention and pleasure, and that you are still equally willing to read it. I had done so too, and I supposed I knew sufficiently its general scope and tenor, though not the precise meaning of every particular passage. But I find I had more to learn than I thought of. And whatever measure of knowledge I may have yet attained, I am sure I have still much to learn, and have no doubt but that I may derive more light and knowledge from these sacred books every day I live. As we are both but learners, what should hinder us from pursuing, as formerly, our studies together? If I should happen to think myself a lesson or two ahead of you at our outsetting, we may go on as fellow-students notwithstanding. One preliminary step, I think, would be very useful, that is, to revise those arguments by which the inspiration of the scriptures is evinced. There is very ample and convincing proofs that those books we call inspired, were certainly written by divine direction and superintendency. And it is of consequence, when we read them, that that conviction should be fresh and lively, in order that every word we read may be received, not as the word of man, but of God. I read lately, along with ——, Doddridge's *Dissertation on the Inspiration of the New Testament*, in the third volume of his *Family Expositor*, which I think plain, judicious, and impressive. His three sermons on the *Evidences of the Gospel*, are also plain and convincing. Either of these performances, or both if at hand, might, I think, be perused with advantage, before entering on a course of scripture reading.

'You might be sensible, dear Madam, that to search the scriptures with care, is not the business of divines exclusively. All are equally interested in knowing what God has revealed to man. It would therefore be highly desirable to associate with us in these sacred studies, as many as we can persuade to join us. Might not you easily engage Mr —— to accompany you in your reading? Or, if he should not read along with you, he might read the same book at home to Mrs —— to whom I understand he is in the use of reading for their mutual entertainment, and thus you could talk over the subject at meeting, and see which had profited most.

'When —— would see you in earnest about such an object, he too might be induced to join you. At any rate, I hope A—— would willingly attend you in each stage of your progress. And thus you might be the means of bringing others, as well as yourself, to the knowledge of those facts and doctrines on which depends the everlasting happiness of their souls and of yours. So it appears, that when I can scrape together a little time, I can still write a long letter on a subject which interests me. I wish, dear Lady, your bodily health and ease were such as to allow me to expect a long letter in return. I remember the time when neither of us counted paper or postage. And what was the subject?'

In answer to another letter in which Mr Stewart had attempted to explain the condition on which men stand with respect to the divine dispensations,—she writes as follows:

'*July* 14. 1798,

'I have repeatedly and attentively read over your last letter, also the distinction that you make between the covenant of works and the covenant of grace. I have looked out all your quotations, considered all with the utmost attention I can command; and have also talked over the subject with our mutual friend Mr ——; and after all, I am no more inclined to give up the covenant of works, than you are to give up the covenant of grace. Your argument, in my opinion, strikes at the root of all moral virtue, and must prove the ruin, not the salvation, of mankind. My creed is that we must strive what we can to take the advantage of both these covenants, by the strictest attention we can pay to our moral duty; and when our nature fails us, we are to trust to the covenant of grace and mercy, through our Redeemer.

'Your new creed appears to me to lean strongly towards the doctrine of necessity. Some of your quotations are necessity as strong as can be worded;—"that the elect were chosen before the creation of the world," etc. I believe that the worthy and the good were the elect chosen, but not that they were picked out individually. Sure I am, that you are no such enemy to morality in your conduct, as you are in your doctrine. Give up the covenant of works! No, surely, never while I retain my senses.'

Mr Stewart's answer shall close this correspondence.

'*Moulin, July* 21, 1798.

'I am happy that I have an opportunity of acknowledging thus early your very valuable favour of the ——. I am much indebted to you for the patient attention with which you have studied my letters and *quotations*; and for your full and candid avowal of the result. This avowal is to me very satisfactory. The common error of weak minds, with respect to religious doctrines, and which I meet with every day, is that they fancy they believe such or such propositions, and aver that they do believe them, when in reality they do not. Your clearer head, and more solid judgment, have saved you from this error, for you seem to have ascertained distinctly what you do, and what you do not believe. The experiment is now fairly made, how far a person's natural understanding will admit the truth of scripture doctrines on the authority of divine testimony. The result corresponds exactly, in your case, with what scripture itself tells us must always happen (1 Cor. 2:14). I think, too, you must observe the truth of what I remarked some time ago, that there were facts asserted in the Bible which you probably did not yet know, and which, when you should be told them, you probably would not believe. The experiment is, I think, decisive, and proves the necessity of the agency of a superior power to turn men from "darkness unto light," from a state of blindness to a state of vision (Acts 26:18, and John 9:39-41), before they will believe, or distinctly apprehend, many truths relative to salvation. This point being ascertained, I expect no more from argument; and I am perfectly willing, with you, to put an end to controversy on the subject. I would only request you to fix your attention occasionally on the proofs of the divine origin of the Christian religion, and the inspiration of the scriptures; and also on the difference between the points therein asserted, and your own creed; and to observe how far the difference is trivial or important. It will be worth-while to observe, what are the effects of our respective creeds. Whether mine will prove the destruction of moral virtue, as you apprehend its tendency to be, time and trial must show. I dare not make professions, nor hold myself up as a model. My feelings and affections have been all my life remarkably cold, and my constitution very phlegmatic. However satisfied I am with my principles, I cannot say the same of my temper and practice. I am convinced, however, that the direct tendency of the truths of the gospel, so far as they actually influence the mind, that is, just as far as they are actually believed, is to make men honest, kind, generous to others, humble, devout, obedient toward God, patient, contented, happy in themselves. And I know that the grace of God is sufficient to make me feel the influence of these truths; so that my temper and conduct shall be more and more formed by their influence, and on that I found my hope of improvement. I know, too, that the same power can give you a new heart (Ezek. 11:19, 20), to believe and submit to his way of salvation. I thank you for your kind admonition with respect to rash or unwarrantable judgment. I am convinced such a temper must be very different from the true Christian spirit. You see, however, that in the present case I do not judge of you so rashly as you may have supposed, for I do not give you up as lost forever. So far from it, that I have an earnest hope (and I do not this moment know any earthly price for which I would give it up), that the Holy Spirit, who hath brought one of us to the knowledge of the truth, when we were both alike strangers to it, and averse from receiving it, just like the rest of the world (Eph. 2:3), will, in his own time and manner, bring the other likewise (2 Tim. 2:25). I am far from despairing that we shall yet agree more cordially than ever, though for the present we differ. In the meantime, let us by all means study mutual forbearance and kindness. I am sure I have much reason to admire yours, which has been long tried, and continues undiminished. I am by no means for giving up corresponding. I shall only beg this much allowance for my peculiarities, considering how I am impressed with the importance of religious truths, and the necessity of having all my feelings, purposes, and actions, regulated by a regard to religious principles, in the minutest, as well as in the most important particulars, that you bear with me, whenever my letters, or my conversation, happen to discover that spirit. Indeed, I cannot endure the thought of being ashamed of my Master, or of shrinking from avowing my attachment to him.'

CHAPTER 4

REVIVAL!

WE deemed it worthwhile to turn aside for a little, to notice those indirect exertions made by Mr Stewart, to diffuse the good which he himself had freely received. These earnest exertions demonstrate the reality of the change he had undergone, and beautifully illustrate the benevolence inseparable from Christian character. But it is now time to introduce Mr Stewart in his altered character, ministering to his own people, and the happy effects cannot be so well represented, as by laying before the reader his own narrative of the events subsequent to Mr Simeon's visit.[1]

[1] This narrative, so often referred to, was given to the public in 1800, in form of a Letter to Mr Black. That it was well received by the friends of religion, it is hardly necessary to state. Indeed, a

'From that time, I began to preach Jesus Christ, with some degree of knowledge and confidence. From August 1797 to January 1798, I preached a course of sermons on the fundamental doctrines of Christianity; following, for the most part, the selection and order of texts in the tract entitled *Short Sermons*.[1]

---

work like that at Moulin had for years been unknown among our languishing half-dead congregations. Nor would it be easy, among publications of a similar kind, to name one of greater interest, whether we consider the candour, modesty, and intelligence of the writer, or the intrinsic importance of the contents. Letters from entire strangers, both in England and America, bore testimony how well the narrative was received; and, among others, we may mention the venerable Newton, who, both at the time of its appearance, and several years after, expressed a most favourable judgment of the publication.

[1] The texts in the above-named pamphlet are as follows:

Matt. 16:26. What is a man profited, if he gain the whole world, and lose his own soul? Or what shall a man give in exchange for his soul?

1 John 3:4. Sin is the transgression of the law.

Rom. 3:23. All have sinned, and come short of the glory of God.

Gal. 3:10. Cursed is every one that continueth not in all things that are written in the book of the law to do them.

Rom. 6:23. The wages of sin is death.

Acts 16:30. What shall I do to be saved?

Mark 1:15. Repent ye, and believe the gospel.

1 Tim. 1:15. This is a faithful saying, and worthy of all acceptation, that Jesus Christ came into the world to save sinners; of whom I am the chief.

John 6:37. Him that cometh unto me, I will in no wise cast out.

Rom. 5:1. Being justified by faith, we have peace with God through our Lord Jesus Christ.

'I was now enabled to show, from scripture, that all men are by nature enemies to God, disobedient to his law, and on that account exposed to his just indignation and curse. I therefore addressed them, not as persons who were already, from education, birthright, or local situation, possessed of saving faith and other Christian graces, but as sinners, under sentence of death, and who had "not as yet obtained mercy." I did not, as before, merely reprove them for particular faults or vices, and urge them to the practice of particular virtues; but told them, that the whole of their affections and inclinations needed to be pointed in a new direction, and even their virtues to be new-modelled. I showed, that this, supposing it done, could not atone, however, for past offences, nor wipe away guilt already contracted; and that sin could not be remitted without satisfaction made to the broken law of God; that neither could purity of heart, and constant obedience in future, recover their title to the reward of eternal life, which

---

1 Peter 2:7. Unto you which believe he is precious.

Heb. 12:14. Follow holiness; without which no man shall see the Lord.

Titus 2:13. Looking for that blessed hope, and the glorious appearing of the great God and our Saviour Jesus Christ.

Luke 11:13. If ye then, being evil, know how to give good gifts unto your children: how much more shall your heavenly Father give the Holy Spirit to them that ask him?

Heb. 9:27. It is appointed unto men once to die, and after this the judgment.

Heb. 2:3. How shall we escape, if we neglect so great salvation?

had been at first conferred as a free gift by God, and was now wholly forfeited by sin: yet that their case was by no means desperate; for we had the glad tidings to tell, that God had made provision for the complete salvation of sinners; that he had appointed his own eternal Son, in the human nature, to procure for sinners the pardon of sin, and a title to glory, by his own obedience and sufferings; that, in conferring these blessings, God acts as the sovereign dispenser of his own gifts, not in consideration of any merit (for there is none) in the person on whom he bestows them; that a conformity of our will to the law of God, which I formerly considered as the ground of our acceptance, was itself a gift bestowed by God, in consequence of his having first justified, accepted, and adopted us to be his children; that in this great salvation wrought out by Christ for sinners, love to God and man, an abhorrence of evil, and a disposition to what is good, were included as essential parts, inseparably connected with the rest; insomuch, that if a man is not renewed in the spirit of his mind, neither are his sins pardoned, nor his person accepted with God. I urged them to attend to what the word of God declared to be their condition; not to be deceived with vain hopes of recommending themselves to his favour by their own exertions; but as humble needy supplicants, to apply to him, through the merits of Christ, for pardon, and the gift of his Spirit to make them serve him with fidelity and delight; to be diligent in studying the word of truth, which alone can make us wise unto salvation; and having obtained grace from God, to practise diligently every active and every self-denying duty, and to abound in good fruit, to their own advancement in holiness and comfort, to the temporal and spiritual benefit of their fellow-creatures, and to the praise of him who had called them out of darkness into his marvellous light. I thought it right often to caution them against judging of their state by transient impressions or emotions of which they might be conscious; but only by a prevailing habitual preference of God's honour and service to their own gratification, appearing in the uniform tenor of their purposes and actions.

'The novelty of the matter, and some change in my manner of preaching, excited attention. People began to think more, and sometimes to talk together, of religious subjects, and of the sermons they heard. But I did not yet know of any deep or lasting impressions having been made. The two persons before mentioned as earliest converted, had by this time got clearer views of the gospel, were enabled to derive comfort from the word of salvation, and began to bear their testimony to the grace of God their Saviour. They were in use of visiting occasionally a poor infirm woman, who had long walked with God, and who now lived alone in a mean cottage in the neighbouring village. It was proposed that they should come together to her house at a time appointed, and that I and some of my family should join them, and spend an evening hour or two in reading, conversation, and prayer. In process of time, different persons, who were inquiring after the one thing needful, hearing how we were employed, and believing that God was with us, were at their own request admitted of our party. In this poor woman's little smoky hovel, we continued to hold our weekly meetings, to August 1799, when she was called away to join the general assembly of the first-born above. Her growth in grace had been very conspicuous, and her death was triumphant.

'In summer 1798, the Lord's supper was dispensed in our congregation, at the usual time of the year. For some weeks before, I endeavoured in preaching to explain more fully, and with more application to the conscience, the nature of the ordinance, and the character of those who, under the denomination of disciples, were commanded to keep it. The exhortations and warnings then given, appeared to be accompanied with a divine blessing. Some of the ordinary communicants, judging themselves to be in an unconverted state, kept back, of their own accord, from partaking of the sacrament. Others, after conversing with me privately on the subject, took the same resolution. Many of those who might otherwise have applied for admission, forbore to apply. I inferred this from the comparatively small number of persons applying. For some years before, the number of candidates for admission each summer amounted to thirty, forty, and sometimes near fifty. In summer 1798, there were not above twelve; of whom nine were admitted. The sacrament was dispensed the same year again in November, on which occasion there were only six more new communicants admitted.

'Although the number of communicants was thus for the time diminished, yet the number of those who were brought under concern about their eternal interests was increasing. This concern showed itself chiefly among the younger people under twenty-five or thirty. Their knowledge was yet imperfect. A natural shyness often hindered them long from discovering to others what they thought or felt. They had as yet no friend or intimate whom they judged able, from experience, to understand their situation, or to give them counsel. Some of them began to visit one of the two earlier converts formerly mentioned, from whose reading and conversation they derived considerable benefit. By means of this common friend, they were brought more acquainted with each other. One might now observe at church, after divine service, two or three small groups forming themselves round our few more advanced believers, and withdrawing from the crowd into the adjacent fields, to exchange Christian salutations, and hold Christian converse together; while a little cousin, or other young relative, followed as a silent attendant on the party, and listened earnestly to their religious discourse.

'As the sacrament of the Lord's Supper had been much abused, by admitting, without strict examination or special instruction, all candidates who could give a tolerable answer to common questions, and who were free from grosser immoralities; so it must be confessed, that the sacrament of baptism had been still more profaned. Nothing but one kind of scandal was understood to preclude a man from admission to this ordinance. Gross ignorance, or immoral behaviour, only laid a man open to some admonition or reproof; or at most laid him under the necessity of procuring another sponsor; but hardly ever hindered the baptism of his child. Nothing subjects a man to greater disgrace and obloquy among us, than to have his child remain unbaptized. The dominion of custom in this matter is so despotic, that most parents would choose rather to carry their children a hundred miles to be baptized by a Popish priest, than to be refused baptism when they demand it. The superstitious notions, and other abuses attending our celebration of this sacrament, called loudly for reformation. Last year, I preached a short course of sermons on baptism. At the same time, agreeably to a recent resolution and recommendation of the presbytery to which I belong, I revived the laws of the church which had fallen into disuse, relative to this ordinance, particularly that which prohibits private baptism (*Acts of Assembly*, 1690, X). Whenever I baptize a child on a week day, whether in the church or elsewhere, I give previous intimation of sermon; and, after preaching, I administer the ordinance in the presence of the congregation.[1] By these means, many have been brought to understand better the nature of this sacrament, and to attend to it with more reverence. It had been long customary for the parent to give an entertainment, according to his station, to his neighbours and connections, immediately after the baptism; by which means this sacred ordinance, instead of being regarded as a most solemn religious service, had degenerated into an occasion of carnal mirth and festivity. The more religiously disposed amongst us have set the example of discontinuing this practice.

'The following month, March 1799, I began a course of practical sermons on regeneration, which I continued to the beginning of July following. These were attended with a more general awakening than had yet appeared

[1] 'In process of time I found that this practice needed some restriction. It was always desirable that both parents should be present at baptism, as being parties peculiarly interested in the solemn transaction. They could rarely attend on the ordinance in church, without risking the health of the newborn infant, and of the mother not yet fully recovered. It was likewise inconvenient for private families, especially in such circumstances, to have a mixed congregation of people assembled at their houses; nor could many be accommodated. Therefore, instead of intimating sermon, I have now been long accustomed to allow the head of the family to ask such friends or neighbours as he chooses to have present; and I read and expound a portion of scripture, in presence of the parents and the company assembled. This private exposition and application of the word of God, I have found profitable, as well as the more public preaching of it.'

amongst us. Seldom a week passed in which we did not see or hear of one, two, or three persons, brought under deep concern about their souls, accompanied with strong convictions of sin, and earnest inquiry after a Saviour. It was a great advantage to these that there were others on the road before them; for they were seldom at a loss now to find an acquaintance to whom they could freely communicate their anxious thoughts. The house of one of our most established Christians became the chief resort of all who wished to spend an hour in reading or conversing about spiritual subjects. Some who had but newly begun to entertain serious thoughts about religion, and who had not yet come so far as to speak out their mind, would contrive an errand to this person's house, and listen to her talk. She was visited at other times by those who were drawn only by curiosity or a disputatious spirit, who wanted to cavil at her words, or draw her into controversy. Such visitors she did not avoid, and at last they ceased to trouble her.

'Other experienced Christians among us have been extremely useful to their younger brethren and sisters. Their conversation and example have been principal means of turning the attention of the young to religion, and of edifying those who have been already awakened. Such persons I find most serviceable auxiliaries. If they be neither *prophets*, nor *apostles*, nor *teachers*, yet their usefulness in the church entitles them to the appellation of *helps* (1 Cor. 12:28). Nor do I think an apostle would hesitate to acknowledge them, both men and women, in the relation of *fellow-labourers* (Phil. 4:3). Nor has success in this divine work been confined to instruments raised up among ourselves. The same happy effects have in a certain measure attended the preaching, the prayers, or conversation of pious brethren, who have assisted at the celebration of the Lord's supper, or made us other occasional visits.

'It is observable, that the work of conversion has been begun and carried on among this people, in a quiet manner, without any confusion, and without those ungovernable agitations of mind, or convulsions of the body, or shrieking, or fainting, which have often accompanied a general awakening in other places. One young woman was so much moved in church, in March 1799, that she wept bitterly, and her friends thought it prudent to convey her out a little before the congregation was dismissed. She was for five or six days unfit for going about her usual work. In June following, at the time of our sacrament, she felt emotions of joy for a few days, to such a degree as to withdraw her regard, in a great measure, from sensible objects. Spiritual affections were unusually strong in her, and spiritual objects appeared visible and near; but her sentiments were quite correct and scriptural. A few days afterwards, when her emotions had subsided, she told me that she was at the time sensible that her mind was somewhat unsettled, but that she found comfort in recollecting the apostle's words, "If we are beside ourselves, it is to God." This was exactly her case. She continues a humble lively Christian, and, except these two short intervals, she has regularly performed her ordinary work, as a maidservant, to the satisfaction of her master and mistress, in whose service she still remains. Another woman, the mother of a family, in April last, was so much moved in hearing the sermon, that of her own accord she left the church. Excepting these two instances, I know of none whose emotions under the preaching of the word discovered themselves in any other manner than by silent tears.

'Having lately made an enumeration of those of our congregation, whom, to the best of my judgment, I trust I can reckon truly enlightened with the saving knowledge of Christ, I find their number about seventy. The greater part of these are under thirty years of age. Several are above forty; six or seven above fifty; one fifty-six; and one above seventy. Of children under twelve or fourteen, there are a good many who seem to have a liking to religion; but we find it difficult to form a decided opinion of their case. Of persons who have died within these twelve months, three we are persuaded, and we hope two or three others, have slept in Jesus.

'A very considerable number are friendly to religion, and countenance and defend the truth, even while they do not as yet appear to live under its power. A few among ourselves did for a while jeer and deride the godly; but such persons are left in so small a minority, that they have ceased to be troublesome. The scriptures, too, are so generally read and referred to, that the truth itself serves to stop the mouth of scoffers. We are sometimes told that the sentiments and language of our people are much misrepresented, and are the object of much wonder, and ridicule, and invective in other places. But we only hear of such things; they are hardly permitted to come nigh us. The chief opposition arises from those who possess superior scholarship, and acquaintance with the scriptures. These contend, that there can be nothing substantial or necessary in that experimental knowledge which illiterate persons may pretend to have attained; and that it is mere arrogance in them to imagine that they can have a larger share of saving knowledge than men who are greater scholars, and better versed in the scriptures. "Are we blind also?" has ever been the indignant language of carnal wisdom, of literary pride, and of self-righteous presumption.

'It is evident, that the scriptures represent all mankind as divided into two classes. These are distinguished from each other in the most explicit manner; and the distinction is marked by the strongest language, and the most significant comparisons. They are called the children of God, and the children of the devil (1 John 3:10); the children of the kingdom, and the children of the wicked one (Matt 13:38); the just and the wicked (Matt. 13:49); they who are dead in trespasses and sins, and they who are quickened together with Christ (Eph. 2:1-6). They are compared to wheat and tares (Matt. 13:25); to good and bad fishes (Matt. 13:47, 48); to sheep and goats (Matt. 25:32). In the general tenor of my preaching, especially in discussing the important doctrine of regeneration, I have endeavoured to keep in view this distinction, and to exhibit it clearly to the notice of my hearers. Many have been not a little offended at such a discrimination; have found fault with the preacher; have complained of uncharitable judgment, pleading that it was God's prerogative to judge the heart; that they hoped theirs was good, though they did not make such a parading profession of religion, etc. The truth has prevailed, however, and some have confessed to me, that their first serious thoughts about the state of their souls arose from the surprise and resentment they felt on being classed, under the character of unbelievers, along with murderers and idolaters (Rev. 21:8). But in giving such offensive, though necessary warnings, I had much need of the Spirit of Christ, to repress all asperity of language and manner, to awaken tender compassion for those whom I addressed, and to enable me to speak the truth in love.

'I observe among our young converts a considerable variety of frames, but a striking uniformity of character. They are dejected or elevated, according as their regard is more fixed on their own deficiencies and corruptions, or on the glorious sufficiency of Christ. But all of them are characterized by lowliness of mind, by a warm attachment to each other, and to all who love the

Lord Jesus, and by the affections set on things above. I know no instances among them of persons trusting for comfort or direction to dreams or visions, impulses or impressions; and hardly an instance of seeking comfort from external signs or tokens, arbitrarily assumed by the inquirer, after the example of Abraham's servant (Gen. 24:14), and of Gideon (Judg. 6:36-40).

'We have not yet to lament any great falling off in those who appeared to have once undergone a saving change. There may be persons who were for a time inquiring with some apparent earnestness, and afterwards fell back to their former unconcern. I have reason to suspect that there may be several in this situation, though I have not access to know the exact state of their minds. May the Lord discover it to themselves in time! But all, so far as I know, who seemed to have been once truly humbled for their sins, and made to feel in their hearts the grace of God in the gospel, continue thus far to maintain a humble, spiritual, conscientious walk. They have a constant appetite for the sincere milk of the word, and for Christian fellowship with one another. The younger sort have lost their former levity of speech and behaviour, and are become devout and sober-minded; those more advanced in life, have laid aside their selfishness and worldly-mindedness, and are grown humble, contented, and thankful. The external effects of a general concern about religion have appeared in the behaviour even of those who do not seem to have experienced a change of heart. While the younger people attended a Sabbath-school, those who were grown up used to spend the evening of that day in sauntering about the fields and woods in gossiping parties, or visiting their acquaintance at a distance, without improving their time by any profitable exercise. Now there is hardly a lounger to be seen, nor any person walking abroad, except going to some house or meeting, where he may hear the scriptures read. Swearing, profane talking, foolish and indecent jesting, have in a great measure ceased.—At *late wakes*, where people assemble to watch by the body of a deceased neighbour, the whole night used to be spent in childish, noisy sports and pastimes. Even the apartment where the corpse lay was the scene of their revelry. This unnatural custom, which is still pretty general over a great part of the Highlands, is almost wholly discontinued in this part of the country. They still assemble on such occasions, but they pass the time in reading the Bible, or some religious book, and in sober conversation.

'In reply to your request of relating a few of the more remarkable cases of conversion, which have occurred among this people, I must say, that I have little uncommon to communicate. I have mentioned already, that almost all our converts have been brought to serious concern and inquiry, in a quiet gradual manner. To an intelligent observer, the change in the conversation, temper, deportment, and the very countenance of individuals, is striking; the change, too, on the general aspect of the manners of the people is conspicuous. The effect is thus, on the whole, obvious; yet there are few particulars in the case of each person, which, taken singly, will appear uncommon, or worthy of being detailed in a separate narrative. We have no instances of persons remarkable for profligacy of manners, or profaneness of speech, who have been reclaimed from such enormities, because there were none of that description to be found in our society. The change has been from ignorance and indifference, and disrelish of divine things, to knowledge, and concern, and spiritual enjoyment. Neither are there among us examples of persons suddenly struck and impressed by some alarming event, or singular interposition of Providence. The word of truth proclaimed in public, or spoken in private, has been almost the only outward mean of producing conviction of sin, and confidence in the Saviour. In every single case, the power of God is visible in the effect produced; but there is little "diversity of operation." Instead of endeavouring to paint the beauties of holiness in the scene around me, I rather wish to prevail with you and other friends, who know how to enjoy such a spectacle, to "come and see."'

Without making any remark on this interesting statement, we shall insert a few letters written while the great work was going on.

He had met with a severe domestic trial in the loss of Mrs Stewart, who, at the time of Mr Simeon's visit, was affected with the pulmonary disorder that brought her to an early grave. And to show how a Christian can bear the bereavement of the dearest creature-comforts, we shall insert the letter he wrote to Mr B. announcing her decease:—

'*Moulin, Feb.* 7, 1799.

'Now, my dear brother, have I joyful news to tell! My Louisa is safely arrived at her heavenly home. Her passage was remarkably smooth, and her exit speedy. Yesterday morning her spirit took its departure about 10 o'clock, and long ere now it is with God who gave it. Her strength had been declining every day,—she could speak but little and with difficulty,—but her speech was full of her Saviour's kindness and love to her soul. Two or three days before her death, she was threatened with some degree of suffering, from the feebleness of her frame, but it came no farther. The Lord was pleased to deal most tenderly with her and us, for she breathed her last without a struggle, or a feature discomposed.

'But a few years ago, my address to my friends, and to you, I remember, in particular, was "rejoice with me," on what we all reckoned a joyful occasion. Through the grace of God vouchsafed to my dear partner and myself, I am enabled from my heart to repeat the same address. I do not forbid you, my dear friends, to weep,—it is the expression of many a tender and spiritual emotion,—but I do call on you not to grieve or mourn for me as for one without hope. Rather let us praise the Lord, and exalt his name together, for his many loving-kindnesses and tender mercies, saying with Job, "Blessed be the name of the Lord!"'[1]

Thus strongly did Mr Stewart enjoy the consolations of Christ in the season of nature's tribulation!

To assuage the grief of his friend for the loss of a loved son, Horace,[2] among other expedients, advises him to divert the mind from the object lost, and fix the attention on the new conquests of Augustus:—

'————————Desine mollium
Tandem querelarum: et potius nova
Cantemus Augusti trophaea
Caesaris, et rigidum Niphatem
Medumque flumen gentibus additum
Victis, minores volvere vortices:
Intraque praescriptum Gelonos
Exiguis equitare campis.'[3]

[1] Mrs Stewart left two children,—Alexander, about to become a preacher, and Catharine, married to the Rev. H. Allan, minister of Kincardine, Ross-shire.

[2] [Quintus Horatius Flaccus (65–8 BC), commonly known in the English-speaking world as Horace, was the leading Roman lyric poet during the time of Augustus (also known as Octavian).]

[3] ['Come now, do put a stop to these unmanly lamentations, and let us rather sing of Augustus Caesar's latest victories, of ice-bound

But if attention to the victories of Caesar could afford a suitable diversion to the labouring mind, Mr Stewart had a much nobler field of relief presented to him in the conquests of Christ, whose victorious grace was subduing many hearts around him, as the extracts that follow set forth more particularly than was compatible with the plan of his general narrative.

'*Moulin, Oct.* 20, 1800.

'To Mr Black.

'O my dear brother, had you but been with us for a week past, how your heart would have rejoiced! Such hungering and thirsting after communion with God! such genuine humility and contrition for sin! such devotedness to the Saviour! old converts quickened, and new ones added to the Lord! Yesterday was, I trust, a great day of the Son of man. I almost felt my own nerves, rigid as they are, touched, and my sympathy (my admiration I am sure) excited, in various private conversations which I had during the week. Glenbriarachan, which I visited on Tuesday, I found blossoming like the rose. I had observed, for some months past, a kind of concern, a kind of "voluntary humility," appearing among them, rather bordering on ostentation; but now

---

Niphates and the Persian river rolling its waves less proudly now that it has joined the conquered nations, and of the Geloni who gallop their horses within fixed boundaries on plains that have suddenly dwindled' (Horace, *Odes Book II*. Translation from Loeb Classical Library).]

their expressions of concern and humiliation were fewer, more unaffected, and seemed to come more directly from the heart. But I must refer to sister's journal, as I am called to speak with one of our new *evellíes* (awakened), and our hour of worship is not distant. One after the other is calling, but I must defer them till after worship.'

To the same.

'O for the pen of a ready writer to tell of the Lord's abundant goodness! One lad in the parish of Blair, whom I visited a few days ago, and who seems to have walked with God for many years, appears to be going home bearing ample testimony to the grace of God his Saviour. Several called here yesterday, hungering and thirsting as much as ever. Widow M. entered joyfully into her rest. But what chiefly engages our praises at present, is the case of a Robert R——, tenant in Glenbriarachan (still a favoured spot). His wife was among the firstfruits in the glen; and now the husband, laid on a sickbed, has been visited with the joys of salvation, and proclaims the freeness and fulness of divine grace. It is a singular sight to see his wife, with the near prospect of widowhood, and a family of small children, his two sisters, brother-in-law, etc. all rejoicing by his bedside. Mrs B. or you, I am sure, will not fail to make our dear brethren partakers of our joy.'

To the same.

'I have to inform you how much we have been gratified by a kind visit from Mr ——. He preached here the last Sabbath of December. I had been in the pulpit twice before; once to salute my people, and request their prayers and thanksgivings in my behalf; and another time to baptize a child. The day Mr —— preached, I succeeded him, and gave briefly in Gaelic the substance of his discourse, which had been a long one. He stayed here Monday. That day, he and I took a walk to see John C——, mentioned by sister in her last letter to Mrs Black. This man had been brought, a few weeks ago, to a clear and comfortable knowledge of the gospel, chiefly by means of a young woman, whom he had hired for the five weeks of harvest, on purpose to enjoy her religious company. About a month ago, his wife was in great bodily distress; but it was a season of love to her soul. She was enlightened with the knowledge of her Saviour, and enabled to trust and rejoice in him. Margaret K——, the young woman whose conversation had been blessed to the husband, was their constant attendant. The wife has been much distressed since her illness, and her recovery very doubtful. Mr —— and I found her in a very weakly state; but both she and her husband were quite resigned and cheerful. Unfortunately, neither of them can speak a word of English, so that Mr —— had no conversation with them, but he was much delighted with the man's animated and heavenly countenance. A heavy fall of snow, which prevented all intercourse for some days, has occasioned our not hearing accounts of the woman's health for five days. I have had calls from two young women, who spent one or two half-years in service in this parish. They were in that time awakened, I trust effectually, and pretty well instructed in the truth. At Martinmas,[1] they quitted their service, and returned to their native parish of Blair Athole, where they lived in the same village, and are mutual aids and comforts to each other. They read and converse much together, and not seldom bear their testimony against the profanity of swearers and Sabbath-breakers in their village. Their unusual manners and sentiments draw upon them many taunts, and on the Moulin people, among whom they learned such odd notions; but they have been enabled to abide stedfast, and I hope humble.

'Such things having now, by the peculiar blessing of God and his abounding grace, become pretty frequent, are much talked of. They have excited the attention and wonder of many, and the diversion and hatred, of some,—just as might have been expected. I hear of few scoffers among ourselves, where the behaviour of our young converts is seen and known; but I hear they are the

[1] [Martinmas, the feast day of St Martin of Tours (d. AD 397), was widely celebrated on 11 November in medieval and early modern Europe. Martinmas also marked the end of the harvest season and beginning of winter.]

subject of much obloquy in the neighbouring parishes, where, on account of the distance, there is more room for misrepresenting their sentiments and conduct, and where they are grossly misrepresented. Hitherto the Lord has watched over them most tenderly, so that I have not heard of one who has fallen off, or brought a stain on his profession. On the contrary, those who live nearest to this place, and whom I know best, appear evidently to be growing in grace and knowledge. We have many inquirers after the truth, who are yet but exploring their way; and some who, from opposing and reprobating its doctrines, are brought to listen to them with acquiescence, at least, if not with a desire to learn. S—— is attended every day, and almost at all hours, by persons of every description. She and a tradesman in this village, W.W——, a Margaret K——, are my principal "helps" (1 Cor. 12:28). Expositors would be at no loss to understand that term, if they were a few weeks among us.

'What a treasure has been distributed among us! and in what frail earthen vessels! Truly the excellency of the power is of God, and not of us. O that our hearts were more enlarged, and our tongues more ready, and our voices more tuned, to praise him who hath made the dayspring from on high to visit us! But how dry! how barren! I used to give little credit to the complaints of good men, such as Mr Newton, when lamenting their want of love, and their indisposition to labour; but now I give them full credit. I am sure they said no more than they must have felt, and I dare say they felt no more than was real.'

Referring to these communications, his correspondent inserted the following reflections in his diary:—

'*Edinburgh, July* 20th, 1800.

'Felt a little quickened by a sweet letter the other day from dear brother Stewart, containing an account of the wonderful things that the Lord is carrying on in his parish. O may the Lord's work still continue and increase exceedingly, that there may be joy in heaven over more repenting sinners, and that the thanksgivings of many upon earth may redound to God on their account! And O that it would please God to visit all our congregations with the refreshing influence of his Spirit, that sinners everywhere may be seen flying to Christ as clouds, and as doves to their windows! God of all grace, send a plenteous rain!'

When the news of those things had spread abroad, it excited an uncommon interest among all who loved Zion's prosperity. Good men and good ministers could hardly be satisfied without repairing to the scene; and it was after a visit of Mr Black to Moulin, he thus wrote in his diary:—

'*Aug.* 24, 1800.

'Returned from St Madoes, Perth, and Moulin, where I spent the last two weeks, upon the whole, I trust, profitably to my own soul, if not to the souls of others. My visit to Moulin was peculiarly gratifying. Such a revival I never witnessed before,—it is truly the doing of the Lord, and marvellous in our eyes. Much as I had heard of it before, it far exceeded expectation. I preached on Matt. 22:42; the congregation attentive, and some of them much affected. Had a great deal of conversation in private with many of those under religious concern, and considerably under the influence of doubts and fears. They spoke feelingly of the hardness of their hearts, and of their indisposedness for everything that is good. At the same time, their hearts seemed to be much alive to God. They have a keen appetite for the word of God, and an evident love for the Saviour, though they will not allow it themselves. A deep sense of their own unworthiness, and a strong affection for one another, are the most prominent features in their character. Some are more advanced and greatly enlightened in the knowledge of divine truth. These serve as guides to the rest, and are made exceedingly useful by their example and conversation.

'Dear Mr Stewart himself is mercifully preserved humble amidst all the honour that God is conferring upon him. O may the good Shepherd watch over him, and the dear flock committed to his charge! And may the divine influence be spread abroad throughout all our congregations, that everywhere there may be a shaking among the dry bones, and that a great harvest of souls may be gathered to the Saviour!'

'*Sept.* 28, 1800.

'Dear brother Stewart spent eight days with us, and his company and conversation were truly enlivening.'

'*Jan.* 18, 1801.

'Amidst the complaints of deadness and unprofitableness, two things have done me good,—the reading of Mr Pearce's Memoirs,[1] a sweet and precious testimony to the power of divine grace; and the accounts of the success of the gospel at Moulin, communicated from time to time by dear brother Stewart.'

'*April* 19, 1801.

'Returned from Perth last week, where I had been assisting in dispensing the Lord's supper. Had a sweet day on the Sabbath. Preached on Gen. 32:26 with much comfort, and was greatly refreshed next day with hearing dear brother Stewart on Col. 3:15.'

'*Sept.* 6, 1801.

'After being considerably feverish, and much weakened, it pleased the Lord mercifully to restore me,

[1] [Samuel Pearce (1766–99), an English Baptist minister whose *Memoirs*, edited by Andrew Fuller, were first published in 1800. There is a sketch of his life in *Sound of Trumpets* by Faith Cook (Edinburgh: Banner of Truth Trust, 1999).]

so that, before I went to Moulin, I enjoyed my usual state of health. I preached there the following Lord's day, and truly it did my heart good to see so many friends of the Lord walking in truth, and in love to one another.'

'*April* 25, 1802.

'Preached at Moulin to brother Stewart's affectionate and highly favoured flock. Some things I heard lately respecting them, gave me concern, and I was afraid I saw in these things (small and inconsiderable as they seem at present), the beginnings of dissension. But from conversation, and further inquiring, I trust my fears will prove groundless. O may the Lord keep his good hand about his dear people in that corner, and maintain what he has wrought.'

It is pleasing to contemplate Mr Stewart in the fidelity and in the success that accompanied his public ministry; but, in order to give the reader a more complete idea of his character, it is necessary to exhibit him in some of the more private walks of duty. There were two things that pervaded his ministerial intercourse with his parishioners,—an affectionate desire to benefit them, and the faithful application of the most probable means to do them good. From the day he knew the grace of God in truth, his heart was opened with undissembled love to genuine Christians, and with tender compassion for the condition of men living without hope and without God in the world.

As an instance of his kindly affection to those around him, it may be mentioned, that at the hour of evening worship, a bell rang to give notice to the bordering villagers of the evening sacrifice, when as many as were disengaged and willing-hearted, repaired to the place, and in the kitchen, or in fine weather before the door, listened to the opening up of some passage of scripture, and joined in prayer and praise.

His attention to the cases of the newly awakened was unremitting; and if some trial, or some unlooked-for mercy, exercised the hearts of his more established converts, their minister took a lively interest in the dispensation. The connection betwixt them was such, as can neither exist nor appear desirable to the merely professional guide and his professed followers, the one teaching a way he neither knows aright nor loves, the other listening to his directions without the least intention to obey them, or to make progress. The one would think Mr Stewart's attention to his flock a miserable bondage; the other would view the affectionate respect and assiduity of his people as the effects of superstition and credulity.

As to the interest which Mr Stewart himself must have felt in the spiritual birth of so many sons and daughters, no man can describe it, but a parent of souls, if we may be allowed the expression. That minister who has beheld none converted by his means,—who, when he looks around his congregation, sees no man that owes his soul to him,—whose faithfulness has perhaps only irritated many, who, when he goes abroad, follow him with eyes that watch for his halting, and treat his name and character without deference, and without sentiments of filial regard;—such an one knows nothing of the endearing attachment that binds together a faithful pastor, who has won their souls to Christ, and a deeply-indebted flock. He may go or return without exciting any other interest than the interest of good neighbourhood among one class, or the interest that arises from the calculation of probable gain or loss among others more dependent. What a fine picture Mr Stewart draws in some of his letters, when, after an occasional absence, on drawing near to the habitations of his beloved people, now one, and now another, on discovering his approach, hastened to salute him, and to welcome his return! and how interesting must those Sabbaths have been, in which the Son of man showed his power, and sent forth the gospel invitation with an influence of grace the called could not resist! No wonder many resorted to such a highly-favoured spot, and that many were anxious to procure to their own congregations the benefit of Mr Stewart's occasional ministrations.

CHAPTER 5

ONGOING WORK IN MOULIN

OF Mr Stewart's prudence and spirit, both in the walks of humanity, and in efforts to guard his parishioners from the influence of temptation, the following extract of a letter to Mr Black affords an instance.

After apologizing to his correspondent for not paying a distant visit, he adds:—

'Matters occur almost weekly at home, which could not be so well done in my absence. By a concurrence of two or three providential circumstances, we have at last got R——, late schoolmaster at St Madoes, elected and settled here, a man who, I hope, will prove a valuable acquisition. But if I had been from home, and the election deferred, I suspect another might have been introduced not nearly so proper. A family, or rather two families in one house, consisting of a man, his wife, a widow lately deprived of her husband, and not a fortnight delivered of a posthumous child, with two or three other children, were all laid up at once in a fever, without a creature to attend them. The neighbours were willing to contribute anything to their support, but none would go near them for fear of infection. The families of Lude and Urrard offered any hire to a woman who would wait on the wretched invalids; a woman was found who was willing to undertake the unpleasant and dangerous charge. But her neighbours, and particularly the farmer from whom she rented her cottage, threatened her, if she went near the infected house, that they would turn all her furniture out of doors, and never admit her again among them. The miscreants were not of my parish. As soon as I was told of these circumstances (for the people resided in the extremity of this parish), I visited the sick family; found the man delirious, his wife next to insensible, and a crying child between them in one bed; in another, the widow with her young infant. Notwithstanding the open window, it was difficult to remain even a few minutes in the apartment. Accompanied by an elder and a tenant, I went in quest of the woman proposed for a nurse. We expostulated with her landlord, engaged the woman, carried her with us, and introduced her to her charge. By the direction of a surgeon, who had just called, the poor invalids were shifted and laid more comfortably in bed. Cordials were administered, and I left them quiet. Indeed, I had much reason to adore the goodness of the Lord in giving me such an opportunity of being useful, and in prospering the means employed. I expect to see the poor creatures again tomorrow, as I purpose to preach in the neighbourhood.

'Another occurrence, last week, called for my interference. Some of the young volunteers had planned a ball, and engaged some of the lightest girls in the neighbourhood to attend. I learned that they were contriving among themselves to spend the day abroad, and to attend the ball without their parents' knowledge. I have thought it my duty uniformly to discourage those foolish revels which increase youthful levity, and apply artificial heat to ripen the fruits of folly. I repaired first to the woman of the public house (her husband died the other winter) where the ball was to be kept. She assured me it was not agreeable to her, nor done with her consent. I then took my elder Mr W—— with me, and called on every young woman in the village. After a few words of introduction, I asked each, in presence of her father and mother, if she intended to go to the ball; taking at the same time my pen and ink, and writing the person's name and answer I received. Everyone answered me without hesitation, that she was not to go. I then made her give me her promise in the presence of her parents and the elder, that she would not go. This they all readily did, and I wrote it down. This was on the morning of the day appointed for the dance. The lads were abroad at drill. I called on two or three of them in the afternoon, and remonstrated with them. The result was, that there was no ball. It would have been extremely rash to set about any measure of this kind, without asking special direction from God. I trust I was directed. People learn soon to disregard admonitions from the pulpit, if they are not followed up in some way that shows the monitor to be in earnest, and concerned in the counsel he gives.'

It may be proper, in this place, to advert to the manner in which he acted in his ministerial capacity towards a class of his parishioners, with which, in general, it is very difficult to deal faithfully, without provoking an enmity that may obstruct one's usefulness to his people in matters of secular and public concern. It is *Heritors*[1] we mean, who, when openly irreligious, are not likely to strengthen a serious minister's hands in the work of his office. This it were unreasonable to expect; nor has any man just cause to complain of not finding it so. But what affords a ground of reasonable complaint in such cases is, that if they nominally belong to the Established Church, they judge themselves exempt from all

[1] [In a Scottish parish a heritor was a proprietor of lands or houses who was liable for the payment of such things as the minister's stipend and the school teacher's salary.]

jurisdiction as to religious character, and resent the refusal of privileges as a personal injury.

As soon as Mr Stewart had right views of the spiritual nature of the sacraments of the church, he became solicitous to see suitable character in those to whom they were administered. This led him to exercise much strictness in the examination of candidates for communion at the Lord's table; nor was he more negligent in the matter of *baptism*, not respecting the persons of poor or rich, when the glory of his Master, and the right administration of his ordinances, were concerned.

One of his heritors having the prospect of a family, and seeming to entertain no doubts of his qualifications for standing sponsor to his child, Mr Stewart, who had different views of his character and competency, anticipating the occasion, wrote him the following letter:—

'It must give pleasure to all your friends to find, that Mrs —— is likely to bring an addition to your family, and to continue the line of your forefathers, who have been so much respected in the country in which they lived. My sincere wish is that she may be preserved to be the happy mother of a thriving child. It is a serious matter to become a parent, to have an immortal soul committed to your care and keeping, to be trained up in the knowledge and service of God. If it be his will to bring your child alive and safe into the world, you will of course choose to have him baptised, according to the universal custom of our country. Permit me, my dear Sir, to remind you that this is a most solemn religious service; that a person ought never to go about it for the sake of custom, or fashion, but in order to please God, who has appointed it. At the same time, we cannot expect to please him in this service, unless we do it with proper views, and in a proper spirit. This implies, that we have a distinct knowledge of the several articles of the Christian religion to which baptism has a direct reference, and that we feel their influence in our hearts. Allow me, then, to suggest to your own consideration, how highly requisite it is that you should apply your mind seriously to this important subject, before you engage in such a solemn transaction between God and your soul. I wish with all my heart I could be any way assisting to you in this inquiry. Shall I write more fully on the subject? Shall I send you any books? Or will you give me leave to call upon you at ——, with the design of conversing about the things that are revealed in scripture? Indeed it is no vain or idle matter, but much the reverse; and it is especially necessary to be in earnest concerned about religion, when one has the prospect of engaging in such a solemn service as devoting his child to Christ in baptism, lest, for want of attention and knowledge, he should be found to deal falsely with the great God, who knows the heart.

'I hope I need make no apology for the freedom of this address, as I am sure it is prompted by the truest friendship; and I cannot suppose that you will take amiss what proceeds from the best intention. It would give me the highest pleasure to know that it had obtained your serious attention, and that of Mrs —— also, for each of you has a soul that will exist forever, and you are both equally concerned in the welfare of your offspring.'

This letter being well received, and a willingness to receive instruction expressed, Mr Stewart, on the birth of his child, addressed him once more; and, after compliments and inquiries, wrote:—

'My anxiety for your best interests, induces me to send you the Form of Baptism which I always use, in hopes that you will take the trouble to read it with attention. You will find shortly mentioned in it those peculiar doctrines of our religion, which every person who partakes of either of our sacraments professes to believe, and which, therefore, he would need to have studied thoroughly. You may compare it with the doctrines asserted, and the duties inculcated, in the office of baptism laid down in the Book of Common Prayer of the Church of England. You must judge, after considering the enclosed paper, whether you can faithfully and explicitly make the declarations and promises contained in it. In a solemn transaction like this, a person would need to be sure of what he says, and what he promises. It is not enough for a man to go through a form, and satisfy himself that he has done like others. If others go through the same form, without sufficiently considering what they are about, that may be partly their own fault, partly that of their teachers, but their neglect cannot excuse us. Be assured, my dear Sir, in one word, that unless you be yourself renewed by the Spirit of God, and heartily devoted to Christ, you cannot devote your child to him in baptism with that sincerity, and faith, and cordiality, which will make it an acceptable service to God. And if it be not an acceptable service to him, it were better not done at all. I wish and pray God, that these things may obtain your most serious consideration.'

This was an instance of ministerial faithfulness, which it is worthwhile to record, and it may be proposed as a pattern to others in like circumstances, who, from want of similar spirit, cannot bring themselves to deal conscientiously with persons of superior rank, and thus do violence to their own judgments, and lose opportunities for benefiting those whom they want resolution either to admonish or to instruct.

That none, however, may be surprised, if in some cases of this nature, disappointment be the result, we shall mention that Mr Stewart, with all his address, and fidelity, and acknowledged *purity of design*, did not always succeed in his endeavours. For, to another of his heritors, having written in the following terms:—

'While your friends and neighbours are all making kind inquiries about your health, which has been so poorly of late, may I be allowed to step forward among the rest, to express my anxious concern on your own account, and also on account of your dear lady, who must be painfully affected by your present indisposition. But indeed I come not to amuse or to flatter, but in a serious way to wish you well. It is a wish I strongly feel, but it is not confined to your bodily health, or your prosperity in the world. My wishes, believe me, extend much farther,—to a state of existence beyond the present. Perhaps an absence from the cares and objects which require so much of your attention at home, may allow you some leisure to extend your views in the same direction. And when your journey is taken in quest of health, which the blessing of God alone can give, it is a fit season to apply to him for a still higher blessing, which he alone can bestow also. I doubt not that you will get the best medical advice, and I do wish and pray that it may be of benefit to your health. But where, my dear Sir, shall we find the physician who will prescribe for your soul? or will you be prevailed on to follow the prescription? That your soul is diseased, sick unto death, and in danger of perishing, there cannot be a doubt, if God speaks true; and that there is but one remedy, and that an infallible one, is equally true. My fear is, and what induces me to write, that you do not suspect your danger, nor know your remedy. I wish I could think there was room to me to be mistaken—I wish I may hereafter find reason to form a different opinion,—what joy would it give me! But, with regard to the present state of your soul, I cannot help saying that my fears greatly predominate. Consider, dear Sir, have you ever studied the word of God as the rule of faith and practice? and are you sure you do believe it, and that your life has been conformed to it? or have you considered it as the standard by which we must all be tried and judged? and are you prepared to stand such a trial? Unless an invalid *take* the medicine prescribed, it can be of no benefit to him. So, unless you understand, and approve, and apply to your own case, the doctrine of the gospel concerning the salvation of sinners, Christ's salvation can be of no benefit to you. I will pursue this no farther, but only to take the liberty of urging the strong necessity of inquiring and attending to these most important objects, while life and ability are given; especially when divine Providence is reminding you that life is uncertain, and eternity approaching. It is possible you may not be provided with proper helps. There are many fashionable sermons, which contain many good and useful things, but which do not explicitly declare the way of salvation, nor teach the knowledge of Jesus Christ. I wish I knew how I could be useful to you in this way. The enclosed letter came lately in my way, I think it worthy of more than one serious perusal. Let me now, my dear Sir, wish you a safe journey, that your health may be restored and prolonged; but, above all, that you may *know*, and *love*, and *serve* the blessed Redeemer, and through him obtain eternal life and happiness. That you and Mrs —— may be joint partakers of this blessedness, is the sincere prayer of,' etc.

The answer contained little more than a request, that Mr Stewart will in future give his advice when asked *only*.

Previous to the above correspondence, the same gentleman had sent Mr Stewart notice to 'be at —— on Friday at half past five o'clock, to perform the ceremony of giving a name to his son.' Mr Stewart having sent word, that 'on such a solemn occasion as that of devoting a child to Christ in baptism, it was requisite to have some previous conversation concerning the principles of the Christian religion, which a parent ought to know and believe, and the religious duties which he ought to practise, before he can with sincerity make the professions, and come under the engagements, which are required in dispensing that sacred ordinance'; the following was the laconic reply; 'Mr and Mrs —— do not require Mr Stewart to attend at —— this evening.'

Mr Stewart's heritors had concurred with him in various expedients of his proposal for effecting reformation in the parish, being satisfied of the reasonableness of his plans, and of the wisdom of supporting him in carrying them into effect for the common good.

Among other abuses which he aimed to have corrected, he made an attempt to abolish Sunday proclamations, relative to sales and other secular business, of which, in many parishes, it is still customary to give audible notice in the churchyard, by the beadle[1] as a public crier, immediately on the congregation being dismissed. This palpable relic of the barbarous age of Popery, during the full sway of which, the Sunday was a busy day among pedlars and chapmen, in places distant from market towns, who exposed their wares in the churchyard, it is high time to interdict; for what more unseemly, than to come directly from the publication of salvation, to be informed of what is to be sold throughout the district in the progress of the week.

In most parishes, however, the crier's proclamation has given place to advertisements, often placarded on the very walls of the church, the resort to which is a painful sight to one that cares for the sanctity of the place and day; while so little respect is paid to the Lord's day and service by the public authorities, that sometimes, on our pronouncing the valedictory blessing on the

[1] [The beadle, sometimes called the church officer, was an official appointed by the kirk session to care for the place of worship and to perform other similar functions. '"Minister's man," custodian of church buildings, guide, philosopher and friend to old and young alike, he has figured in more anecdotes and been etched by more pens than anyone except the minister himself.'—*New International Dictionary of the Christian Church*, ed. J. D. Douglas (Grand Rapids, MI: Zondervan, 1974, p.113.)]

congregation, the sound has hardly ceased to vibrate on the serious ear, when every feeling of duty and propriety is outraged, by the sudden eruption, from the precentor's desk,[1] of an official mandate to pay taxes, under penalty, at time and place prescribed.

The laws of our country we respect, but we cannot approve their spirit and tendency, when they bear on the practical abrogation of the law of God. Surely other expedients might be devised for giving notoriety to public or to private transactions of a secular interest, without encroaching on times set apart for higher concerns, and without lessening the sanctity of a day, the contempt of which has a most demoralizing influence on society.

In Moulin, the old practice of intimating the public business of the week at the parish church-door was in use. Aware of its inconsistency with the proper business of the day, Mr Stewart, who, it seems, had not the power to suppress it himself, addressed the resident heritors on the subject in the following circular:—

'I beg leave to request your attention to a subject which has for a considerable time engaged my thoughts.

'It is evident that by the establishment of Sunday schools, under the patronage of the heritors, and by discontinuing the practice of drinking on Sunday after

[1] [A desk or lectern at the front of the church at which the precentor led the singing of Psalms without musical accompaniment.]

marriages, christenings, and funerals, the morals of the people have been, at least in some measure, improved, and the profanation of the Lord's day has been in many instances prevented. A strict observance of the Sabbath has ever been found closely connected with the interests of religion and morality. It is an important point to preserve a sacred regard to the Lord's day, whether we respect the good of the people, or the authority of him who instituted the Sabbath, and commanded us to keep it holy. Now, it appears to me that there is one practice still prevalent among us, which is a direct breach of the Sabbath, and I wish much to have the countenance and assistance of the gentlemen of the parish to get it abolished. The practice I mean is that of making proclamations on Sunday relative to country business, etc. This is as contrary to the religious observance of that day as transacting secular affairs, which, you know, is expressly prohibited. At the same time, however, that I earnestly wish this unlawful custom to be set aside, I would like to have some other expedient proposed to be adopted in its stead. Suppose that some public conspicuous place were appointed, on which advertisements might be posted, either in Moulin or Pitlochry, or both; and that the church officer should have the charge of taking in advertisements, posting them up, and preserving them from damage, every day except Sunday. The number of persons who can read and write is now such, that the contents of these advertisements would be easily known, and soon spread over the country. When once this method was established, it would become customary for every person who passed through the village, to inquire if there was anything new on the advertising post; and would have this advantage, that an intimation could be made at any time of the week, without waiting the return of Sunday.

'Particular cases may indeed occur, especially in what relates to the defence of the country, in which it may be warrantable not only to make public notifications, but even to arm, to march, and to fight on Sunday. I would have no scruple to stop in the middle of a sermon, in order to make an intimation of that kind. I speak at present only of proclamations relative to common affairs, and secular business.

'As to the practicability of carrying on country business without Sunday proclamations, I know country parishes where the practice has been long unknown. And I know, that in our own parish, roups[1] have been made, and sufficiently well attended, which never were notified by proclamation; and that some tenants and others, for upwards of two years past, have never caused a proclamation to be made on Sunday, on any account whatever.

'I have thought it best, Sir, to submit these things to your consideration by letter, that you may have time to attend leisurely to the subject on which I have taken the liberty of addressing you. If the matter strikes you as it

[1] [That is, auctions.]

does me, I hope you will approve of making the experiment how the proposed substitute of written advertisements, instead of proclamation, will answer. Or if any better mode occur to you, or to any other heritor, I shall be happy to receive your instructions about it, and to join with you in recommending and carrying it into effect.'

After two months deliberation on this memorial, the heritors to whom it was submitted sent word to Mr Stewart, 'We all concur in one sentiment, that proclamations shall continue to be made in the same manner as at present.'

During the greater part of Mr Stewart's continuance at Moulin, his country, in common with the rest of Europe, felt the vast shock which almost the whole civilized world received, from the revolutionary frenzy that so long agitated France.[1] And it is proper to remark, that he was by no means an unconcerned spectator of passing events. Indeed, it appears from his correspondence with Mr Black, that both these individuals watched the varying aspects of Providence towards the nations of Europe, with a pious and most ardent observation.

[1] [A reference to the events of the French Revolution of 1789–99, which included the overthrow of the French monarchy, the subsequent 'Reign of Terror,' and seizing of power in a military coup led by Napoleon Bonaparte.]

Let it not be thought, however, they so far forgot their calling as to become immersed in the political theories of the day. Their Lord's kingdom is not of this world,—a fact too little adverted to by many among the professed subjects of his grace, who plunge into political discussion with intemperate zeal. Mr Stewart formed his *political* principles on the spirit and precept of the gospel institute; and he who brings an unbiased mind to the subject, with the New Testament before him, will seldom be at a loss what line of conduct to adopt and to pursue. In what a serious light Mr Stewart viewed national providences, and the relation that subsists between rulers and subjects, will appear from the following extract of a letter written in 1803.

'For some weeks past, I have been assailed with a trial rather new to me. I have thought it my duty, since the commencement of the present war,[1] to try occasionally to explain to my people the circumstances of the country, and the object of calling out the people to take arms, etc. I was happily successful, and my services proved highly gratifying to the gentry. They were not backward

[1] [Britain declared war on France on 18 May 1803, ending the peace ushered in by the 1802 Treaty of Amiens after just fourteen months. The immediate cause of the rupture was the status of Malta, which Britain refused to evacuate in accordance with the terms of the peace treaty. It is generally understood that behind Britain's refusal was a sense of loss of control, as well as loss of markets, and the threat posed by Napoleonic France to Britain's overseas colonies.]

to acknowledge this. After consulting with his brother officers, Colonel B—— wrote me a letter bearing very ample testimony to my patriotic exertions, and offering me the appointment of Chaplain to the Athole Regiment of Volunteers, under his command. This I did not hesitate to accept. It gave me access, *ex efficio*,[1] to all the men of the several companies, to give them advice without being chargeable with officiousness. All this, however, I found a snare. Even in doing what I thought became me to do, I ever found motives of vanity mixing with those of duty. The people, too, were ready to ascribe much of what I said to an undue compliance with the wishes of the gentry. From this suspicious situation, I was in a good measure relieved by a compliment I did not expect. On the very evening before the public fast, I received a card, written in the name of Colonel —— and the other officers, inviting Mrs Stewart and me to a ball and supper at the next inn, on the following Tuesday. This appeared very unsuitable and unseasonable an entertainment, at such a juncture, that I animadverted in my fast-day sermon on all manner of levity, as a disregard of the divine rebuke, and introduced Isaiah 22:12-14. And as it was necessary to answer the card of invitation, I wrote a letter to Colonel —— stating my views pretty freely. I really found it a relief to have something to do in the line of duty, that did not flatter the inclinations of carnal men. The day of the said ball was to be a field-day

[1] [That is, by virtue of his position as chaplain.]

with our corps. I thought it my duty to appear on the parade. The Colonel took civil notice of me as usual, and asked me to take my station along with the officer on the right of the line, in saluting the General. This was the whole of my exhibition, and when the exercise was over, I came home. I hope I have been divinely guided in this matter, for however my mind may have wavered, and my motives been greatly mixed with carnal and selfish views, yet I do not yet see that my outward conduct has been improper.'

Whether Mr Stewart, or those light-hearted warriors, were the better friends of their country, and which of them exhibited most of patriotism in their views, it is not difficult, on the principles of Christianity, to decide. On the eve of a public fast, to appoint a ball, was a bold challenge to public opinion; but to invite to their assembly a man of Mr Stewart's known sanctity of habit, and the uniform reprover of such levities, was surely carrying complaisance to an extraordinary height.

Mr Stewart had accepted the military chaplaincy, which was without emolument, in order to be useful to the men composing the Volunteer Battalion, being always intent on means for advancing the interests of his Lord. An address he delivered in this new capacity was afterwards published, and could not fail to be read with much interest at the time, as it was written on the supposition, then very prevalent, that an actual invasion would be attempted, and contained precepts adapted to such an emergency, not overlooking the aspect of Providence, nor forgetting to warn every man to flee from the wrath to come. But it is enough just to advert to these matters, in order to exhibit Mr Stewart's character as it bore on the civil government of his country, and to show how far he stood removed, on the one side, from servile unchristian compliances with the prejudices of the high or low, and on the other, from unchristian indifference to the political circumstances of his country, or an hostility to the powers that be.[1]

[1] In this Address, after proving the lawfulness of defensive war, and vindicating the power of the magistrate to call forth sufficient means for repelling aggression, he adds:—

'We go on sure ground, while we thus see that we have the command of God to authorise us to take up arms at the call of our rulers, to defend our civil rights against an assailing enemy. It is with the highest satisfaction, my friends, I observe that you have undertaken this important duty, with an alacrity and cheerfulness which do credit to yourselves, and to your country. While most of the French troops have been dragged like slaves to the camp, and compelled to follow a standard which they detested, to feed the insatiable ambition of a tyrant; you rise to oppose lawless depredation, and *voluntarily* flock to the standard of your Landlords, to guard from brutal outrage your Sovereign, your Country, and your Homes. The name of VOLUNTEERS, with which you are dignified, testifies to the public the readiness and good-will with which you stepped forward to occupy the post assigned you.

'In this kind of military service, there is no room for jealousy between gentry and common people. We know how ready some persons of pretended wisdom are, to fill your heads with suspicions of the gentry, as if they always rolled the burden off themselves on

As a minister of an ecclesiastical establishment, it concerns us more to put the reader in possession of his sentiments and views on the religious polity to which he was attached. He entered the church under the auspices of the moderate party, as it is called, some of whom, and particularly Professor G. Hill,[1] afterwards so well known in church courts, interested themselves in procuring his settlement at Moulin. With Dr Hill he appears to have been in habits of intimacy at the time of his ordination; and, with the exception of his correspondence with Mr Black, his intercourse lay wholly with men of moderate principles, prior to his own decided change of heart. Then, as was to be expected, he ranged himself under other banners, and without the least tincture of bad feelings towards his former associates, passed over to men of congenial ardour in the cause of Christ. We have seen how earnestly he sought the acquaintance of evangelical ministers in the city; and with those around him, or within a visiting distance, he cultivated the closest relations of brotherly love.[2]

---

your shoulders, and exposed you to toil and danger, while they saved themselves. In the present case, it is plainly the reverse. The gentry take an equal share of the toil, and more than a double share of the danger; for it is well known, that an enemy would wish rather to kill one officer, or take him prisoner, than six privates.'

[1] [George Hill (1750–1819), minister of St Andrews (1780–1819) and a professor in the University of St Andrews.]

[2] Among these may be particularly mentioned, the late Mr Scott of Perth, and Mr Willison of Forgandenny, as much esteemed by Mr Stewart, and deservedly dear to him.

In the business of church courts, he was the farthest possible from affecting to lead; and though he had diligently studied the laws and constitution of the Established Church,—and from his uniform self-possession, and ready copiousness of elocution, and power of argument, few were better qualified to make a figure in ecclesiastical causes,—he does not seem, during his settlement at Moulin, to have taken a prominent place in any court, supreme or subordinate.

There was one part of his conduct at Moulin which tried the forbearance of his moderate co-presbyters, and which some of his warmest friends thought needed to be excused. About the period of his decidedly embracing the truth, a great impulse had been given to the Christian community by the spirit of zeal which burst forth in the south, and which bore down before it the mounds which party names and prejudices had erected, to mark the peculiarities of their own narrow grounds of distinction. All men who held the essential truth, awakened with surprise to a conviction of their past supineness and inactivity, and looking abroad on the vast extent of the unchristianized world (feeling alive at the same time to the obligations of duty, to seek the enlargement of Christ's kingdom, and the salvation of perishing mankind), wide and generous combinations were formed, for calling into action the general resources of the well-disposed of all denominations. The formation of the British and Foreign Bible Society will be a monument to after ages, both of the wisdom and the zeal then abroad in the Christian community of England.

But what had given the most sensible impulse to the Christian feeling in Scotland, was the formation of the London Missionary Society, which, comprehending in its general plan Christians of every denomination, irrespective of lesser differences, or external modes of worship, opened a channel of exertion to the zeal of all.

Evangelical ministers of the Church of Scotland hailed the institution, and gave it their utmost support. The flame of zeal which had been kindled for foreign missions, lighted on laymen as well as on the clergy; and home missions were undertaken, which at first were carried on by pious laymen. In a little time it appeared that some ministers in the church, feeling themselves straitened by the constitution, or actual regimen of the national establishment, had begun to think such establishments at variance with the fundamental rights of Christian men, united in the fellowship of the gospel; and several withdrew themselves on the ground of the unlawfulness or inexpediency of national churches, which owe their establishment and support to the civil power, and which they scrupled not to denominate branches of the mystical Babylon. These having gradually receded from connection with the Establishment, had places of worship erected in the principal towns, and formed societies on the principles of those called Independents. As Mr Stewart was on friendly terms with some of those who took the lead in separating from the Establishment, he continued to maintain his former Christian intercourse; and as lay-preaching was extensively practised among them, and their missionaries spread themselves over the country, he often came in contact with their agents.

Probably some of them thought no minister, who himself knew the truth, and walked uprightly, could conscientiously remain in communion with the national church; and some expectations were perhaps entertained of Mr Stewart's secession; at least, attempts to shake his principles in the article of national churches, were not wanting.

'I had a very kind letter,' says he, 'from your neighbour ——, which drew from me an answer of some length. He is such a good man that I cannot behave shyly towards him; yet I am almost afraid of being entangled in a correspondence with him. My dear brother —— too, would not care to draw me into a friendly debate about the shackles of establishments, and the freedom and advantage of independence. He wrote me a few weeks ago, applying roundly to myself a text on which he had heard me preach at Dundee, "Loose him and let him go." I answered him in such a decided manner, that I suppose he will hardly think of resuming the subject.'

In another letter he writes:

'Mr S. cautions me not to encourage —— too much. It is right. It is impossible to go all lengths with ——. I must stop short somewhere, and then he will be as much hurt as if I had yielded nothing.

'I could find in my heart to write on confessions, as it is a subject on which my mind is quite clear and settled, and on which a deal of stark nonsense has been said, which is not worth combating, but the effects of which might be easily obviated by a plain statement of the end and use of confessions.'

Situated as Mr Stewart was, amid a people called under his ministry, and among whom he had every facility to preach the gospel, and to exercise discipline to the utmost desirable extent, one would be at a loss to find out a justifiable reason for throwing up his pastoral charge; yet it seems others wondered at his blindness, in not seeing it unlawful to maintain the station he held, and seemed to construe his civilities to their agents, into a proof of his disaffection for the church. Even some of his friends were alarmed at the countenance he gave to the itinerants; and though less interest now attaches to the discussion, yet amid the activity of conflicting sects, as others may be placed in circumstances not very dissimilar from his, it may be useful to hear one, who had much of the mind of Christ, explain the principles on which he acted, as they are stated in a letter written to one of his brethren of the presbytery. This letter is worthy of preservation, for other reasons than any connected with the question of lay preaching.

'If I could have accepted your kind invitation, and stayed at D—— last Tuesday night, I should have wished for a half-hour's conversation with you about the itinerating missionaries. If you will have patience to read a long letter, I shall endeavour to state now, what I would have said then. I have long been desirous to explain myself on this subject, wherever I thought I might not be misunderstood, especially to you, in whose candour I have the fullest confidence, and from whom I have experienced much kindness, and unwearied civility. I cannot but regret, that the peculiar circumstances in which I have been placed, have given occasion to any person to hold me up as a contrast to the neighbouring clergymen, and made me almost an eyesore to my brethren. Indeed, I have, for a considerable time past, reckoned myself much indebted to the forbearance and delicacy of my co-presbyters, in not taking me roundly to task, for giving such countenance to men whom they considered as actuated by the most unfriendly intentions. Perhaps I am not far mistaken in supposing, that you, in particular, may have incurred reprehension from some of your acquaintance, for continuing to treat as a friend and intimate, one who had become such an apostate. I assure you, my dear Sir, I feel my obligations to you on this account.

'I think I hinted to you some time ago, that it is not many years since I came to understand what are the peculiar doctrines of our religion. My views of Christianity were till then very imperfect and confused, and my apprehensions of the importance of its doctrines were proportionally obscure. I had no solicitude about my own, or my people's eternal state. A certain constitutional mildness of disposition recommended me to their esteem, but neither they nor I had discernment to perceive that I was doing them no good. In these respects, my mind did certainly undergo a very material change. It was accompanied neither with melancholy nor with ecstasy, but I understood and perceived things which I had not understood or perceived before. It was then first I saw the vast importance of the ministerial work, and felt an anxiety about the spiritual concerns of my people. This took place before I had seen Mr ——, or any of his present associates. The more important the truths of Christianity appeared to myself, I became the more desirous to have them explained and inculcated on others. Both the matter and the manner of my instructions were changed, in private as well as in public. I believe the bulk of my parishioners soon observed this; but it was some time before they went along with me. By degrees, however, many of them became more or less acquainted with the doctrines which they heard from me, and were impressed with them accordingly. By this time I had formed a personal intimacy with Mr ——. A similarity of views and feelings on the most interesting of all subjects, strengthened that intimacy. When he came here, I knew that his exhortations on religious subjects would be such as I could recommend to my people; and I judged that a pertinent address from a stranger could not fail to excite attention, and would probably make a lasting impression. Sensible how very inadequate my individual labours were to the work assigned me, I was willing to avail myself of this occasional aid. My people perceived at once the striking coincidence between what they heard from the stranger, and what they heard from their minister. They judged that both were much in earnest, and seriously concerned for the souls of their hearers. They had already remarked that this manner of preaching was essentially different from what they had been accustomed to hear from me during seven or eight years of my ministry. This coincidence in doctrine and manner of instruction between me and the itinerants who occasionally passed this way, served to recommend both parties to the esteem of my people,—I speak of the majority of the people only; for I believe there are some among them who dislike me and my preaching, as much as they do the itinerants. I have the fullest reason to believe that none of these itinerants have spoken anything in this parish but what was agreeable to sound doctrine, and free of every tendency towards sedition or disaffection.

'I have neither sagacity nor address for a politician; but I believe, that in countenancing these missionaries, so far as I have done, from much better motives than political ones, I have just done what good policy would have suggested. These men would have assembled the people, and would have been listened to whether I pleased or not. Had I kept aloof, and showed them no countenance, while they spake nothing but what was useful and acceptable to the people, my people would have become jealous of me, and suspected me of partiality and hypocrisy. But now, by having showed my approbation of what appeared good in these men (and we have seen nothing else), my people are the more disposed to give me credit, if I should hereafter find occasion to warn them against individuals who may appear to me suspicious. I have not failed repeatedly to caution them in general against giving themselves up to the guidance of strangers, who may come, just like these itinerants, with the Bible in their hands, and the scripture in their mouths, and yet may really be impostors. And, on the same principle, I have always vindicated our landed gentlemen, for keeping a watchful eye over strangers, who come about in such a questionable shape.

'As these men have excited much attention, and are "everywhere spoken against," it will of course happen, that much more is said against them than is true. This makes me very slow in giving credit to the many unfavourable reports that I hear about them. Their leaders are suspected of the most mischievous designs.

Of this I have seen no evidence; and so long as it is only matter of conjecture and opinion, I must say that my opinion is widely different, and that all they have actually done, setting aside exaggerated reports, and unsubstantiated charges, appears to me sufficiently accounted for, by the motives and objects which they have avowed. It was necessary to state this as my opinion explicitly, else you must have thought me shamefully inconsistent, if I continued to keep any correspondence with these men, while I concurred in opinion with those who think them the enemies of their country, and of their species. It is possible, indeed, I may be mistaken, and, when well authenticated facts shall show it (for while so many mouths are opened, I can give little credit to flying report), I think I shall be as ready to believe solid evidence, and acknowledge my mistake, as another.

'I wish everyone who concerns himself any way about me, and you, my good friend, in particular, to be assured, that I am most cordially attached to the Church of Scotland—to her faith, worship, etc.; nor would any earthly bribe, as I think, induce me at present to desert her. I am likewise convinced, that if we, her clergy, possessing the many advantages we do possess, were in general as enlightened, and faithful, and zealous, as many of our predecessors, no sectaries could run away with her people, nor any way endanger her prosperity. But I well know what a lame support I should have proved to the church a few years ago, and how little the personal attachment of my people, and my skill or influence, would have availed to keep them from deserting me and my temple, and following to the field sectaries who should have at that time introduced among them the vital truths of Christianity. And I have no doubt that a defection in favour of the Itinerants would have taken place here before now, if it had not been providentially ordered that I myself first taught these truths, and that my people heard them from me, before they heard them from strangers. Convinced of the need there is for my labouring more incessantly among my people than I had been accustomed to do, I have endeavoured to take a lesson of diligence from these Itinerants, and to obtain a portion of their zeal. And if I am enabled to labour with fidelity, and if I succeed in teaching my people true religion, I am sure I shall have done more to keep them united together, and attached to the church, than by inveighing against men in whom they have seen no evil.

'*Me voilà,*[1] as the French say, I have surely laid my case and sentiments before you. I was anxious to do it, partly that I might not appear worse than I am in the estimation of a brother, on whose good opinion I really put a high value, and partly to guard against any misunderstanding which might arise from the casual interference of our parishioners, or from the officious commendations of Itinerants, or others. I have told honestly the grounds of that favour which I seem to

[1] ['This is me.']

have shown to the society for propagation of the gospel at home, and of which their missionaries seem to have vaunted in this part of the country. The incidental agreement, if it may be called incidental, between me and the missionaries of that society, in religious doctrine, in the object we both profess to pursue, and in our method of pursuing it, together with my known intimacy with some of its members, may have induced a persuasion that I am connected with the society, and an abettor of all its measures. This is a mistake. I have no connection with that society,—I know but few of its members,—my favour, so far as a little civility went, was shown only to two or three of its individuals, and that on the ground of their being Christian brethren, who laid themselves out, according to their ability, to press on the attention of all sorts of people the leading doctrines of Christianity,—a labour which appeared to me by no means superfluous or unnecessary, as I thought, and still think, these doctrines are in general little attended to or understood.'

But while Mr Stewart vindicated his conduct with respect to the Itinerant teachers, he was far from being indifferent as to what opinions his flock should form on the minor points of church order.

'I happened to call one day,' says he, 'on ——. She told me she had a book that was sent her to read, but she was half afraid to tell me what it was. She did tell me, however, that it was Letters by ——, that she had read but little of it, and that she did not like to read more, for it only made her unsettled and uneasy. I said I had no doubt of Mr ——'s sincerity and good intention in what he had done and written, but that there were many men of the first eminence for piety and usefulness, who were as decided in holding a different opinion from Mr ——, and adhering to the Church of Scotland. I named Boston, Willison, Rutherford,[1] and others, whose character and writings she was acquainted with. She said, "I wonder what way Mr Newton is of?" I told her, to her great surprise, that Mr Newton was of a different way from them all, and that he had examined, leisurely and deeply, all the ways of them, and made a most deliberate choice, and that he had never seen reason to repent or regret the choice he had made. When I came home, I looked out and marked several parts of Mr Newton's *Apologia*,[2] which I carried to ——, and read to her. She acknowledged, with much thankfulness, that she had heard nothing which so perfectly satisfied and composed her mind.'

It is no new thing for such men as Mr Stewart to be stigmatized as enemies to the church to which they belong,

[1] [Thomas Boston (1676–1732), John Willison (1680–1750), and Samuel Rutherford (1600–61) were all outstanding ministers of the Church of Scotland— Boston in Simprin and Ettrick, Willison in Dundee, and Rutherford in Anwoth.]

[2] [*Apologia: Four Letters to a Minister of an Independent Church* by the Rev. John Newton (1725–1807).]

though, like him, they cordially embrace the original principles of her polity, and act according to the spirit and the tenor of her fundamental laws. Those laws had his deliberate approval; the manner, however, in which they were administered frequently met with his undissembled reprobation. The enactment which prohibited the employment of such a man as Mr Simeon, to whose ministry he was indebted for his own soul, could hardly commend itself to his enlightened judgment; as it went to preclude the possibility of any other deriving a similar benefit in the same way. And some of the measures devised about that time, to strengthen the guards and fences of the church, he thought, had an obvious tendency to expose her weakness, and lay her more open to assault.

But in his happy retirement from the metropolitan arena of discussion and of contest, he never entered into consultation with a calculating and a worldly prudence, how far Christian love should be shown to those who loved Christ, and who, though on somewhat different views, sincerely sought the conversion of souls, and the glory of God. His heart and his house were open to them, and he had no mean jealousy lest their success should eclipse the lustre of his own; and though the zeal of many of those men was soon diverted into a variety of little channels, that narrowed into straiter charity as they ran; it must be confessed, that impressions were then made on a number of careless people, with a name to live, the effects of which, doubtless, caused joy in heaven, and afforded new incentives to praise him, who worketh according to the counsel of his own will.

Whatever approbation may be yielded to the motives and the zeal of the Itinerants, however, it is difficult to assign a reason for their activity at Moulin, where such a labourer as Mr Stewart was already in full employment, and while so many places were confessedly in greater need of evangelical cultivation. He seems to have acted on a different principle, who said, 'Yea, so have I strived to preach the gospel, not where Christ was named, lest I should build upon another man's foundation. But, as it is written, To whom he was not spoken of, they shall see: and they that have not heard shall understand' (Rom. 15:20, 21).[1]

[1] 'It was the apostle's ambition (so the original word signifies), to carry the glad tidings of salvation to those who had not before heard of Christ; and thus to face the dangers and hardships of making the first assault on the kingdom of Satan, in every place. Nor was he disposed, in general, to build on the foundation laid by other ministers, who were competent to carry on the work which they had happily begun; but rather to fulfil the scripture, which foretold that many nations and rulers would see and understand such things, as they had before been strangers to (Isa. 52:15). Probably, in mentioning this, he may glance on those false apostles, who crept into churches which he had planted, and endeavoured to establish their own reputation and influence there, by alienating the hearts of his own converts from him; while, like some in our days, they built on his grand and noble foundation, an edifice of wood, and hay, and stubble.'—Scott's Commentary.

CHAPTER 6

A CHANGE OF PASTORATE

BUT we must now return to Mr Stewart's more personal history. In the month of August 1802, on the invitation of several ministers who had sought his fellowship in consequence of what they had heard of the doings at Moulin, he took a journey to Ross-shire, being led by a way he knew not, and for purposes which, when he set out, were most foreign from his thoughts. Among other esteemed brethren in that country, he visited Mr Charles Calder of Urquhart, a minister, whose father and grandfather had shone as stars of the first magnitude in the church, and who himself in no wise diminished the lustre of the name and office transmitted to him from such ancestors. Mr C. had none of that constitutional vigour, which enables a man to throw into his public appearances the interest and the attraction which arise from decision of *tone*, and power of action; yet there was in his gentleness something so *saintly*, and in his aspect such an air of indescribable *benignity*, while his doctrine was *Christ*, and his aim evidently to win souls to the Saviour he preached, that, in the absence of voice, gesture, and artificial oratory, no man could regard him in the pulpit without being overawed by the calm and sober majesty of his appearance, and few could resist the simple, yet deep-felt strain of his address. In his church was to be seen an auditory collected from many adjoining, and some distant parishes, listening with the most compressed attention, yet not listening to *admire*, nor, with high-worked passions, intent on the wondrous man, but each one sitting as intent on himself, and as if none besides were interested in the preacher's address. And while the tones of the speaker scarcely struck on the ears of a careless stranger, who went in casually or from curiosity, and complained of an inaudible preacher, they reached the inmost soul of the serious and devout. Mr Calder's ministry was eminently successful, and, though meek and modest almost to timidity, he was bold for Christ. In his family, the daily topics of conversation were, the general interests of Christ's kingdom, and the joys or sorrows of individual Christians, in whose vicissitudes he exquisitely sympathized: glad, or grieved, as others of the Lord's people felt around him. Mrs C. who was of one of the first families in the North, moved and shone in her own sphere with equal constancy and grace.

To this family Mr Stewart was directed, intending only a wayfaring man's abode.

'When I came to his house,' says he, 'on Wednesday last, I supposed that it might probably occur to him to ask my assistance at dispensing the Lord's Supper, the time of which was at hand; and I had made up my mind to resist every solicitation of the kind. When he accompanied me to my bedroom, he pressed me earnestly on the subject, but I steadily refused. Next day before dinner (for I stayed till the evening), Mr and Mrs Calder both renewed their entreaties, not at all in the way of mere urgent importunity, but in the most tender and spiritual manner. Mr Calder appears to be a man not so old in years, as he is debilitated by much labour, and an infirm constitution; Mrs Calder is a very superior woman for piety and intelligence. I cannot now relate all they said to prevail with me. After talking, we separated, and thought, and prayed, and cried, till we were half ashamed to appear to each other. I was to go on that evening to P. R——'s. We got early tea. Mrs Calder shook me by the hand, but could not take a final leave. Mr Calder had ordered his horse to be saddled, and accompanied me nearly four miles to a ferry, in hopes that I might yet be directed to consent to stay. It occupied much of our thoughts, as we rode silently together. I at last thought, that if it were indeed the Lord's will to keep me here to assist at Urquhart, it could not be perhaps more expressly intimated to me, than by such continued earnest entreaty made by his dear servants, not on their own personal behalf only, but on account of their people. If any society, or Christian fellowship, could afford the prospect of spiritual advantage to myself, it would be such as I enjoy in this country, where the savour of divine things is so strong. I trust I shall engage a strong reinforcement of prayers here, in behalf of my dear people. Before parting with Mr Calder, I did, in dependence on the Lord's good pleasure, settle it, that I should spend the preaching days at his house, and assist as I should be enabled, and the dear man left me full of gratitude to God.'

Mr Stewart was afterwards connected with this family by a closer tie, the eldest daughter of Mr Calder having been united to him in marriage, with the cordial approbation of all friends; on which occasion he wrote Mr Black, 'that it had pleased the Lord to enrich him with one of the most precious temporal blessings he had to bestow.'

Of this union, it is sufficient to say, that to the end of his life, Mr Stewart regarded it as a special blessing. And were the letters he wrote to Mrs Stewart, during an occasional absence, nearly twenty years after the period of their marriage, to be submitted to the reader, it would appear, that Newton was not singular in the strain of ardent, yet respectful affection, which runs through *Letters to a Wife*.

As Mr Stewart's family was increasing, it became evident to all, how inadequate the emoluments of his parish were for their support. These emoluments, I believe, seldom exceeded £70 a year; and as he withheld not his contributions from institutions that had lately sprung up in the Christian world, for the diffusion of Christianity, and was both hospitable by inclination, and peculiarly exposed to have his hospitality put in requisition by the numerous visitants whom his character and operations attracted to Moulin, it could hardly escape the observation of his friends, that some accession to his income was become necessary. There was a general feeling in behalf of the Moulin people, and almost everyone revolted from the idea of being necessary to a separation. However, an impartial and unprejudiced view of the case reconciled many to the prospect; and in 1805, it appears, various plans were in agitation for effecting his translation to Edinburgh,—plans, into which Mr Black entered most warmly. In the midst of these, the parish of Dingwall, adjoining to Urquhart, became vacant; and a very general desire was manifested in that town, to obtain a presentation for Mr Stewart to the charge. This prospect was hardly opened, until he was informed by Mr Black, that another had been appointed. Then he seriously took into consideration his proposed removal to Edinburgh, and wrote to Mr Black the exercises of his mind on the subject.

'I shall now, my dear Sir, submit to you what has thus far occurred to us, in considering the question of removal to Edinburgh. As to the state of the people here, there has been no gross declension nor scandalous falling off, among those who appear to be truly enlightened. But we cannot reckon on any accession to their number for many months past. There is, or appears to be, a diminution of liveliness, and a dullness of spirit hanging over the most of us. A still uniformity prevails throughout our manner of living and outward circumstances, which furnishes nothing to interest us in behalf of each other. I do not think our attachment to each other is abated, but it is less excited and kept in exercise than it was formerly. The real Christians among us are well established in faith and knowledge. Some years ago, I should have thought it more dangerous to have left them exposed to the various winds of doctrine, than now, and I believe they would have been more hurt at the thought of a separation. Indeed, if they should get a young evangelical minister in exchange for me, I am persuaded the affections and interests which would be excited, would enliven their devotion, and prove of material advantage. But, if they got one of a different description, the consequences would be melancholy.

'As to temporalities, there is no prospect of my emoluments being increased. The stipend cannot be augmented; the manse is growing more uncomfortable every season; and with wars and taxes, it is very uncertain when the Heritors may be prevailed upon to build a new one. I used to shrink from the idea of living in Edinburgh; my aversion to it, I own, is abated. In Edinburgh I would find plenty to do, more, I ween,[1] than I could accomplish. I have not yet mentioned the proposal that divine Providence has brought under consideration, to any besides my sister and Mrs Stewart. I intend to communicate it, however, to some of our pious neighbours, to request their prayers, and to see what impression it shall make on their minds.

'We had a discussion with Mr K. about Edinburgh schemes, and tried to take a large view of the question. As I had been looking most to reasons for remaining here, Mr K. and sister (and I believe Mrs S. joined them), stated the arguments on the other side,—that it was not withdrawing from my Master's service, but only transferring my labour from a more confined to a more enlarged and diversified field;—that the variety of duty, together with the opportunities of improvement attending a residence in Edinburgh, would bring into exercise talents which at present are dormant for want of scope and cultivation;—that one's powers are kept

[1] [That is, I think, suppose.]

more awake, and one's labour more productive, when directed into different channels, than when moving in one unvaried track;—that providing for the maintenance and education of one's family, is itself a duty of no little moment; and that it is much more consistent with duty to embrace a provision of this kind, when providentially offered in the way of ministerial service, than to go in quest of it by engaging in farming, and other secular employment in the country;—that if the present proposal (supposing it realized) be rejected, there is no probability of a similar opportunity occurring again; and though it should occur at the distance of some years, yet, as rustic habits would be gaining strength, and mind and body losing vigour, I should be less qualified then than now, for discharging duty in a new sphere;—that, in yielding to the united force of all these reasons, and complying with a providential call, which I had never thought of soliciting, I needed not fear that I was doing injustice to my present people; but having brought them past their nursing-time, I might safely leave them to the direction of that spiritual wisdom and knowledge which they have already attained, in the confidence that the Lord will take care of his own. It appears there is something to be said on both sides. I have thought and written on the subject till I am tired of both. Much do I now need spiritual wisdom, to teach me to profit by what has already occurred, and to guide my judgment in whatever path may lie before me. Do write me when you can, what has occurred in your prayers and meditations on the subject.'

From this state of fluctuation Mr Stewart was in a little while relieved, by providences, the bearings of which he regarded as sufficiently clear for his direction.

'*Moulin*, *March*, 1805.

'Prepare, my dear Brother, to hear what will surprise you. Our times are in the Lord's hands, and his counsel shall stand. When every prospect and symptom of a change of place was removed, and when my people and I were set down again quietly and comfortably together, a new and unexpected turn has agitated us afresh. The post brought me a letter subscribed by the whole town-council of Dingwall, stating the general desire of the parish to have me called to minister to them the word of life,—the providences that had frustrated the views of other candidates, and promoted those respecting my appointment,—and containing a cordial and a pressing invitation to accept the charge.

'Besides this, I had a letter from some of the serious inhabitants of the place, narrating the various turns of providence, the offers made to other ministers connected with members of the council; their refusal; the persevering prayers, and other means employed by the godly all over the country, to gain the council; the delays, alarms, and disappointments, and at last the complete success of their wishes.

'You will learn everything more particularly, when I show you the correspondence in Perth, if it please God we meet there. When I considered all the steps and circumstances,—a worldly engine put in motion by the breath of prayer, the "iron gate opening of its own accord,"—I could not but acknowledge the divine call, nor hesitate to accept it. I have accordingly written my answer, accepting the council's invitation. How to manage with the poor Moulin people, is the present difficulty. I took a number of them into my room last night, after worship, read my letters, and conversed with them. They were indeed sorely grieved, yet they did not deny the call being of God, and nothing but their personal attachment to me hindered them from fully acquiescing in it. We have the example and the success of the D—— people, to encourage us to be instant in prayer, that the Lord would send a faithful pastor to Moulin, who may feed them with strong meat, for babes' milk is all that I could give them. Now that the people in Ross have obtained their desire, I must engage them to help their poor Moulin brethren with their prayers.'

But, although the town-council, and the parishioners at large, were very zealous to procure his nomination, the majority of the Presbytery of Dingwall looked on it with no fond anticipations, and were well disposed to throw as many obstructions in the way, as private influence, and the tactics of church-courts, could bring into action. 'My business in the North,' he writes more than two months after the above, 'met with difficulties and obstacles to the last. The issuing of the presentation was retarded, till it was almost too late. There appeared reason to suspect, that even after it was signed in London, there was an intention of keeping it up, till it should prove ineffectual. Mr —— had a short conversation with two young ministers of Dingwall Presbytery, who were hastening homeward to exercise the Presbytery's right of presentation in favour of ——. After some spirited letters from Dingwall to the Provost in Edinburgh, it was promised, that the Provost's brother, who was coming to D—— about "Borough Election," would certainly bring the presentation in his pocket. He came, however, without it, but seeing the town so dissatisfied, and a certain interest likely to suffer, he immediately wrote to Edinburgh, or to London, and the paper was produced. A meeting of Presbytery was held, just three days before the six months elapsed. Yesterday, I received a letter, that everything went on smoothly, and that the moderation of the call was appointed. I trust the Lord will glorify his own wisdom and power, in making the truth to triumph, while he baffles the "schemes of its enemies."'

Thus was determined a step on which much of the usefulness of his future life depended, and which involved, in its consequences, the spiritual interests of many.

With respect to the propriety of resigning the Moulin charge, a charge endeared by the most tender associations of spiritual kindred and affinity in Christ, different opinions will be held, according to the principles, means of information, and capacity to judge, which meet in the individual who brings the matter into deliberation.

That removal is absolutely unlawful in cases, no man will maintain, or if he do, he will involve, in his rash censure, many a distinguished servant of Christ besides Mr Stewart. That a minister, like other men, is at the disposal of his Lord, is unquestionable; and his will is to be learned by the intimations of providence, concurring with the intimations of scripture and of conscience, concerning duty. When a man is satisfied on these points, he is not to be blamed on slight considerations, and on superficial views and regrets for some concomitant inconveniences. That Mr Stewart was fully satisfied on the point, is well known to all who enjoyed his intimacy; and it were rash in others possessing very incompetent means of forming a judgment, and not actually the subjects of similar providences, to pronounce him mistaken in the conduct he pursued. If one place before his eyes the interesting flock at Moulin, going forth under his pastoral care, finding pasture to their full content under his direction, and feeding on the mountains of Zion in peace and concord under his eye, who but grieves at the removal of their guide, and the consequent dispersion that awaits them? But if the circumstances of Dingwall be considered,—the destitution they were in,—the desire for a shepherd which they felt,—the worth of their souls, and the interest the good Shepherd takes in the whole of his flock collectively,—we shall probably pause before we condemn Mr Stewart's resolution to pass from the care of a well-pastured part of the flock, to tend another division of it that wandered as sheep without a shepherd. That the change was beneficial to himself, as to temporalities, will not alter our judgment; for that benefit was needed, and was the very circumstance that gave preponderance to other motives respecting Dingwall, purely spiritual, when they hung in a condition of suspense. Certainly, had the matter of temporalities been reversed, it would have so far detracted from the wisdom of his determination, and the reasonableness of his change.

While Mr Stewart saw that it was his duty to suffer the relation in which he stood to the parish of Moulin to be dissolved, it was not without feeling for them a concern truly paternal.

'Now that the time of my departure is almost at hand, you will be anxious to know how it fares with us all. There is really much composure and quiet acquiescence that prevail. Some weeks ago I used only to make distant allusions to the situation in which we stood. Of late, I have thought proper to speak of our separation more explicitly, and make the mention of it somewhat familiar to our ears, so as to be able to think and talk of it without overpowering emotions. Our evening readings are crowded. The people seem to swallow the word greedily, considering that their time may be short.'

Mr Stewart's anxiety for the future prosperity of that people, led him to take a deep interest in the appointment of a successor. The nomination was in the hands of a nobleman, who has been long distinguished in that country for his zeal in supporting established order, and for giving stability to the existing constitution in church and state; and as Mr Stewart had lent his influence to compose the minds of the people in times of considerable agitation, and had with ample effect stood forth the firm advocate of loyalty and social order, on Christian principles and in the fear of God, it might reasonably be expected, any representation he should make, relative to the good of the parish, would be entitled to consideration, and have some weight with those most concerned in maintaining the public weal. At least, he thought it became him to use every probable expedient in such an emergency, and therefore submitted the following statement to the patron:—

'My Lord,

'As his Majesty has been pleased to present me to the church and living of Dingwall, and I have received a call from the magistrates, heritors, and inhabitants of that borough, it is probable that my settlement will take place in September. In that event, I shall have to resign into your Grace's hands my present living, which I have enjoyed for a considerable period by your bounty.

'I willingly take this opportunity of submitting to your Grace's consideration, a fact which consists with my knowledge, namely, that during my incumbency, no person residing in this parish has left the established church, to join any dissenting connection whatever. Indulge me, my Lord, in expressing an earnest wish, that in the case of a successor, the same union and harmony may continue between minister and people, which are so essential to the happiness of both. I am induced to take this liberty in addressing the noble patron, from the deep concern which I feel for the peace and improvement of a people among whom I have happily spent many years of my life, and to whom I must ever retain a warm attachment, though duty now calls me away from them.

'I am sure the people ought not, and I believe they will not be forward to make any application in favour of an individual candidate, unless they understood that it would be agreeable to your Grace to know their mind. Yet it would be affection to conceal, that, in their own judgment, they must give a preference to one before another. But I presume no farther than simply to hint, how much the quiet and peace of this parish depend on your Grace's choice of a minister, who, possessing qualifications which must recommend him to the esteem of the heritors, may also be qualified to gain and retain the confidence of the people.

'I hope your Grace will not charge me with going beyond the line of my duty, in thus respectfully representing the state of the parish I am now about to resign to its noble patron, who has always shown a judicious attention to the interests of his people.'

I am afraid it will disappoint many to be informed, that a representation so unassuming, and in a matter affecting the clearest interests of a whole parish, met with no reply. The elders of the congregation, too, wishing to leave nothing untried, sent a representation to the patron, setting forth their great respect for him as their superior, and expressing their unwillingness to make divisions, or to separate themselves from the Establishment; and that they might not be compelled to do so, petitioning that a person should be presented to the parish whom they could conscientiously receive as their minister.

This representation was not more successful; and Mr Stewart having entirely failed in his attempts to obtain for his people a pastor to his own mind or to theirs, was obliged to devolve them on the care of the chief Shepherd, and took leave of them somewhat in the way described in Acts 20:36, 37.[1]

[1] On considering the above representations, one cannot forbear

'We had a favourable journey north,' he writes to Mr Black; 'I fancy sister may have already described our parting from Moulin, and the deep yet composed grief of the dear sisterhood. We had many an anxious thought about them on our way. On our arrival in this country, we took up our residence with worthy Mr and Mrs C. The 26th September was the important day that loosened my connection with one flock, and bound me to another. My reception here has been warm and cordial in the highest degree. Every neighbour is more kind than another. Besides offering and sending us many articles of furniture in loan, till we should get our

---

reflecting what a fine opportunity was here lost for benevolence, to make many happy,—for patriotism, to attach men to wise institutions,—and for religion, to promote and cherish among a well-affected people the virtues of growing piety! Meanwhile, we are far from insinuating that the Noble Patron acted arbitrarily, and without bringing into exercise a deliberate judgment on the case. His determination was doubtless the result of mature thought; but, at the same time, it was probably influenced by that ancient prejudice which views evangelical principles as necessarily allied to political insubordination. Even the tried loyalty of Mr Stewart and his people, could not, it seems, dissolve the imaginary association in the minds of some. It is on this erroneous ground, that when two candidates for a presentation have offered themselves, the *moderately* religious has been generally preferred.

Heritors, however, are at length beginning to act on better principles; and in his own neighbourhood, the writer is happy to perceive a growing solicitude among those possessing influence to promote the spiritual interests of the people in the settling of vacant parishes.

own things, we have got presents, etc. etc. etc. I have preached now two Sabbaths, to a crowded and attentive congregation. I have met and conversed with several serious men and women. Simple warm-hearted Christians they appear to be. In short, I have every encouragement at present. A great door seems to be opened. If the Lord would but move the hearts of the people to receive my message, as they have so cordially received myself, how we should then rejoice together.'

Mr Stewart, in his new parish, had to break up ground over which the gospel-plough had not for some time passed. That country presented a scene not often to be seen,—a people of the simplest habits,—when religious, of the sublimest piety,—when not enlightened, addicted to low immoralities, and a prey to debasing superstitions. In no part of the world, perhaps, will be found a clergy more orthodox than those called the popular ministers, and nowhere are the effects of Calvinistic preaching more broadly exhibited, than in the character and views of the more serious among the people. Experimental religion is there well understood; and it is no uncommon occurrence, at public meetings for religious conference, to observe a plain peasant rise with all the modesty of retiring diffidence, and on surmounting the visible reluctance of an unassuming mind to obtrude itself on the attention of other men, enter into the discussion of some point of casuistry, or penetrate into the marrow of some doctrinal subject proposed for consideration, with a power of discrimination, and a copiousness of argument, truly surprising. On these occasions one might imagine an Owen revived, having lost nothing but his Greek and Latin quotations.

Their religious views are generally profound; and in no place is the discrimination betwixt converted and unconverted more observed, or more observable. In parishes that have for a long period enjoyed adequate training, the religious standard is high, and the general aspect of the people is plainly as if they sought a better country, and looked on this world as a scene not desirable. They are grave, watchful, and intent on serious thought; and he who would take the oversight of them, had need not to be a novice.

In a letter to Mr Willison, written on his return to Moulin, after his former visit, Mr Stewart thus describes his first impressions:—

'I was greatly refreshed with what I saw and heard in Ross-shire and Inverness; numerous devout congregations, many lively Christians, and a great door of utterance. I was struck with the contrast between the general cast of religion in East-Ross, and at home. Here, religion is in its youthful state; there, it seems rather in its declining age. Here, we are warm and affectionate, simple and unsuspicious; yonder, they are rather indifferent about plain fare, fond of casuistry, and each occupied about his own particular experience. Yet their religion is far from being an unfruitful profession. They are exemplary, moral, kind, and charitable.'

But this description would not apply to parishes under the care of unpopular ministers, in which predicament the parish of Dingwall had for some time stood. Their former clergyman was a man of taste and learning, made a good figure in ecclesiastical courts, was a ready and polite preacher, and lived in good terms with the genteel neighbourhood, for which Dingwall is noted. Of his pastoral fidelity not much is known. There were a few pious people in the town, who, as the manner of that country is, travelled far on a Sunday to enjoy evangelical ordinances. But the general aspect of the place was certainly not religious; and though, on his settlement there, Mr Stewart found many willing to hear the truth, not many were found who knew its power. The Sabbath was little regarded; many were not only lax, but accustomed to draw topics of merriment from the gravity, the devout composure, and the strict lives of the few who professed godliness; and as for the populace, the same levity and thirst for diversion, and inattention to Christian morality, characterized them, which commonly prevail in that class, when not accustomed to the subjection of religious restraints.

That there was much ignorance among the people, was apparent to all who had opportunity, and sufficient knowledge to judge. But it was obvious there was no suspicion entertained by themselves that they were deficient; and, I believe, the assertion of it would have exposed a man to very pointed expressions of resentment. However, their minds were generally disposed, at the period of Mr Stewart's coming among them, to receive both him and his testimony with abundant respect; nor had he been long settled, until a visible alteration took place on external conduct. One instance of which he has pleasantly described in a letter written not two months after his induction:—

'You will be overjoyed to hear something of gospel news from Dingwall. Our serious people already remark an evident shaking among the dry bones. There is, in various instances, a melting under the word. The house of an experienced Christian in the town, D—— M——, which used to be open on the Sabbath evening to a few who attended to his reading and prayer, is now crowded. A mason in the neighbouring parish, who was anxious to send a letter in haste to his son, about a piece of work he had undertaken, on a Sabbath morning applied in vain to different persons to write for him. One had cut his thumb, another was not at home. He came to Dingwall to try to get his letter written there. From this he was led to go to Dingwall church. He was much impressed, and next day confessed, to a serious acquaintance, the steps by which he had been led, and that he thought the sermon he heard was all levelled at himself. We have a precious select party, who meet every Friday evening for prayer and conversation at D——M——'s. We have had some special meetings in the Manse, for prayer about Moulin. The brethren here are preparing a letter to be sent to their brethren at Moulin, to encourage them.—Poor Moulin!'

The concluding part of the above extract will painfully recall the reader's thoughts to Moulin. Their pastor was hardly removed, until sectaries began to preach to them the duty to come out from the Established Church, and be separate. 'There has a great change taken place about Moulin,' one of them writes, 'which gives me many a sad hour and day, when I consider how, formerly, everything was going on prosperously among us. But, perhaps, for our sin in the misimprovement of former privileges, our enemies triumph over us, and we go mourning because of the oppression of the enemy all day long; but with God there is mercy and deliverance.' And only three years after Mr Stewart's removal, the same person says, 'All things about our place are growing worse and worse,—iniquity abounding and practised without restraint,—the Sabbath much profaned,—and things turning to their old course; only the few who love the Saviour are still holding on, like Gideon, "faint, yet pursuing."'

Such accounts must have been a grief to Mr Stewart, for no man was more susceptible of religious sympathy than himself. He did what he could to alleviate the distress, by correspondence and advice, and by prayer, in which he got the religious people around him to engage on their account. And as a specimen of his counsels, we insert the following letter in answer to a desponding one he had received:

'My dear Friend,

'I have been wishing for many weeks to send my blessing and best wishes to you, and my dear brethren and well-wishers in the parish of Moulin. But it is really little I can write to anybody, as my eyes do not bear to do much by candlelight, and there is but little daylight for other purposes. Your very welcome letter of the 2d January came to hand, and awakened anew my affectionate remembrance of you all, and quickened my poor prayers for your comfort and edification. I see the Lord continues to try you with a scarcity of spiritual bread; but while he leaves you the blessed word, and his Holy Spirit to dress the food for your use, and to prepare your souls to receive it, you must not think that you are starved. God wrought a miracle before he would allow the widow of Sarepta[1] to starve in time of famine. If he feeds even the fowls of the air, will he not much more feed you by sending you spiritual food? I am unwilling to add, "O ye of little faith!" but still I feel

[1] [Another name for Zarephath (1 Kings 17:9).]

much for your situation, and indeed my heart and my affections often go out towards you in secret, and I feel, like Paul, a strong desire to see your face in the flesh, and if the Lord would honour me so far as to stablish your faith, and impart to you some spiritual gift (Rom. 1:11). But, O what a precious privilege is it to have a Saviour to whom we can express our desire, and commit all our cares!—to whom we can commit each other in prayer, and trust all our concerns!—an ever-watchful Shepherd, who knows the wants of his sheep, and their weakness!—and although he sometimes lets them feel the cold, yet he stays his rough wind in the day of his east wind. Many a saint now in glory was on earth destitute, afflicted, tormented, wandering in deserts and mountains (Heb. 11:37, etc.), who are now convinced that it was good for them to have been afflicted. Is it not a mercy for you that you are not like the poor Christians at Ephesus, when Paul left them exposed as a prey to grievous wolves, not sparing the flock? and that there are not persons arising among yourselves speaking perverse things? (Acts 20:29, 30.) But I acknowledge it must be a grief to your heart, to see so many around you unconcerned about eternity, careless about the one thing needful, not minding the gospel, nor thinking about it. But as it was in our Saviour's days, so it was in the days of the apostles, and so it will be until the Spirit be poured out from on high.'

Of his proceedings at Dingwall, he writes to his sister, seven months after his settlement, this account:—

'Our Sunday operations continue, and we hope with some effect. The practice here had been to have but two discourses, one in each language, all the year round, without any interval, beginning at a quarter past twelve. About a month ago, I changed the hour of meeting to eleven, which gave me time for a Gaelic lecture and sermon. Then I have an hour of interval, and an English discourse beginning at two. About the same time, having got some length of daylight, in the evening I began a diet of catechising in church at half past four, which continues to six. I find all this just as much as my strength will bear. But as my discourses are not long, and the church does not require great exertion of voice, I hope I shall be able to continue. The catechising diet is well attended, and the church quite full, just as it used to be at Moulin, with this difference, that we have here several of the gentry, who understand Gaelic, that attend regularly. As soon as this meeting is dismissed, our Sabbath schools begin, of which we have now three, besides D—— M——'s open meeting for notes and reading, and another in R—— N——'s house. These various diets fill up the day, and afford opportunity of improvement to many who can neither read nor think to any purpose at home. When we recollect the opposition that was made to the introduction of a gospel ministry in this place, and now see the freedom with which various means of improvement are employed and countenanced, we are encouraged to hope that they will be productive of good. D—— M——, my town catechist, has gone over the greater part of the families in town, in the way of catechetic instruction, on week-day evenings. I have occasion to be called to baptize children in the town. I always make it a practice to read and expound a portion of the scriptures on these occasions. I think it has as good an effect in this way, as though I brought them to church. Yesterday, in the house of ——, I had an opportunity of reading a sort of chamber-lecture to about twenty ladies and gentlemen, from Luke 10:8, 20. It must be seen that the kingdom of God is come nigh unto them; and we hope the Lord will gather some into it. Though some weeks have now elapsed since the event, I cannot yet write or think with a dry eye of the sore bereavement which I, in common with many, have suffered in the unexpected removal of our dear brother Black. It is, indeed, an awful token of the divine displeasure, as Mrs C—— expressed it, of a hostile disposition in the court of heaven, when its ambassadors are thus suddenly recalled. Edinburgh has lost more than half its attraction for me. I could not find myself at home there any more. Indeed, there is very little probability that I shall see Edinburgh for a while.'

The event so deeply deplored by Mr Stewart, had taken place on the 25th February 1806; and as Mr Black was only in the forty-fourth year of his age, and had written ten days before, stating his family and himself to be in ordinary health, the sudden and unexpected change must have added to the poignancy of his grief. Of this friend and guide of his youth, he continued to bear the most tender recollections to the close of his own life.[1]

Among other expedients which Mr Stewart was on the alert to devise for improving his people in religious knowledge, he states, that he had lately begun a sort of private lecture for the benefit of some of his female parishioners. 'It was suggested to me,' says he, 'by some young women applying for admission to the Lord's table, whom I could not encourage to proceed, and persuaded to stay back. As they were of that rank that I could not always have access to them at their own houses, nor examine them at a public diet of catechising, I thought it was best to invite them to my own house. Others have been at their own request admitted, so that I have a party of nine or ten ladies. We propose to meet once a fortnight. We had our second meeting yesterday (Friday), at one o'clock. When you entreat the Lord for your great family, pray that he may also send a blessing on me and my little hospital.'

[1] For an interesting sketch of Mr Black's life, see Memoir prefixed to his published Sermons.

A few months after he writes to his sister:

'I should have saluted you last Friday on your birthday, but it was the day of my female meeting, and I need Friday afternoon as well as Saturday, to prepare for the Sabbath's work. I am still getting new accessions to my female meeting; about seventeen attend now. In my lectures to them I find Halyburton's[1] *Great Concern* of principal use. What the fruits may be we do not yet see, but I trust the Lord will, in his own time, bear testimony to the word of his grace. I had occasion, two or three weeks ago, to protest against an evil which was meeting with encouragement, and likely to grow if not checked. For some seasons past, a company of players spent two or three months in Inverness, and made a visit to Dingwall before leaving the country. Our town's people were passionately fond of the entertainment. At my next meeting, I took the opportunity of discoursing pretty freely to my ladies about the evil of such entertainments. Only three of them had gone to see them, and none of them went any more.'

While on this subject of theatrical amusement, we shall insert another instance of Mr Stewart's resolute and successful exertions to keep his parish free from

[1] [Thomas Halyburton (1674–1712), Professor of Divinity in the University of St Andrews.]

those demoralizing exhibitions, though it occurred four years after the above-mentioned attempt.—

'We have had some stir this week,' says he to his sister, 'about theatrical amusements, of which the detail would entertain you, but I fear I must confine myself to outlines. A man of the name of T——, with his son, came to the town last week, waited on Mr ——, the senior Bailie, with an introduction, requesting the use of the town-hall for a party of comedians. Bailie —— consulted Mr ——, the leading man in the town, who readily agreed, and the hall was granted. Workmen were immediately employed to place seats, etc. All this passed before I was aware of what was a-doing. It was Friday evening. I was afraid it was already too late to attempt stopping the players, as they were in possession of the hall. However, I called on Bailie ——, and remonstrated against the measure of giving the hall. He told me it was done with Mr ——'s concurrence, but regretted, as he saw me so much hurt by it. I then went to Mr ——. I found him much disposed to support them; but at last prevailed with him to send a message to Mr ——, that if he chose to recall the grant of the room, *he* would have no objection to his doing so. His message I delivered to Mr ——, who undertook to send for the player, and let him know this. A little before 9 o'clock, I called again on Mr ——, and found him writing me a long letter, saying, that he might expose himself by breaking his engagement with the player, unless he was supported by the Town-Council, and proposed to call a meeting of the Council. I approved, and a meeting was accordingly called. Though late that evening, I called on these counsellors, and got them to engage heartily to oppose the players. Next forenoon, the result of the meeting was officially communicated to me, viz. that two were for giving the hall, and four against it, unless I consented to an exhibition for one night only. I could not, consistently with my decided and avowed judgment, give such a consent; of course the man was told that he must give up the hall, on being repaid his expenses in fitting it up, which were but trifling. He afterwards called on me himself, to endeavour to gain me, but it would not do.'

But while Mr Stewart acted as a Christian, he was alive to every claim of humanity, and the following note will show, that though he opposed Mr T——, he was not his enemy, and was not without the most benevolent concern for his best interests:—

'Sir,

'I truly feel for the embarrassment to which you must have been subjected by your disappointment in this town. So far as the enclosed guinea can go to relieve you, I give it with perfect good-will. I cannot forbear to express my strong regret, that a man of education and talents, of character and respectable connection, for all which I am willing to give you credit, should stoop to the degrading condition of picking up a precarious subsistence, by the mean arts of mimicry and buffoonery. I sincerely wish you and your son had a more creditable profession. I wish I could first persuade you, and then assist you to follow some other line, in which you might have a more comfortable and respectable subsistence in this life, and enjoy the prospect of a happy eternity in the life to come; neither of which advantages you can expect to possess in your present occupation. May God Almighty impress this admonition on your heart, and lead you to think seriously of your everlasting concerns before it be too late.'

The union of generosity and religious principle manifested in the above communication, could not fail to commend itself to the conscience of Mr T——. However, in his answer, after making suitable acknowledgements for the donation, he could not refrain from some reflections on the 'bigoted sophistry of those, who make no allowance for appearances they do not comprehend, and condemn what does not immediately suit their particular way of thinking, or have not refinement or sensibility enough to discriminate.' And 'as for theatrical representations,' he observed, 'have they not for ages tended to reform mankind? are they not supported by the best regulated governments in the world, as well as the most enlightened; and attended, as a part of education, in almost every seminary where religious tenets are instilled, and principles established?' And then he goes on to show, that to represent a bad character, must rather be subservient to the interests of morality, than injurious; defending his profession, as it can only be defended, on principles from which true religion revolts, and which Christian morality expressly disclaims.

It is not known that any good was produced on the mind of T—— by this incident. His subsequent proceedings in Dingwall, showed no respect for the judgment of his monitor, and the lovers of pleasure sympathized with him on their common disappointment. 'As a little ferment was excited by T——, I thought it proper, next Lord's day, to make a short address after divine service, highly approving the conduct of the Council in excluding the players from the town, and urging all who regarded the interests of religion, good order, industry, and sobriety, to join me in discountenancing their admission now, and on every future occasion. The few serious people are pleased and thankful that such an engine of vice has been stopped. The majority submit to their disappointment with sullen murmuring.' However, the delicacy and yet determination he manifested on the occasion, and the known inflexibility of his purpose to set his face against such spectacles on the ground of Christian principle, had the effect to deter other bands from invading the land for the following seven years, or at least wrought on the minds of the borough magistracy to refuse all applications of a similar kind.

CHAPTER 7

CHALLENGES OF DINGWALL MINISTRY

IN 1808, Mr Stewart received a very animating letter from a clergyman in Staffordshire, who, having heard of the revival at Moulin, and having had a like honour put on his own ministry some years before, was induced, though entirely a stranger, and of a different branch of the Christian church, to open a correspondence with his fellow-servant, to gain additional information respecting the Moulin people, and strengthen each other's hands in their common work. This new friendship Mr Stewart delighted to consider as seasonably provided for him by his divine Master, in order to solace him for the recent removal of Mr Black; and in warmth of piety, and strength of attachment, though no personal interview ever took place, he seems to have been all a friend could wish. The first letter of Mr D—— was addressed to Moulin, on the supposition Mr Stewart was still there. Mr Stewart's answer is dated,

'*Dingwall, Ross-shire, June* 23d, 1808.

'My dear Sir,

'Seldom have I been favoured with a more gratifying communication than that which I unexpectedly received, some days ago, from your hand. Among the precious tokens of love with which the Lord has been pleased at times to revive my sluggish soul, I have found reasons to distinguish particularly the expressions of regard which I have received from some of his dear children. I assure you, my dear Sir, that your brotherly salutation was a cheering cordial to my dull spirit. I am sure I felt it such; and I wish, in my poor way, to acknowledge it, and to bless the Lord who put it in your heart to address me, and stir me up to thankfulness to that gracious Master who has, in various ways, helped his unworthy servant. I wished to return you an answer immediately, but some avocations hindered me for a week. I now gladly seize the first vacant day to endeavour to make you some return.

'That short printed account which introduced my name to your notice, contained some particulars of my own history, and of the Lord's gracious visitation of my dark soul, as well as of my benighted parish. In giving a brief continuation of that account, I must again have recourse to egotism, for my own story is closely interwoven with that of my parishioners. The interest you have taken in me and my people will naturally excite a curiosity to know what led me to separate from my beloved flock, and to remove my residence to the town from which I date this letter.

'During two years subsequent to the date of my printed account, we continued, on the whole, in a flourishing and progressive state; and the influences of the divine Spirit were apparent in the heavenly walk and conversation of those whose hearts he had renewed. I shall here refer to a few pages of appendix which was subjoined to a third impression of my letter, and which I enclose. From this period, however, there did not appear any accession to the number of converts. The bulk of the people appeared satisfied with lending their approbation to what they saw and heard, and attending regularly to ordinances, but there was no more pressing into the kingdom of heaven. The heavens appeared to be shut up, and the showers were withheld. Of those who formed our little Christian society, some were in Providence removed to a distance, and others were called home by death, so that our numbers began to lessen, rather than increase.

'My removal proved, as I expected, a stimulus to the minds of the people, as well as to my own. It was painful, indeed, but I am persuaded it was salutary. Some attempts were made to influence the Duke of Athole, patron of the parish of Moulin, to present a man of evangelical principles to the vacant living, but without effect. The consequence is, that some have withdrawn from the ministry of the present incumbent, and some have removed out of the parish. I hear but melancholy accounts of the greater part of the people. They are growing careless and licentious,—I fear against their better knowledge and conviction. But the few godly keep close together; they continue to meet often together, for prayer and conference, and love and cherish one another. I have visited them repeatedly since my settlement here, and found them "sorrowful and rejoicing." Two or three of Moulin parish, and a good number of the neighbouring parishes of Blair, Logierait, and Dowally, who were seriously disposed, have joined a sect of Independents, whose founders are pious, zealous men, but over-attached to congregational government, and to an ideal purity of communion. I wish I could give you any agreeable account of the few congregations of Scots Episcopalians in Perthshire. We have a small congregation of the same connection in this town, very worthy decent people, withal very frank and friendly to me. I am acquainted with one of their ministers, who occasionally officiates here, a man of learning and respectability. But how inferior to the burning lights among your English brethren,

Cadogan, Milner, Newton, Cecil,[1] etc. whose names are justly dear to us.

'I have not time nor room at present, to add much about the state or character of the people with whom I am now connected. As to my own situation, I certainly enjoy privileges and advantages far beyond what I possessed in my former station, particularly from the society and example of pious ministers, and the conversation of experienced Christians. That my "profiting" under these advantages, should "appear" so little, is, alas! matter of sore lamentation! But enough of myself. Let us adore that Saviour who, I trust, does guide us both, and will keep that we have committed unto him against *that day*.

'Let me hope, my dear Sir, that you will find time and inclination to favour me with the continuance of a correspondence so auspiciously begun. It will be most gratifying to me to hear of your dear spiritual children at C——, and what the Lord has done for their souls. I remember Mr M. well, and am under particular obligation to him for encouraging you to write to his remote, secluded countryman. I will be happy to hear that the Lord gives him employment in his vineyard. I sympathize with you on your weak state of health. I bless God my health is pretty sound and uniform, though I am by no means robust or equal to great bodily exertion. A

[1] [William Bromley Cadogan (1751–97), Joseph Milner (1744–97), John Newton (1725–1807), and Richard Cecil (1748–1810) were all prominent evangelical ministers of the Church of England.]

circumstance I need to mention in my first letter, which may make me sometimes a tardy correspondent, is a stiffness or imbecility in my fingers, which commonly makes writing a tedious and laborious operation. But it is a mercy to be able to use my fingers at all.'

To the same.

'*Dingwall*, 29*th July*, 1808.

'My very dear Sir,

'From my knees, where I think the Spirit of God has been trying to stir up a little my dull sluggish spirit, I repair to my desk, to express the very high gratification I received, in various ways, from the repeated perusal of your favour of the 23d instant. Verily, I cannot sufficiently admire the tender dealing of our God with his most unworthy, ungrateful servant. When I deserved, for my inactivity and carelessness, to have been severely chastised, instead of the rod, he makes me to hear an unknown voice from a distance, sweetly awakening me, and inviting me to arise and call upon my God. What shall I render to the Lord for all his benefits towards me? Truly he is the good Shepherd who calls the wanderers home, and furnishes supplies in the wilderness. To your affectionate invitation to "go to pray before the Lord, and to seek the Lord of hosts," my heart most readily replies, and I trust with sincerity, "I will go also" (Zech. 8:21). I do not know that you could have named a *more convenient hour for me*, than the one you have already chosen. I can confidently assure you, my dear brother, that no difference in rituals or government shall make the smallest separation between us. If you and Mr M. could unite so cordially together, I, who occupy a kind of middle place, may easily coalesce with both. Indeed, to confess a secret, I incline much more to Episcopacy than to Independency. But I believe that a sincere disciple of Christ may faithfully follow his Master, and get to heaven either way. I do feel a warm interest in your esteemed friend Mr E——, and sympathy for his sufferings; at least, according to the measure of my feelings, which, if you knew them, you would reckon extremely moderate. The circumstances you are pleased so frankly to communicate in your own situation, serve to give me a nearer and more distinct view of my newly acquired friend, and (to adopt Mr Wilberforce's language) to bring our hearts into *closer contact* together. You have already most kindly adopted me as your associate in the oratory; and you are in a fair way of finding me your companion in the parlour, the study, and the sanctuary. Yesterday's post brought me your letter, and this day, being *Friday*, I would make no delay, but in my poor feeble manner, I essayed to join myself to my two kind beloved fellow-disciples of B—— and W——, that we might warm our hearts together at the fire of the same altar. To assist you in performing the kind brotherly service of intercession in behalf of your favoured new associate, I must beg your attention to some particulars in my situation. I wish to imitate, if I can, your amiable frankness; and judging from myself, I think I need make no apology for minuteness. Behold me, then, the father of six young immortal creatures, not unpromising in their dispositions and capacities, but *everyone* dead in trespasses and sins, waiting to be quickened by the Spirit of him who raised up Jesus Christ from the dead; blessed with a partner, pious, intelligent, active, indefatigable in her attention to the interests, both temporal and spiritual, of her children; pastor of a flock nearly 1,500 in number, a great majority of whom are very ignorant and unconcerned. We have a small number of pious experienced Christians, who associate together, and strengthen each other's hands, and we find a very few who feel desirous to know the truth, and seem beginning to feel somewhat of its impression. One of my own greatest wants, which I much need to have supplied, is the want of zeal and activity in my blessed Master's cause. Indolence and unconcern weigh me sadly down, and make me an unprofitable servant. Ask for me greater earnestness in my Redeemer's service, and more solicitous concern about the miserable state of my poor perishing people; along with this, more spiritual and experimental knowledge, that I may adapt my counsels to the different conditions of my people. I want, besides, spiritual wisdom and discretion to rule my *house*, that I may bring up my children in the fear and knowledge of the Lord, and have them in subjection in all *gravity*, a quality in which, even at my time of life, I am not a little deficient. You will ask for me, likewise, my dear friend, more firmness in opposing or reproving what I disapprove, for I am sadly enslaved to complaisance. I want—but I may say with you, what want I not? I am an expensive, yet useless workman. Indeed, it would surprise you, if you knew the person whom you have distinguished by your favour, how the Lord should have made him successful, or ever employed him at all. But the Lord's ways are not our ways. By committing his invaluable treasure to coarse, clumsy, earthen vessels, he secures the glory to himself, and all is as it should be.'

To the same.

'*Dingwall*, 23*d July*, 1810.

'Your last letter, my dear Sir, brings much delightful and encouraging intelligence; our dear brother E—— restored to a good measure of health and ability in his Master's service,—your own strength rather improved,—your congregation listening with attention, and not in vain, to the glad tidings you bring them,—the number of evangelical clergymen increasing,—and the kingdom of our gracious Redeemer enlarging. What reason have we for hope and joy! Yes, my dear brother, let us encourage ourselves in the Lord. He hath not left, and he never will leave himself without a witness. I, who have not been led through deep waters, am perhaps on that account less apt to view things in a gloomy light, than others who have known the depths of Satan. I am not sure whether this may be the cause which makes me consider as a favourable omen, a thing that gives much uneasiness to the pious people here, I mean a new species of persecution which is just making its appearance in the church. When, by the rigid enforcing of the law of patronage, the approbation of the people came to be entirely overlooked in the settlement of the minister, it often happened that a minister was placed in a parish, at the sole pleasure of the patron, neither acceptable to the people, nor faithful to their interests. In this case, the only resource left to those who earnestly desired to be edified under a gospel ministry, was, either to join a Dissenting congregation, or to become the stated hearers of an evangelical minister, wherever they could find one, in the Established Church. The former mode was often out of their power, for there are few Dissenting churches in these northern counties, and the people are too poor to maintain them. As they are cordially attached to the Established Church, they greatly preferred attending a faithful parish minister, though under the inconvenience of travelling many miles to hear him. Accordingly, it was no uncommon thing for persons to leave their own parishes, and go from ten to fifteen miles on a Sunday morning to church, and return in the evening. Our *moderate* brethren, jealous of the popularity of some of their neighbours, and irritated against their own people, took their measures, and obtained the sanction of our most Venerable Assembly to a rule, subjecting to the heaviest censures, all who should be guilty of the horrid schism of withdrawing from their parish church, and hearing sermon regularly in a neighbouring church. Whether this rule will be rigorously enforced, may depend much on the tempers of particular ministers; but I have no doubt that it will in some parishes in this county, and it is easy to foresee, that it will be productive of very serious hardships. But we are assured, that any suffering to which our dear people will be subjected for righteousness sake, will be graciously overruled for their growth in grace, and for the spread of the gospel.'

The hardships that result from exercising an arbitrary patronage, without regarding the circumstances or inclination of the people, to which Mr Stewart alludes in the above letter, have been long felt, and grievously deplored in those parts. By a judicious and Christian exercise of the light they claim, the patrons had it in their power to attach the people to themselves in a manner known only in places where hereditary chieftainship obtains. But by forcing upon them spiritual guides they could not receive, as being in their opinion unqualified, and unworthy of their confidence, men of rank have, on too many occasions, done what they could to dissolve the spell which hereditary distinctions and traditionary influence had cast over the minds of the plebeian orders.

If it be said, the opinion of the people is only to be contemned when it differs from the judgment of their superiors, this is a sentiment which Christianity never taught, and which political wisdom never approved; and on fairly meeting the question at issue betwixt a reclaiming parish *refusing* to acknowledge a pastor imposed on them, and the patron insisting on his legal right to impose, it will perhaps in general be found, that the judgment of the people is not so unsound or irrational as their opponents allege, and that, if there is any truth in religion, and any benefit to be derived from its ordinances, a man of reputed piety and circumspect life, is much more likely to lead them to the benefits of religion, than one whose principles are without character, and his life without sanctity.

In that country, so high is the opposition to an exceptionable presentee sometimes carried, that almost the whole parishioners abandon his ministry, and refuse the sacraments at his hand. Under the influence of this scrupulosity of conscience, the ordinances of religion are not neglected, but painfully resorted to in places far distant, if no popular clergyman is near; and on a Sabbath morning, the roads leading to a well-esteemed preacher, are thronged by strangers from a distance. Of these wanderers, many resorted to Dingwall during Mr Stewart's incumbency; and as they were generally persons of at least professed religion, there was something very imposing in their numbers, in the solemnity of their gesture, and in the apparent devotion of their worship.

No law can restrain the attendance of the people on ordinary means, to receive instruction, where they list; but the desertion and implied disesteem of their people, is very galling to their own pastors, how much soever they pretend to undervalue the taste and opinions of the vulgar; and, of course, the objects of their preference do not escape censure, as encouraging those secessions by flattering the popular prejudices. However, as the ecclesiastical law strictly prohibits any minister from administering Baptism or the Lord's Supper to extra-parochial hearers, a watchful eye is kept on the conduct of the popular clergy, to detect any infraction of the established order; and where found, no pity is shown to the offender. Mr Stewart was sufficiently circumspect in these points. As to the article of marriage, however, he refused to be limited; and to a neighbouring minister, whose parishioners had left him, with the exception, it is said, of those officially bound to attend (viz. the schoolmaster and beadle), and who had sent him a remonstrance on that subject, and charged him with an intended violation of his rights, in proposing to marry a couple whom he knew to be on their road to Dingwall for that purpose, he replied:—

'I received your letter this day about half an hour after marrying J—— M—— and C—— A——. I apprehend you are quite mistaken in supposing, that in doing so, I am guilty of an undue interference between you and the people of K—— parish. Many people in this parish have been married by other clergymen than their parish minister, without lines from me; nor would I ever think of such an odious and unconstitutional measure, as depriving people of their civil right of being married by any minister they chose, after the banns have been regularly published.

'Indeed, I have all along given my people to understand, that they have no occasion to ask my leave to be married by whom they please; for the law requires only proclamation of banns, but astricts[1] the parties to no particular minister. I will go farther and say, that I have ever reckoned it very unbecoming a conscientious pastor to oblige his parishioners, by compulsory measures, to receive baptism from his hand, if they were unwilling to take it, and preferred another. And anyone who knows human nature, will not expect to extend his usefulness by arbitrary restrictions, or compulsive impositions. These are the maxims on which I have hitherto acted; nor do I wish any of my brethren to act otherwise towards me. And however reprehensible or unneighbourly you may think my conduct toward you,

[1] [Astrict: to bind by a moral or legal obligation: constrain, restrict, limit.]

I assure you I am not disposed to make you an exception in the license that I would allow my people; for if any parishioner of mine shall apply to you for marriage or for baptism, I give you full liberty to celebrate the one, and to administer the other, upon the parties producing the ordinary certificates under the hand of the session clerk.'

Several of his co-presbyters were disposed to keep a watchful eye on his proceedings; but, as he both knew his own rights, and was not to be intimidated in doing his duty, and was fully competent to meet his moderate opponents on the arena of debate, he was not often molested in church courts. Indeed, his character was so uniformly consistent, and the popular favour so meekly sustained, that he gave no occasion of blame, except what sprung from the offence of superior zeal and sanctity.

In one parish, Mr Stewart had two congregations, perfectly distinct and dissimilar in character. Those who attended the Gaelic service in the forenoon, were chiefly of the lower class, and many of them from remote places. Of this audience, the aspect was deeply serious; a solemn stillness pervaded the multitude, and nothing was heard but the tones of the preacher's voice, unless now and then a sigh, or a groan, confessed the inward emotions of the full heart. In addressing this auditory, Mr Stewart had usually great enlargement and freedom, and to them his gospel came not in word only. But in the afternoon, the congregation consisted of the neighbouring gentry, and those who held official situations in the town, together with such among the lower classes as understood English, in which not many, except those in business, were competently versed for profiting by a discourse in that language. That Mr Stewart had little satisfaction in this department of duty, he often confessed and lamented. Not but that attention was paid, and many compliments lavished on the preacher's performances; but what are the civilities a minister receives from a people who refuse to be won by his ministry to Christ? Shall attention to himself make him overlook the injury done to his Lord? If abundance of respect could have satisfied Mr Stewart, he would have been satisfied; but he looked to their souls, and to the affecting brevity of a day of grace; and that many of them were concerned for improving that day, very little evidence appeared.

'I do not know,' writes Mr Stewart, on the approach of a sacramental occasion, 'I do not know that I ever felt the burden of duty heavier upon my mind, than in the prospect of administering the Lord's supper here next Lord's day, to the English congregation, so careless do they appear. It was a matter of anxious concern and prayer with me, how I should preach to them on the preceding Sunday, and how I should preach on the communion day. I was directed on the two last Sabbaths to these texts, Matt. 15:26, "It is not meet to take the children's bread, and to cast it unto the dogs"; and John 7:37, "If any man thirst, let him come unto me and drink." I trust I was enabled to be faithful in exhorting every man, and warning every man. For my action sermon, I have fixed on that verse, Luke 20:13. "Then said the Lord of the vineyard, what shall I do? I will send my beloved son: it may be they will reverence him, when they see him."

'To your queries about the state of religion in this parish, I fear I must answer in a complaining tone. Irreligion, indifference about spiritual concerns, attachment to the world, the intemperate use of spirituous liquor, prevail to a melancholy extent. The doctrines of the gospel are heard, in the main, I think, with indifference rather than dislike, which I ascribe to their not being understood or attended to. Some weeks ago, on occasion of preaching on the necessity of regeneration with close application, a strong and general dissatisfaction was openly expressed in many companies during the ensuing week, and some declared they were on the point of quitting the church. I thought there was something hopeful in this movement. They seemed at last to have felt a little the sword's point. But, alas! it went no farther. They only knit their brows, muttered something against the preacher, and then sat as composedly on their seats as ever. But still, amidst this abounding aversion and resistance to the truth, the good seed appears not to have altogether perished. There are several, among the lower ranks, who show an earnest desire for religious knowledge, and the company and fellowship of pious persons, and appear to receive "the truth in the love of it." Our advanced Christians bring me some encouraging intelligence of this kind, from time to time. While I am ready to cry, almost in despondency, "Who hath believed our report?" one or two instances of awakened souls encourage me to say, Behold, is not here the arm of the Lord revealed.'

But though Mr Stewart mourned the state of lukewarmness in which his English congregation generally lay, there were among them a few names of distinguished excellence, in whom he had great delight; and if he had some griefs, he had also many times of refreshing among his Gaelic people, and especially on sacramental occasions, the wonted solemnities of which he thus describes:—

'Three weeks ago, the Lord's supper was celebrated in this place. This is a season of more than ordinary solemnity in these northern counties. We have divine service performed on three several week days in English and in Gaelic, and two discourses preached in each language on all of those days. Four or five ministers are invited to preach, besides the parish minister; and where the pastor is himself a faithful evangelical preacher, he employs none but persons of the same description to officiate along with him. Serious Christians, from a distance of thirty or forty miles, assemble with many others, to the number of some thousands. These are lodged and entertained by the inhabitants of the parish. After attending the public services of the day, the remainder of them are employed partly in secret devotion, partly in private social worship, where some more aged, experienced Christian presides. Altogether it is a great solemn festival, of four or five days continuance. Believers are greatly refreshed and edified with the various talents which are brought into exercise, among so many preachers, and the various matter which is carried home to their souls, suited to the cases of each; and also by the pleasing and animating intercourse with Christian acquaintances, old fellow-pilgrims, whom perhaps they seldom or never meet with, except in these periodical solemn interviews. In such a large and mixed multitude as then comes together, there is always a great proportion of the ignorant and graceless. These, too, are particularly noticed in the addresses from the pulpit, and often with strong effect, and merciful success.

'On the late sacramental occasion here, we were favoured with very fine weather. This is very desirable, for all the Gaelic service is in the field. We had some excellent ministers, who were well helped in the discharge of their duty.'

These assemblages are often reprobated by inattentive observers, and censorious judges; and though it were hopeless to expect universal correctness, as some baser elements may mix in the purest stream, yet the general character was unimpeachable, and the general effects of those religious festivals were evidently beneficial on life and morals. Perhaps northern hospitality, so much vaunted, is at no time seen displayed to such an extent of disinterested kindness as on these occasions, for no man is so poor, but he will then lodge a sojourner for a night; and the conduct of the strangers is usually such, that to entertain them is thought becoming even in the irreligious themselves, who, though they think their piety fanaticism, are not unwilling to hear the prayers they offer up in terms of lively gratitude for their benefactors.

We have seen how Mr Stewart succeeded in maintaining his position against the players, and he was not less successful in reforming the ordinary Christmas immoralities.

'I have been a good deal occupied of late,' says he, 'in holding diets of examination in the church, and in preaching holiday sermons,—on old Christmas, a missionary discourse, when we got a respectable collection for the spread of the gospel; and also on New Year's Day, to young persons. On both these days, which used to be devoted to noisy revelling on the streets, and promiscuous parties for dancing and drinking all night, I had the satisfaction of seeing the town as quiet and regular as on a Sabbath, and no public balls.'

These pious attempts to suppress revellings, and the levities which infallibly ripen into confirmed distaste for religious duties and spiritual enjoyments, will appear to the carnal mind nothing better than the energies of an irrational zeal, exerting itself to extend the gloomy reign of fanaticism over the provinces of harmless mirth and cheerful indulgence, which, it is alleged, belong of right to human nature. But while the world sneered and resented those aggressions, there was a greater than the world, no doubt, ready to say, 'Well done, good and faithful servant!' And it is to be hoped, that some of those for whose souls he so faithfully watched, though little sensible of their obligation at the time, and perhaps judging them an encroachment on their happiness, have long since viewed his strenuous exertions to keep them from the snare of the evil one in a proper light.

These exertions of Mr Stewart deserve the consideration of his brethren in office. It is not enough to denounce theatrical exhibitions, and carnal levities, from the pulpit. If we believe they are pernicious, ought we not to employ counteracting means? Preaching against sin is so much a thing of office, that it is little heeded by the world. But when we are seen carrying on an active warfare against it in private life, by a timely application to individuals in danger, to warn and to exhort them, it shows us to be in earnest, and, if done in the spirit of wisdom, it will impress. Sin may raise an outcry for a while, but meek perseverance will in due season reap its expected fruits. Mr Stewart took the only effectual method to correct periodical levities,—he substituted serious engagements, and left not the mind to the dangers of vacancy and idleness.

But, leaving Mr Stewart prosecuting the course of his public duties, in the manner of an able and faithful minister of Christ, we may with propriety advert to his domestic scene, on which he appeared with singular grace. As his family increased, a considerable portion of his time was allotted to their improvement; and having in Mrs Stewart a person of excellent judgment, and unwearied assiduity, to co-operate in the work of 'training the young idea how to shoot,' and in forming the plastic disposition of ingenuous youth to proper habits, the result was in proportion to the means. Mr Stewart had a very correct knowledge of human nature; and while he investigated its principles as a philosopher, he brought to philosophy the light of divine revelation, which gave to his researches a certainty otherwise unattainable. He had known human nature in its twofold condition,—first in the degenerate state, previous to renovation, and afterwards in its regenerated form; and, with this complex experience, was the better qualified to devise suitable modes of early culture. He had likewise a perfect habit of self-government, preserving his mind calm and unruffled to a degree rarely witnessed, so that some, who had opportunity of seeing him for years together at home and abroad, confessed they had not beheld in him any irregularity of temper, or passionate expression of bad humour. His children, therefore, always saw in him the same authority of reason, and the same command of temper, and the same sanctity of parental character. How happily this must have operated in conciliating esteem is obvious, while in his manner there was nothing severe or repulsive, but rather a manifestation of kindliness never withheld, unless to signify moral disapprobation. Mrs Stewart, on the other hand, had the maternal tendernesses in a copious measure, but so tempered with wisdom, and sanctified by religion, that not a fault met with indulgence; and if good qualities were apparent, instead of diminishing them by praise, they were assigned their appropriate sphere of exercise, and left to shine apparently unheeded.

The united care of such guardians was not without its reward. In a numerous family, not a *spoiled child* was to be seen. There was entire subjection and subordination, with no apparent restraint; an air of happiness, and even gaiety, animated every face, and no domestic scene could be more delightful, than to witness the well-disciplined group. What Cecil says of the frequency of parents groaning under the vices of their children, is true; but in many instances these very children have been first made to groan under the vices of their parents, being in infancy used for sport, and when their spoiled humours have made them troublesome, being then subjected to the alternations of *harshness* and *indulgence*, and both alike unreasonable and pernicious. Under such injudicious treatment, what wonder that many should embitter the peace of domestic life, and, as they grow up, multiply sorrow to their friends.

Mr Stewart had great skill in communicating knowledge, in a way adapted to varying ages and capacities; and when he found the demand made on his time, for domestic tuition, incompatible with attention to the duties of his ministry, he called in help, and, for several years previous to his removal from Dingwall, employed a governess and preceptor of approved qualifications, to carry on the business of education.

He had a deep sense of the importance of a right fulfilment of the parental obligation recognized at baptism, to train up children for the church; and it may easily be supposed the inculcation of religious truth was a serious part of education in his house. He did not think it enough to have the memory stored with right principles of religion; he inquired, he examined into the exercises of their minds, with respect to those principles; for he justly reckoned it to be a great inconsistency in a minister, to do less for promoting religion in the souls of his own family, than he does for the souls of strangers. He was aware, too, that the formation of character begins in early life, and hence his assiduous attention was directed to their habits, principles, and manners. Such knowledge as was essential to secular usefulness, he took care to have carefully instilled. And as he always calculated on an early removal from his family, of which many growing infirmities furnished painful admonition, he justly considered a proper education as affording to his children, if they should suffer an early bereavement of himself, the most probable means, under Providence, for procuring them an honourable sphere in life. In their proficiency he was not disappointed, nor will their future conduct, it is presumed, be unequal to the expectations formed from the first fruits yielded in youth.

In his intercourse with his parishioners, Mr Stewart was frank and accessible; but from his first settlement in Dingwall, he resolved to abstain from general society. In conformity with this plan, he rarely dined abroad, unless when officially necessary. There were a few families in the neighbourhood where he could introduce his Lord, and there he occasionally spent an evening, and among these few, were found *some noble*, by whom his society was much prized. But, in general, he was rarely to be met with, unless at home, and in the engagements of professional duty. He possessed social talents of a high order, and which, if freely indulged, would have delighted any company, but might have proved a snare to himself among the irreligious, and he wisely withdrew from the pleasing danger. Of the proprieties of social life he was an accurate judge, and a diligent observer; and in his own deportment, both at home and abroad, was exhibited no inferior model of graceful manners, and unaffected politeness.

In his own family, his conversation was fraught with useful remark, and pious reflection; with confidential friends, he was rich even to affluence in the stores of profitable discourse; and the writer of this, having lived several years in his neighbourhood, will never lose the remembrance of the many happy hours spent in his company. Hardly a week passed without one evening at least devoted to his society; and though the only guest, as much treasure of communication was poured forth as though many had been present.

The advantages which he enjoyed in this free access to Mr Stewart, made him often revolve how much general good eminent ministers might do to students in theology, by admitting them freely to their society and conversation, and by giving the sanction of their countenance to the well-disposed,—though, it must be confessed, few men possessed qualifications equal to his, either of a moral or intellectual kind.—He was alike fitted either to handle the topics of theology, discuss the theories of philosophy, or to expatiate on the beauties of classical learning; while neither did unseasonable merriment, nor the ebullitions of party feeling, degrade the sobriety of his discourse. In his company, one felt in a religious atmosphere, but it was clear, elastic, and enlivening to the spirits, calculated to mature virtuous sentiment, and to invite every generous and holy affection into wider expansion.

Notwithstanding the time devoted to family and ministerial duties, Mr Stewart found leisure to engage in several literary pursuits of considerable difficulty. Besides contributing occasional papers of much value to periodical works, he continued the cultivation of Gaelic, and at length published the fruits of his inquiries in his well-known Grammar. Of the progress of this important treatise, he gives this account to Mr D——:

'Though I could speak Gaelic in my infancy, yet, as I was many years unaccustomed to use it, and my study was all in English, I found considerable difficulty, when I began to preach, in expressing myself with tolerable accuracy or fluency. This constrained me to examine the language grammatically, and endeavour to reduce it to rule. In this labour I had very little assistance; for, though the Gaelic was once a copious and cultivated tongue, it has been degenerating into a rude and irregular state since it became the speech only of ignorant and illiterate people. My notes gradually extended. At last, having been confined a whole winter by a tedious recovery from a slow fever, I employed a part of my time in correcting and arranging what I had written; and I was encouraged to publish my lucubrations in the form of a short Gaelic Grammar.'

The first edition of the Grammar appeared in 1801; and with what industry of research, and patience of investigation, it was prepared, various proofs exist in the correspondence he carried on, for several preceding years, with the best-informed Gaelic scholars, on the philology of that language; and particularly with Dr Donald Smith, of whom mention has already been made.[1]

When the Highland Society of London had resolved to publish the Gaelic originals of Ossian's poems,[2] the revisal was committed to Mr Stewart; and as the manuscripts, from age and neglect, were in a very mutilated state, it required no small labour, as well as ingenuity, to restore them. His emendations, the secretary informed him, were 'literally adhered to by the superintending committee.' And, in addition to the grammatical province of the work, it was assigned him to furnish a view of the internal evidence of the authenticity of those famous poems. 'I know none better qualified to undertake this than yourself,' wrote the secretary; 'you will be animated to the task by your regard to the literary honours of Caledonia; and your labours will not only

[1] [See above, p. 63.]

[2] [In 1765 the Scottish poet James Macpherson published *The Works of Ossian*, a translation from the Gaelic language of a cycle of ancient epic poems. A legendary figure by the name of Ossian is represented as both the narrator and author of these poems. There has been a long-running dispute over how much of what Macpherson translated he himself first wrote.]

confer an obligation on the Highland Society, and the present age, but posterity will be gratefully thankful for the zeal which excites your talents to the undertaking.'

Posterity, however, will owe to Mr Stewart its meed of gratitude and applause, for the revisal of works of higher inspiration, and better authenticated original, than those of Ossian,—we allude to the part he took in correcting the Gaelic translation of the Holy Scriptures. But before noticing his labours in this department, we shall here mention a proposal that was made to him by the Highland Society of Scotland to undertake to supply the grand desideratum to Gaelic students,—a dictionary of the language.

In 1812, he had been induced to send out a new edition of his Grammar, greatly enlarged and improved.[1] To encourage him in the work, Sir John M'Gregor Murray, Bart., a zealous and generous promoter of Gaelic literature, besides recommending the Grammar to public favour, as far as his influence extended, offered to take 600 copies for himself. As this work placed Mr Stewart among the first in the first rank of Gaelic scholars, in the estimation of all competent to judge, the Highland Society having already enrolled him among their honorary members, turned their eyes to him as the person best qualified to execute the Dictionary they had projected.

[1] [*Elements of Gaelic Grammar in Four Parts,* Second Edition, Corrected and Enlarged (Edinburgh: Oliphant, Waugh, & Innes, 1812.)]

Accordingly, the proposition was made to him by Sir John M'Gregor Murray, in the name of the Committee, with an offer of such remuneration, as, in Mr Stewart's family circumstances, was a very considerable inducement to close with the project. He did employ much prayer and deliberation, but at length declined it, chiefly, it appears, on the following ground.

'Here comes the reason,' says he, after discussing the motives for and against it, 'that weighs most with me against the proposed undertaking, that is, the hold which these Gaelic studies take of my mind. If the task were an unpleasant one, unsuitable to my taste or inclination, I might force myself to it as a matter of duty, to bestow upon it an allotted portion of time, and think no more of it till I sat down to it again. But the circumstance of its being congenial to my taste and habits of study, is what makes it a snare. What many would judge a fortunate turn, as qualifying me for the task, and facilitating my progress, I must account the strongest objection to the undertaking. If, indeed, by temporal considerations, I should determine to give a portion (and it can be but a small portion) of my time to this work, and, as I proceed, find the bad consequences I apprehend realized, what am I to do then? Break off my labour in the middle, like a foolish builder, who had not counted the cost? If I should commence the work with the persuasion that my divine Master approved it (and surely I ought to have this persuasion, or not meddle with it at all), then, when trials meet me, how should I know whether these were salutary antidotes against the natural effects of my secular employment, to preserve my soul from catching harm, or intimations of God's displeasure, and warnings to leave off such a carnal occupation, lest a worse thing should befall me?'

Having resisted repeated solicitations, the work was committed to other hands, quite adequate, no doubt, to achieve it. Sometime after, when a specimen of its execution was circulated among the members of the Society, for their opinion, the principal conductor wrote to Mr Stewart, 'That he had received his remarks on the printed specimen of the Gaelic Dictionary, and that they were, as he expected, more than worth all that had been received on the subject.'

Upon the whole, a compilation for which the materials were so scanty, and the drudgery of application necessary to reduce them into form hardly credible to those who have not attempted something similar, was prudently declined by Mr Stewart at the time, and subsequent events more fully justified the propriety of his decision. If he had been moved by the phantom of a name, to have been the first to give a Grammar and a Lexicon to his native tongue,[1] might have held out to literary ambition a strong incentive to the enterprise.

[1] He gave also a Primer, or Spelling-Book.

But he had undertaken another work,—to feed the flock of Christ,—and this was dearer to him than all. In order to fulfil this office, he who was competent for the most splendid exertions in philology, was well pleased to sit down to the obscure but useful work of translating Tracts into the vernacular language.

He had begun his Gaelic publications at Moulin, with a translation of Dr Watt's *Preservative*, etc. etc. Besides the revisal of the metrical version of the *Gaelic* Psalms, the Society for Propagating Christian Knowledge also committed to him the comparing the Gaelic translation of the Prophetical Books with the original Hebrew,—a laborious task, which had become necessary from the frequent instances of disagreement that existed betwixt the original and version; and when a new revision of the entire Gaelic Bible was proposed, the distinguished scholar to whom it was committed, early applied for the criticisms of Mr Stewart. 'I had a letter,' says he, 'in December 1810, from Dr John Stuart, minister of Luss, in Dumbartonshire, requesting my remarks, as he was now employed in revising the translation. I believe philological studies are something of a hobby with me. If I can really be useful in that way, it is well, but I need to remember that a hobby is always a snare,—a favourite may easily become an idol.'

While intent on philological researches himself, he loved to promote them in others; and as an instance of philanthropy, and the interest he particularly took in promoting the translation of the sacred scriptures into the languages of the heathen, it may be mentioned, that having observed, in the reports of the Baptist Bengal Missions, a letter of Dr Carey[1] to Mr Fuller,[2] complaining of the weak state of his eyes, and begging Mr Fuller to procure for him a Vander Hoogh's edition of the Hebrew Bible, which at that time was no easy matter, all communication with the Continent being intercepted, Mr Stewart immediately said to himself, 'I wish the worthy man had my copy,'—and sitting down, wrote, offering it, and desiring to be informed how to have it transmitted. The offer being gladly accepted, 'I with great pleasure followed the direction, wrote a letter of some length to Carey, and sent off my parcel to London. I dare say you remember my favourite Hebrew Bible in two volumes. I parted with it, with something of the same feelings that a pious parent might do with a favourite son, going on a mission to the heathen,—with a little regret, but with much good will.'

His Hebrew missionary had a prosperous voyage to India, and proved the occasion of a very interesting correspondence with Mr Fuller and Dr Carey, whose communications were replete with intelligence dear to Mr

[1] [William Carey (1761–1834), English Baptist minister and missionary to India.]

[2] [Andrew Fuller (1754–1815), English Baptist minister and theologian, who was also a founder member and long-time servant of the Particular Baptist Society for Propagating the Gospel among the Heathen.]

Stewart, relating to the progress of the Christian kingdom. To what amount of missionary good his donation gave occasion, is only known to him, who can trace a moral element through all its combinations, and assign its positive influence on the grand result to which all things tend,—the renovation of the world.

CHAPTER 8

EXCERPTS FROM A DIARY

AMID these multiplied avocations in the parish, and family, and study, it may easily be conceived much labour must needs be expended, and it was hardly to be expected that application so intense, would not prove injurious to health. In fact, though naturally of a firm constitution, its solidity was somewhat relaxed by the assiduity of his literary pursuits at the university; and though his general health, with a few exceptions of occasional indisposition during his continuance at Moulin, was good, he was visited in 1807, two years after his settlement at Dingwall, with an illness of long continuance and severity; from which he rose not only with a countenance much faded, but with a constitution shorn of its former vigour, which it never afterwards regained. Previous to this, his eyes had suffered from the close habits of study in which he had indulged; but during the illness of that period, they were in so impaired a state, as to be unable to bear the action of light, and they continued ever after tender, and occasionally subject to partial defection.

In 1811, an internal disorder of a calculus kind, which had been for years gradually forming, began to manifest very alarming symptoms; causing at times the most excruciating pain, and more than once putting his life in imminent danger. On this occasion he had recourse to the distinguished skill of Dr Gregory, who entered into his case with all the earnestness of a friend, and manifested a solicitude for his recovery, that made a deep impression on the mind of his patient. His disorder for that time yielded to medical treatment; but though it admitted of alleviations and intervals of ease, it could not be radically removed. The symptoms from year to year indicated a more confirmed malady, which, after immense suffering, finally brought him to the grave. It ought, therefore, to be considered, in estimating his doings, that whatever he did for the last ten years of his life, was done amid pain and lassitude, with the rod of disease always hanging over him, and very often painfully inflicted.

To suffer is the common lot of mortality. To suffer as a Christian, however, is not common; and the frame of mind maintained under painful and protracted maladies, puts the solidity of Christian character to a test, and generally affords a correct measure of its actual grace. Of Mr Stewart it may be said, that in the fiery trial, if there was some alloy to be purged away in the process of refinement, there remained a large amount of pure, substantial, imperishable worth of character, on which the flame wrought no diminution. That the Lord was with him in passing through the fire, the meek and exemplary patience with which he trode the painful way, abundantly manifested. Nor was it his object merely to suffer, with a resigned composure and fortitude, the will of God; he thought it became him to employ the most heart-searching scrutiny into his character and state, to ascertain the meaning of the rod; and how he improved seasons of bodily distress, the following memorandum found among his papers will show.

'*March* 11*th*, 1807.—

'After the long indisposition by which I have been confined, and laid aside from duty, it is fit that I should now try to recollect the lessons which the Lord has been teaching me, and seek in prayer to have them impressed and maintained in my mind.

'1. I have been led to see that I have been too remiss in my preparations for the pulpit, not taking due pains to study my subject, to study the scriptures in reference to it, to have my own heart affected with it, and to obtain the Holy Spirit's assistance in enforcing it upon my hearers. It is my earnest prayer that my gracious divine

Master, in whose work I am engaged, if it be his good pleasure to send me out again into his vineyard, would dispose me to be more diligent in these respects for the future; that he would impress my heart with a deeper sense of the importance of the work, and of the value of the precious souls committed to my care; and that he would strengthen my memory and enlighten my understanding, that I may understand the scriptures, and make a proper and seasonable application of them to the consciences of my hearers. It is my purpose, through the grace given to me, to take more time, and to write more of my discourses than formerly, as I think my neglect of writing has been one principal reason of my being superficial and barren in my illustrations and exhortations.

'2. I have been led to consider how very deficient I am in the duty of public prayer, having much formality in my spirit, much barrenness and sameness in my matter and expression. May the Lord give me a more abundant portion of the spirit of prayer, that I may be constant and fervent in that holy exercise in secret, and so obtain a supply both of the grace and gift of prayer in public, so that I may lift up my own heart, and the hearts of my people, to him who is the hearer of prayer.

'3. I have been led to a strong conviction, that one of my greatest snares, and one of the chief hindrances to usefulness in my intercourse with my acquaintances, is complaisance. I have too much desire to say only what is agreeable to others, rather than what may prove useful to them. There may be a mixture of timidity in this complaisance. I suspect there is; may the Lord give me resolution to be faithful in his cause, not to be over-anxious to recommend myself to the good opinion of worldly people, but rather be content to cause some uneasiness, or give some offence, than lose an opportunity of bearing my testimony to the truth.'

Bodily illness is a trial to all on whom it is imposed; but, perhaps, to a minister it comes with an additional aggravation. If he loves his work, it is suspended; if he is concerned for the souls of those around him, they are abandoned to a variety of evils in the absence of his personal superintendence. The consciousness of being for the time useless, or the reflection of past unprofitableness, is not easily borne; and, alas! it too often happens, that offences will spring up among the people, as if to upbraid the inefficacy of his former labours, and loudly to call for redoubled vigour of action, while he must be *passive*. In such circumstances, a faithful minister does not want consolation in Christ; but who need wonder, if, at times, objects present themselves to his mind in colours of despondency? From such feelings Mr Stewart was not always exempt, as may be inferred from the following extract from a letter to Mr D——:

'*March*, 1814.

'I wish I could cheer you with good news from this little town and parish, but, alas! we seem to be doing nothing, almost quite dead. I was laid aside for some weeks, having been seized with a topical complaint, which might have proved fatal, no surgeon being at hand, if I had not been mercifully directed and enabled to use the proper means for procuring relief. I hoped that my own spirit had been softened and warned by this visitation, but, alas! all was like the morning cloud. My own vineyard I have not kept, and now it is growing over with thorns. I have not a heart nor a soul to employ in the honourable service of the most honourable of all masters, but I am to try, at least, to employ my silly body in the work, and am to begin this day a course of parochial examination. Woe is me! for the day goeth away, the shadows of the evening are stretched out over me, and little or nothing done for him that loved me, and gave himself for me,—unprofitable servant!'

To the same beloved friend, he wrote not long after:—

'*July*, 1815.

'One apology for my allowing your much esteemed letter of February to remain so long unanswered, is, that I have been a traveller of late. And were I a man of acute observation, or of quick feeling, I might have many interesting details to give of what I should have seen and felt on my journey. My excursion was not to the next country or province, but to a place which people account "a far country," whereas I found it situated but a few paces from home. You will understand me when I say, that my visit was to the regions on the banks of Jordan, the confines of the unseen world. I seemed to be led to the margin of the stream, and believed that, in a few days at farthest, I must cross the irremeable[1] flood. The prospect was extremely dark; I perceived almost nothing of the beauties of the promised land, or of that goodly mountain, even Lebanon. Like Hezekiah, "I wept sore." I could just with difficulty cast the care of my soul, and body, and family, on the great and good Shepherd of Israel, and, through his tender mercy, I was just kept from despondency. I was, however, sent back into the wilderness, and here I am still a sojourner and pilgrim in a foreign land. To speak without allegory,—in consequence of a long ride in a cold windy day in April, I was seized with a fever, which greatly increased my topical malady, accompanied with alarming symptoms, which did not yield to medicine for several days; and, during that time, it appeared probable that the disorder would soon issue in inflammation, mortification, and dissolution. But the Lord was pleased to spare and restore me, to record his goodness. O for a heart to praise the Lord, for he is good, for his mercy endureth for ever!'

[1] [That is, offering no possibility of return.]

Besides the personal affliction laid on Mr Stewart, his sympathies were powerfully excited by the often indisposition of his beloved partner, who was scarce a step behind him in the path of those tribulations. The decease of her venerable father in 1812, was a trial of great magnitude to both, and occasioned a blank to them in that country, which they never expected to see filled up. The progress of this bereavement Mr Stewart thus describes, in a letter to his sister, dated,

'*Urquhart Manse, Sept.* 30, 1812.

'O my dear sister, what a subject have I got now to write upon, if I could do it justice! Our dear father, Mr Calder, is probably within a few hours of entering into the joy of his Lord! On Thursday last he was seized with an inflammation in the bowels. A physician from Inverness applied various remedies, besides copious bleeding, by which the fever and worst symptoms were much abated. Our revived hopes, however, began to sink again, when we found the disease had only changed its seat, and his suffering became severe and constant. The dear venerable patient has suffered extreme pain, with no rest, except what was obtained by laudanum.[1] His language, during his whole illness, was full of self-abasement, admiration and praise of his blessed

[1] [Laudanum was a 10 per cent solution of opium powder in alcohol, widely used to treat everything from pain and insomnia to female disorders.]

Redeemer, and the most affectionate concern about his family and flock. This morning, particularly, after a pretty long sleep, being more free from pain, and a little revived, we were all drawn round his bed by hearing the sound of his voice; and then he went on a considerable time in the most heavenly strain. His mind was perfectly clear, and his voice distinct. He told us of his good hope of a happy eternity, through the merits of his blessed Redeemer, how much he had us all in his heart,—addressed particularly his dear Margaret (Mrs Calder) and his daughters,—often blessed God for having given him such a partner and children,—and made most affectionate mention of his sons-in-law. He prayed fervently for his dear, dear James, who is far distant. To a respectable elder who was present, he gave it in charge to give his fondest love and blessings to his very dear flock, praying the Lord to send them the bread of life. He had said many such things during his illness,—dwelt upon the beautiful and emphatic image of Jacob's ladder,—observing how the blessed Jesus connected earth with heaven, and how prayers ascended, and blessings descended, through him, as the angels did upon the ladder. I had often read of deathbed scenes in magazines, but never witnessed such a one as this. Even my insensible heart was in some measure affected. It was a great privilege to be present, and especially to be a party in such a scene.'

Several days after.

'After a long interval, I am at last able, and but just able, to resume my pen; for my head and fingers, and especially my eyes, are much fatigued and worn out. We all had the melancholy satisfaction of attending our dear revered father's purified spirit to the gates of heaven. He took his flight on the evening of the 1st October. A few minutes before, he desired Mr M'Intosh and me to withdraw and pray. We did so for some minutes in company with Mrs C——, and then returned in time to hear him pronounce a few words, and then see him breathe his last in a composed and placid manner. The ladies were much affected, but yet were mercifully supported. The female attendants, kind and much attached women, were almost overpowered. The *late wake*, crowded with the first characters for piety in the whole country, mourning as orphans for their father, yet glorifying God on his behalf, was a scene uncommonly solemn and impressive. I cannot enter into a detail of the funeral, which was very numerously attended, and took place on Tuesday the 6th. The Presbytery appointed me to preach in the parish church the following Sabbath; an arduous duty, indeed, which, however, I was strengthened in some manner to perform. From the first, it became a most interesting thought, who should be the man who would be promoted to take the pastoral charge of such a flock. None supposed that the patron, Mr Forbes of Culloden, would act otherwise than to grant the living to the solicitation of some worldly friend. Instead of that, as soon as he heard of the vacancy, he sent an assurance to the elders, that he would present none but a man perfectly agreeable to the parish. He resolutely refused many applications, declaring, that he would not gratify an individual at the expense of distressing hundreds; and when the people presented a petition to him in favour of Mr J. Macdonald of the Gaelic Chapel, Edinburgh, Culloden cheerfully complied, and gave them his letter to that effect. Mr Macdonald has been written to, but his mind is not yet known. All this is matter of astonishment, joy, and praise, to the Lord's people throughout the land.'[1]

'He was removed to glory,' says he, in another letter, 'after seven days illness. This last stage of his journey was indeed a very painful one to the flesh, but he was blessed with perfect composure of mind. While he showed the deepest self-abasement, yet the love, the grace, the fulness, and glory of his adorable Redeemer, were his constant theme. Though torn with acute inward pain, he never uttered a complaining word; not a feature of

[1] If a patron would compare the animating spectacle of a grateful people, expressing 'joy and praise' for the gift of an acceptable pastor, with the discontented aspect of a congregation disappointed in what is to them the greatest solace of life,—surely he would pause and reflect before he made many sad for the interest of an individual, or for the pleasure of a few.

his face indicated a struggle to suppress complaint. The most serene, resplendent luminary of our horizon, is set. His affectionate, bereaved parish, are left for a time as sheep without a shepherd. His pious, venerable widow, bowed down with infirmities and broken health, is left a solitary pilgrim in the wilderness. His tender attached daughters, who doted on their father with almost more than filial piety, have felt a pang in being separated from him, which time alone can heal.'

Thus sustaining no small fight of afflictions, and pressing on in the narrow way, Mr Stewart persevered in the arduous march of a holy life. We have hitherto drawn the materials for narration from letters he wrote to confidential friends. But in 1814, a new door of insight is opened into his character, by the commencement of a diary. It may be regretted, that so much of his active and most important life passed over without a single memorandum of his feelings and views being left on record, excepting what his letters exhibit; as it may easily be conceived, how interesting such memorials would have been in the days of his first illumination, and greatest usefulness, at Moulin. The writer of this, however, had occasion to know, that what deterred Mr Stewart from the practice of keeping these mental registers, was not the opinion of their inutility to the individual himself, for the practice itself, under proper management, he thought favourable to piety; and his having recourse to it himself at so late a period of life, has stamped upon it the approval of his deliberate judgment. He himself accounts for his late beginning, in the introduction to the first record.

'*May 9th*, 1814.—The recommendation and the example of pious men have often suggested to me the utility of keeping a journal or diary, as a short record of providences, experiences, and employments. Different circumstances, not of a trivial kind, have hitherto discouraged me from attempting it. Having now a little more conveniency than at former periods, I am prompted to try a short exercise of this kind, by finding that a great many occurrences have escaped my memory, which ought to have been remembered and improved; and from a hope that the Lord may be pleased to bless this exercise to my soul, by giving me a more thorough knowledge of myself, and of his gracious and bountiful dealings with me in my soul, in my body, my work, and my earthly lot; in giving me a more distinct view of the manner in which my precious time is spent, and the vast important work of the holy ministry prosecuted. Much of my mortal life is past,—much of bodily strength is gone,—my faculties are growing less acute and vigorous,—the day is going away, and the shadows of the evening are stretched out. A growing malady warns me that my stay here may not be long. Yet almost nothing is done or doing in this part of my Lord's vineyard. O useless unprofitable servant that I am! May the Lord be pleased, in great mercy, and for his name's sake, to revive his work in my dull, sluggish, unfeeling soul. Till then, I can scarcely hope to see any good done, by my means, in this place.'

'*May* 8*th, P. M.*—I had this day a call from a judicious tender-hearted Christian, of the parish of Urquhart. She sat and conversed with me some time. She was under much concern about the state of her soul. I felt as if it were a most presumptuous thing in me to attempt to administer counsel or comfort to one so much my superior. I hope the Lord sent her for my good, to give her a greater concern in my spiritual welfare, and to engage her prayers more warmly in my behalf. O that the Lord may stir up many to pray for my poor soul, my family, and my flock!

'Had a strong proof, this evening, how wretchedly I can err when left to myself, and how much I need a constant monitor. Lord, teach me to watch and pray, and set thee always before me, and take the counsel thou offerest.'

'*May* 9*th.*—Had some minutes affecting discourse, this morning, with my son, who came to my study before his brothers. He is naturally tender-hearted and impressible; but I must take care not to mistake natural feeling for gracious impressions. When, O

Lord, will salvation come to this house? When shall we, fond parents, see all our children walking in the truth? When shall we see one of them choosing the good part which shall not be taken from them? Lord, keep me this day watchful and circumspect; teach me to improve occasions, and, if possible, to find occasion of speaking a word for Christ, of reminding sinners of their great concern.

'My time a good deal occupied with ordinary secular matters. I need to learn to keep a strict guard over myself, and to set the Lord before me in all such matters, as my heart is so ready to be untuned and carnalized. Had an agreeable meeting at D—— M——'s in the evening; Question from 2 Cor. 6:17, 18, practical and interesting; my own heart very cold and lifeless. Lord, breathe, breathe on it without ceasing, and make me to pray without ceasing; else the feeble spark of life will not burn at all!'

'*May 11th.*—This morning sound in bodily health, free of pain or trouble, but cold and lifeless in heart. No spirituality do I ever feel, unless when under some painful feeling, some chastening from the hand of God, or some sharp reproof from my conscience. Of all *means*, the rod, applied not to my body but to my mind, has ever proved the most effectual to rouse and spiritualize my dull affections, and stir up anything like a spirit of supplication. But the moment the rod is removed,

I grow cold like iron out of the furnace. When, when shall it be otherwise with me? Lord, perfect that which concerneth me, for thy great name's sake. I endeavoured this morning, but I know not with what success, to lay hold on a promise that was brought to my view. Long has the Lord waited for me with wonderful patience and condescension; may he teach me and enable me to wait only on him, and to "exalt him" in my heart, speech, and behaviour, "that he may have mercy upon me."

'This day visited my much-respected and beloved parent Mrs C.; was refreshed and humbled with her conversation. She had newly received a second letter from her beloved son, written a few days after he had got the first accounts of his revered father's death. His letter was full of filial sorrow, and the most affectionate condolence. He is a dear tender-hearted youth, a child of many prayers and tears, like St Augustine; and like him must be saved. My own mind was unusually empty and unemployed in the way; much precious time lost. May the Lord forgive, and teach me to improve solitude.'

'*May* 12*th*.—An acquaintance called on me today, to represent the case of a neighbour of his own, who had for some time made a credible profession of religion, but for some months back has been falling into a habit of drinking, and wished me to take an early opportunity of admonishing him. I think it is my duty to do so, and would earnestly implore the Lord's direction that I may do it faithfully and in love, and that it may be accompanied with the divine blessing. I have been busied this day about common things, my mind vacant and unedified. Lord, enable me now to close the day with thyself.'

'*May 16th.*—Rode out in the forenoon—the rest of the day employed in ordinary matters—nothing done directly for Christ. This is a shameful loss of precious time. I have often resolved, and I desire to repeat my resolution in the presence of Jesus, "whose I am, and whom I" am bound by a thousand obligations to "serve," never to let a whole day pass without something said, or written, or done, to spread the savour of Christ's name, to stir up some spiritual grace in the souls of others, or in my own. Lord, pardon, for thy mercy's sake, my inexcusable negligence in this respect, and rouse me to greater carefulness in future!'

'*May 20th.*—Visited ——, whom I found still in a state of distress and discouragement, complaining, that though she was persuaded the promises were free and full, yet she was not able to lay hold on them for herself. She complains sorely of hardness, coldness, and insensibility; and, above all, an evil heart of unbelief. She acknowledged she was the better of seeing a person with whom she could converse freely. Though she cannot at present rejoice in the Lord, yet she looks steadily towards him as the God of her salvation. I have no doubt that the Lord is thus preparing her for a fuller manifestation of himself, and that he will soon give her a garment of praise for a spirit of heaviness.'

'*May 21st.*—Having finished my studying and writing for next Lord's day, I purpose, if the Lord permit, to employ some hours of this afternoon (as the day that I am least interrupted) in examination, humiliation, and prayer, particularly in reference to the state of my poor, lifeless, senseless soul, my family, and my parish. It is an exercise which I have sadly neglected, but which I need exceedingly. I know it is difficult and painful. Lord, enable me to begin it, and to pursue it with a single eye to spiritual benefit, and to thy glory. O search thou me, and know my heart!'

'*Evening.*—Having begun what I intended for this day's exercise, with prayer for the divine presence and blessing, and read the 139th Psalm, I was interrupted by a man being introduced by one of the elders, as under great trouble of mind. He is an old man of decent life and behaviour, has been for some weeks under an increasing concern about his soul's state, and is often distressed with alarming fears. Conversed with him some time; then sent for D—— M——, elder, and we conversed with him a considerable time together, endeavouring to lead him to a more distinct view of sin, the true ground of fear, and then to look to Christ as the free and all-sufficient Saviour of sinners. D—— M—— prayed with him before parting. This interview occupied the greater part of the forenoon. Any other Saturday, I should have found it an unseasonable interruption; but this day, the Lord, foreseeing this engagement, had led me to finish my studies, so that I had some hours to spare. Persons applying for spiritual advice is almost a new thing here. May the Lord grant that this may turn to good, and that it may be the beginning of a glorious harvest, to the praise of his free sovereign grace, who worketh when, and where, and how he pleaseth!'

'*May 24th.*—Last night I had a return of an alarming complaint to which I have been long subject. After trying the usual expedients for relief with little effect, I had recourse at last to an expedient that succeeded. I cried to the Lord for help; he graciously heard me, and I succeeded to a wish. I was immediately relieved, and all the troublesome symptoms abated in the course of the day.—How plainly does the Lord warn me to consider my latter end, and not to reckon upon length of days! O that he would be pleased to exert his power, and show me his mercy, by releasing my poor soul in like manner from deadness and inactivity! May this warning rouse me to more constant attention and faithfulness in duty, now that the shadows of the evening are stretched out.'

'*May 25th.*—Occupied about ordinary matters—no spiritual good received or imparted—no progress made in journeying toward heaven—nothing done for the cause of Christ, or the glory of God, a sad return for life preserved, and health restored! Lord, pardon my wretched unprofitableness—make me dread to spend another day so.'

'*May 28th.*—Studied the greater part of the day;—was greatly affected with a letter received in the morning, from my dear and valuable brother, Mr J—— S—— of B—— S——. It was singularly seasonable, and I can scarcely say whether it was more calculated to encourage or to humble me. I must believe, as my dear brother writes, that many Christian friends are attached to me, and concerned about me, and that there was a time when the Lord did make his own word precious to some through my very poor and feeble ministry. But, alas! how is the gold become dim! Woe is me, that I sojourn in Mesech! O that I knew where I might find him!'

'*May 30th.*—In reading the scriptures this morning, and seeking a promise for the day, I am directed to Joel 2:21-27, particularly verses 21, 27, "The Lord will do great things, and my people shall never be ashamed." May the Spirit impress it, enable me to lay hold, and fulfil—'

'*June* 13*th*.—Last week I became acquainted with Mr C——, a pious valuable man, residing in England. I heard him, with much satisfaction, give a private lecture one evening, and preach another evening in the Town Hall. I wish that my hands were often strengthened by such visitors. I have to record the goodness of my bountiful Lord in strengthening me yesterday in body and spirit, in the whole public service of the day. To him be all the glory. Visited three women bed-rid.'

'*June* 14*th*.—Took a ride to Munlochy and Inverness on business. Returned in the evening safe, but fatigued. In Inverness, unexpectedly met Mr C——, who had been disappointed. Exchanged Christian affectionate salutations with him, and took leave, not expecting to see him again in this world.'

'*June* 15*th*.—Most agreeably surprised today, with hearing that a horse had been sent for Mr C——, and that he was expected here today. About two o'clock had a call from the excellent man, and his dear amiable cousin Miss C——. Heard him preach in the evening in the hall with singular power. Assuredly this man of God has been sent on a special message to Dingwall, and particularly to me. O that the Lord would be pleased to send a portion of the same spirit and gift to my dull worthless soul! I am often tempted to ask, "Can the Lord do such a thing? Can he revive my dead insensible heart?" Lord, rebuke me for my unbelief, and quicken me with thy Spirit, before the day pass entirely away, and the night come upon me, wherein no man can work.'

'*June 16th.*—I am disappointed of hearing dear Mr C—— this evening, for the last time. His visit to this town, and particularly his unexpected return from Inverness, is surely a token to Dingwall, either of mercy or of judgment. I may say the same of myself. O! may the Lord bless his dear servant's ministration to some,—to many! What a loud reproof to my careless, heartless, unprofitable services! O! for the breath of heaven! Awake, O north wind! and come, thou south! Amen.'

'*July 13th.*—After a long suspension of my notes, I am admonished to endeavour to resume them. A faithful and seasonable reproof from my conscience, relative to the particular state of my soul, particularly as to the exercise of prayer, warns me, that it is highly needful to search and try my ways. O! may I be enabled to attend and profit by the Lord's rebuke, before his chastening hand fall heavy upon me. I purpose, if the Lord permit, to employ the greater part of this day in retirement, to examine the state of my miserable heart. Lord! do give me light and understanding to perceive my real state, for I fear I have been much misled by the kindness, and the too favourable opinion of others concerning me.

'After spending the morning and forenoon in my room, I have reason to bless the Lord for some little access to himself, which he was pleased to grant me, and one or two momentary meltings of heart; such as to give me a very slight notion of what it is to have fellowship with God, and pour out the heart before him. This I had, particularly in pleading for my very dear children. Lord, continue, review, increase this secret communion with thyself,—no life, no thriving without it.'

'*July 31st.*—Had felt my breast a little inflamed and uneasy in the night, and was concerned how I should make out the service of the day, and having again to preach tomorrow at ——. The Lord strengthened me in person and spirit. I was supported in an ordinary measure in Gaelic, and more so in the English; and when I had finished, I felt my breast quite well, and my voice sound. Well may I say, "the Lord is my helper, I will trust in him, and not be afraid."'

These memorials are short, and interspersed in the original with marks and references, in a character known only to himself. They comprise a space not exceeding three months, and not diversified with any event of importance. His reason for discontinuing them is not known; but whatever induced him to leave off, the little he has given, shows a heart alive to the great concerns of the soul; breathing after the highest attainments in Christian experience, and groaning under the consciousness of deplored infirmities and defects in character, perceptible only to himself, and to his God.

Perhaps some may be led to conceive less favourably of the extent of his attainments in grace, on finding him use the language of complaint oftener than that of approbation, in judging of himself. But to the consideration of such, we would recommend the following sentiments of one of the greatest masters of human reason[1] that has ever appeared in the world; or, if a higher authority be sought, let the 7th chapter of Romans be seriously examined.

'Grace, and the love of God, in the most eminent saints in this world, is truly very little in comparison with what it ought to be; because, the highest love that ever any attain to in this life, is poor, cold, exceeding low, and not worthy to be named, in comparison of what our obligations appear to be, from the joint consideration of these two things, viz. 1. The reason God has given us to love him, in the manifestations he has made of his infinite glory, in his word, and in his works; and particularly the gospel of his Son, and what he has done for sinful man by him. And, 2. The capacity there is in the soul of man, by those intellectual faculties which God has given it,

[1] [Jonathan Edwards (1703–58), *A Treatise Concerning Religious Affections.*]

of seeing and understanding those reasons which God has given us to love him. How small, indeed, is the love of the most eminent saint on earth, in comparison of what these things jointly considered do require. And this grace tends to convince men of this, and especially eminent grace; for grace is of the nature of light, and brings truth to view. And therefore, he that has much grace, apprehends, much more than others, that great height to which his love ought to ascend; and he sees, better than others, how little a way he has risen towards that height. And therefore, estimating his love by the whole height of his duty, hence it appears astonishingly little and low in his eyes. And the eminent saint having such a conviction of the high degree in which he ought to love God, this shows him not only the littleness of his grace, but the greatness of his remaining corruption. It appears exceedingly abominable to him, that Christ should be loved so little, and thanked so little, for his dying love; it is in his eyes hateful ingratitude.

'And then the increase of grace has a tendency another way to cause the saints to think their deformity vastly more than their good; it not only tends to convince them their corruption is much greater than their goodness, which is indeed the case, but it also tends to cause the deformity that there is in the least sin, or the least degree of corruption, to appear so great, as vastly to outweigh all the beauty there is in their greatest holiness; for this also is indeed the case.

'True grace is of that nature, that the more a person has of it, with remaining corruption, the less does his goodness and holiness appear, in proportion to his deformity, in the sin that now appears in his heart, and in the abominable defects of his highest and best affections and brightest experiences.'

If the private records of Mr Stewart had represented him reviewing with complacency his own acquirements, who would not have disesteemed him, and ranked him very low in the kingdom of God? What exalts character is humility,—and that grace dwelt in him richly. He saw more clearly than most men, the intermixture of evil in things seemingly good; and from the comprehensive views he took of duty, the greatest performances of his best times appeared exceedingly little, and unequal to the motives which he at all times possessed. But self-abasement is not incompatible with a sense of safety, or a frame of habitual joy; for it is the privilege of all who fully enter into the grace of the gospel method of salvation, that with the deepest self-abhorrence, they have somewhat wherein to glory, and that is, Christ. And had we Mr Stewart's judgment of faith on record, as we have his judgment of sense, we should doubtless find his heart as full of glorying, as we have seen it depressed with conscious defects. And while he saw nothing in himself corresponding to the holiness of his desires, and the extent of his obligations, in Christ he could say, 'I am complete.'

To overlook self-unworthiness, fosters a ruinous self-complacency, hateful in the sight of Heaven;—to dwell on it perpetually, without 'looking unto Jesus' in the joy of believing, is not more unfavourable to sanctification, than injurious to peace. What Milner[1] observes concerning a sermon of Grossteste,[2] is worthy of remark; that 'it was well calculated to humble the proud, but had very little to encourage the sincere; for that he seemed to have no idea of the attainment of a state of solid peace and joy.' This he attributes to his not knowing 'the just nature of the Christian article of justification by Jesus Christ the Righteous.' This, however, Mr Stewart not only knew himself, but was the instrument of communicating the knowledge of it to many others; and, therefore, though a sense of manifold short-comings caused sorrow, in his righteousness he enjoyed exalted peace and solid comfort, the *sense* of which, however, was to him, as well as to others, liable to be modified by changes in the medium of perception; and it generally happens, that diaries are most resorted to, not in seasons of clear, but of doubtful

[1] [Joseph Milner (1744–1797), was an English evangelical divine, whose work, *The History of the Church of Christ*, was published between 1794–1809.]

[2] [Robert Grossteste (1175–1253), English philosopher and theologian.]

perception. Hence, most memorials of that kind exhibit chiefly the darker shades of experience.

The following sentiments, contained in a letter written several years later than those notes in his diary, breathe the same spirit of conscious unworthiness and self-abasement.

'When I see such living examples as M'L——, and the zealous ministers, and some private Christians around me, I find myself entirely eclipsed, and unworthy of any place in the system. I think this was impressed on me with some force in my late illness. I saw myself a wretchedly unprofitable servant, a withered branch, fit only for burning. I have read of eminent Christians having a strong sense of their own unworthiness; and I have been inclined to think that their state was far otherwise than they themselves apprehended. It is possible that my partial friends may fancy that to be my case. But it is all a mistake. I surely believed that experienced Christians who had the worst opinion of themselves, judged truly, whatever others might think; and so I believe concerning myself, that the worst opinion I can have of my own heart, is short of the truth, however others may form a different opinion. In our present pilgrimage, I believe the valley of humiliation is the most advantageous point of view, from which to behold the Sun of righteousness in his benign and majestic splendour, as well as in his purifying and comforting influence.'

After the death of Mr Calder, the domestic circle of Mr Stewart was frequently enriched with the addition of Mrs C. whose conversation would have been accounted a great acquisition to any society capable of relishing 'the things of the Spirit.'

CHAPTER 9

CLOSING DAYS IN DINGWALL

BEYOND the Christian scene in his own house, he diffused the benefit of his knowledge and advice to many individuals, both in the neighbourhood and at a distance; keeping up a wider epistolary intercourse, than perhaps a prudent regard to the circumstances of his own impaired health might seem to justify. That survivors, however, may yet benefit by his exertion, we shall here insert a few of the letters written posterior to the date of his diary.

In 1815, he received a letter from a gentleman in Edinburgh, with whom a college intimacy had subsisted at St Andrews; and who, like himself, had been led to embrace other views of divine truth, than they ever thought to entertain in those juvenile days. This gentleman having met with his Moulin narrative, not long after he had begun to inquire seriously into revealed truth, immediately opened a correspondence with Mr S. on the subject of religion, and claimed a renewal of ancient friendship on a new and spiritual ground. To this proposal Mr Stewart gladly consented, and thus was restored a connection which had a considerable influence on the comfort and circumstances of his future years. The first letter Mr Stewart wrote to his new correspondent, is dated

'*Dingwall*, 28*th August*, 1815.

'My dear Sir,

'Few things indeed could have given me more delightful surprise than your much esteemed letter, received a few days ago.

'I well remember the agreeable days that we enjoyed together in St Andrews,—how many? thirty years ago and upwards? And I think the only time since that I have had the pleasure of seeing you, was once at Dunkeld House. In this large portion of our mortal life, my course has been a very circumscribed one. I have paced slowly through a small corner of the world, while you have probably occupied a wider range, corresponding to your talents and fortune,—seen much of the world, and been engaged in its busier scenes. Well, I desire to praise God on your account, that he has showed you the world's vanity, and inclined you to seek for yourself and your dear young ones, a better inheritance,—a more fasting and satisfactory portion. And I most affectionately hope, and, so far as my feeble prayers can avail, I do earnestly pray, that he who has turned your attention and desire toward himself, may be your guide and instructor, and lead you to the full knowledge "of the truth as it is in Jesus." The field of revelation is indeed wide, and contains a great variety of objects, and a vast fund of interesting entertainment to a sanctified mind. But the plan of redemption, though immensely grand, is simple, and requires no high cultivation of intellect to comprehend it, but only a humble mind, willing to receive it. And if you, my dear Sir,—and I would always include the dear partner of your joys and cares,—possess this grand requisite, the way lies open before you,—"Search the scriptures, for in them ye think ye have eternal life: and they are they which testify of Jesus" (John 5:39). The word of God reveals some things so strange, and some so unpalatable to our nature, that divine teaching is needful to make us apprehend, and fully acquiesce, in their truth and propriety. This divine teaching is to be obtained by prayer. Everything relative to the reception of gospel truth, the subjection of the will to the authority of God, and thankful acquiescence in the prescribed method of salvation, are all ascribed in the Bible to the influence of the Holy Spirit on the soul. And this influence is freely promised to them that humbly and sincerely ask it. "If ye, being evil, know how to give good gifts to your children, *how much more* shall your heavenly Father give the Holy Spirit to them that ask him" (Luke 11:13). I am well aware how difficult an attempt it is for a man who has lived esteemed by the world, to withdraw from its ensnaring company, its fashions and its habits. Old friends, connections, and companions, will warmly oppose such a separation. A man who quits the "broad road," and enters the "narrow way," must expect to be counted singular, for, in fact, he will be singular; and no little resolution is required to bear the imputation of singularity, to brave "the world's loud laugh." But the grace of Christian fortitude will support a man under any trial, and carry him safely through. You are not ignorant of what the scripture inculcates with respect to separation from the world (2 Cor. 6:17, John 15:19, Rom. 12:2).

'Since receiving your letter, the last report of the Edinburgh Bible Society came into my hands. One of the first things which struck my eye with pleasure, was to see your name added to the list of vice-presidents, and that you filled the chair at the last general meeting. This leads me to think, that you must have already formed an acquaintance with men of enlightened and pious minds, whether clergymen or others, in Edinburgh, who will be happy to cultivate your friendship, and who will be of much more service in aiding your inquiries than ever I could be. But if you were not always acquainted with men of such a character, I confess I should feel exceedingly desirous to answer your and Mrs ——'s kind and gratifying invitation, and fly by land or sea to your happy mansion, to embrace my old, or rather my new friend, and endeavour to strengthen our common faith and hope in the blessed gospel of our Lord and Saviour Jesus Christ. But the wish is all I dare indulge. Though my ordinary health is such as to allow my engaging in ordinary duty at home, yet I cannot venture to move a step from home. But if you honour me with your correspondence, it will give me pleasure to hear what you may be pleased to communicate, and to answer as I may be enabled to do. In reference to my letter to Mr Black, on the state of religion in the parish of Moulin, as you are pleased to say that you think it calculated to be useful, I have no objection whatever to its being reprinted. But, unless you have some special reasons for wishing the names to be suppressed, I think it would be better to allow them to remain. Names and dates give a stamp of authenticity, and create an interest in the perusal, which would be lessened if these were wanting. I have no wish at all to withdraw my testimony to the facts narrated, or the doctrine maintained in that letter, but am ready to renew and confirm my testimony to both, now after an interval of thirteen years from the publication of the last impression. And it occurs to me, that the effect of the narrative might be increased by my adding a short paragraph of that kind, either by way of preface or postscript, to the next impression. If Mrs —— and you think it best to get a small number printed in this way for gratuitous distribution, you have my full consent, and my earnest wishes that your charitable purpose may be abundantly blessed, and your benevolent desires richly gratified.

'I remember your three brothers well, all of them promising young men. I did not know, till your letter informed me, that they were all removed by death, and yourself the only representative of a once flourishing family. A young generation is now springing up under your wing. From what I already know of the parents, I feel no common interest in the children. What a blessing to them to have parents who are anxious to "bring them up in the nurture and admonition of the Lord!" The education of youth, in the enlarged sense of the word, is the most important of all arts. Much has been written on the subject; and I have no doubt that Mrs —— and you have already studied it very seriously. Of female writers on education, Mrs Hannah More[1] is the safest guide, as she takes the word of God for her own guide. In the training of children, rewards and punishments must be employed to a certain extent, corresponding to the good or faulty behaviour of the child. And nothing is more natural than for children to conceive, as they are often expressly taught, that the very same system of rewards and punishments, proportioned to merit and demerit, prevails, without any modification, in God's moral government of

[1] [Hannah More (1745–1833), English philanthropist and writer.]

his creatures. This is the old covenant of works, to which human nature, fallen as it is, strongly and continually leans. This system suited admirably well man's original state of innocence and holiness. But it would now be a most inapplicable and useless rule to address to a weak, depraved, condemned sinner, "If you do well, if you obey the holy law of your Creator, you shall be rewarded; but if you disobey, you shall be punished; be good, and you shall be happy." The propositions are true, but they are truths of no avail to a sinner. What a mercy to us that our salvation is secured by "a better covenant, established upon better promises!" (Heb. 8:6.) Indeed, we need to have perpetual recourse to that better covenant, and to impress on ourselves, as well as on our children, that our only hopes of pardon, acceptance, reward, or future happiness, are to be founded on the merits of another, not on our own; on the sufficient righteousness of Christ, our Surety and Mediator, not on our own, which is of no avail to our justification (Phil. 3:8, 9; Rom. 3:21, 24); that all we hope is from the free love, the unmerited favour, of God our Saviour; yet that the just apprehension, the firm belief of such free love and mercy, cannot fail to gain our love in return, and engage us, by the strongest and most endearing ties, "to live not to ourselves, but to him who loved us, and gave himself for us; who died for us, and rose again" (2 Cor. 5:14, 15). Faith, thus working by love, is the principle of the Christian life. A more efficient principle, or a more delightful exercise, can nowhere be found on earth or in heaven. I ought to feel no ordinary interest in the bringing up of children. I have no fewer than nine of them under my care,—a heavy burden, which I should never have known how to sustain, if the Lord had not blessed me with a partner who is fully as solicitous, and much more able than myself, to guide their childhood, and inform their young minds. My eldest son is at his studies, the rest are under private tuition at home.'

This letter was soon followed by another more open and confidential; and their friendship having been consolidated by a visit of Mr —— to Dingwall not long after, an unbroken intimacy subsisted until death bade the connection for a while to cease.

The interview mentioned took place in 1816, in the course of which year, the following letters were written by Mr Stewart:

'*October* 17, 1816.

'My very dear Sir,

'We all rejoiced very sincerely on learning, from your much esteemed letters, that you had regained in safety your beloved family, and found them well, and delighted, I am sure, at your return. It gives Mrs Stewart and me heartfelt pleasure to find ourselves joined to dear Mrs —— and you in the bonds of Christian friendship; and we hope the union will be not only lasting, but everlasting.

'The packet with the printed pamphlets, came to hand at the same time with your favour of the 7th. I have given them both a hasty perusal, comparing them with Dr C——'s Address. I knew something of W—— before, having seen his Letters on Methodism. His pamphlet is much in the same spirit, dogmatical, overbearing, and ill-tempered; very ill calculated indeed to enlighten or convince an opponent. Even where his tenets are right, his manner is more repulsive than conciliatory. B——'s pamphlet is quite a contrast to W——'s, clear, correct, temperate, and friendly. It is well fitted to be useful not only to Dr C——, but to all who read it.

'It appears to me that Dr C—— had found, or imagined, that an opinion prevailed among his people, that till a man has distinctly ascertained, to his own satisfaction, that he is possessed of true faith, he is under no obligation to break off his sins, or "maintain good works." Dr C—— justly conceives such an opinion to be erroneous and dangerous; but I think he has mistaken the proper way of applying the remedy. He is aware that the law is to be our schoolmaster, to bring us to Christ. And on this ground he urges obedience to its precepts, in order that a sinner may thereby become disposed and prepared to receive the free offer of salvation in the gospel; whereas, the strictness and spirituality of the law are to be held forth to convince men of their sin, to show them that they never did and never can keep it, but are already condemned by it, and so to render them willing to accept of mercy as a free unmerited favour. This willingness is not produced by a consciousness of struggling with sin, but from a conviction that they are dead in trespasses and sins, and that they never can make one successful struggle against the inward power of sin in the heart, without being created anew by the Spirit of God, through faith in his Son.

'I think Dr C—— is certainly mistaken in supposing, that a man may be sincerely and actively inquiring after the way of acceptance with a holy and righteous God, and yet may be at the same time going on, contentedly, in the practice of known sin. If he is anxious for pardon, he must be uneasy under the dread of punishment; and if he be desirous to be freed from the power of sin, he must be uneasy under its dominion. Commonly, the first step of the Spirit's work in the soul, is to convince of sin; so that the sinner is "pricked in his heart"; involuntarily cries out, "What shall I do to be saved?" and then is led to embrace Jesus Christ, freely offered in the gospel. But there are diversities of operations, and I believe there are some, who, in the first instance, have their "understanding enlightened" to perceive the truth, to see the freeness and suitableness of the great salvation wrought out by Christ, the necessity of being interested in that salvation, and that this is to be obtained only and simply by believing the truth; while there is no *powerful* application of these doctrines to their own souls, no *deep* sorrow or humiliation for sin, no *strong* earnest longings of the soul after the favour of God, and the privileges of his children. I would not deny such light came from heaven, but it is only a kind of moon-light, and does not possess the animating warmth of the sunbeam. How desirable is it to have the heart warmed, and the affections kindled, with "the love of God shed abroad in the heart by the Holy Ghost!" This should be our constant prayer; and it is by means of contemplating the love of God in Christ, that we may expect to have this holy affection kindled and increased in our own souls. I am really writing without order or premeditation, so I hope you will excuse the want of connection. I thank you sincerely for B——'s pamphlet. I would thank the writer, if I knew him. Pray, what is he? I remember drawing up a paper on the subject of saving faith, corresponding exactly to Mr B——'s view of it, which was inserted in the *Edinburgh Monitor* for January and August 1807. Many pious persons are not satisfied with this view, and seem to fear that the grace of faith is degraded by reducing it to believing, just as moralists fear that salvation is degraded by connecting it with faith alone.'

To the same.

'*3d December*, 1816.

'My dear Sir,

'I have to thank you for sundry communications. It was very good in you to send me the Glasgow pamphlet in defence of Dr C. On a subject which has attracted so much notice, one is curious to know what is said further. The controversy warms as it proceeds; but though the heat increases, it does not follow that the light increases also. Mr B.'s was a luminous Essay, and threw light on the subject of discussion. The advocate for Dr C. appears rather to throw a shade upon it. He seems not to understand the distinction between the workings of natural conscience, and the operations of true peace. He has learned what the fundamental doctrines of the gospel are, but he errs in applying them for the conviction and conversion of sinners. He appears to me to be a man who, attracted by the charms of Dr C.'s eloquence, has learned from his preaching, for the first time, the leading points of orthodoxy, but has not yet felt their power upon his heart. He is a convert to Dr C.'s creed, but not converted so as to "become as a little child." He likes to have everything rational and free of mystery, and is much displeased at finding fault with his favourite preacher. I am sure he maintains some things in his pamphlet which Dr C. would not assert, for he knows better. See the first line of page 15. "Is not faith imparted to the mind, just as men deserve it?" One who is capable of expressing himself in this manner, must be a stranger to the free grace of God in the gospel. Surely Dr C. "has not so learned Christ." It is vain to attempt to try to divest the gospel of mystery. Our Lord speaks of the "mysteries of the kingdom"; and the apostle Paul "of the mystery of the gospel," "the mystery of faith," "the mystery of godliness," etc. See Cruden's Concordance, under the word *mystery*, and the judicious explanation there given of the term. The apostle farther speaks of things that are "unsearchable, unspeakable," etc. Such things can never be made plain and intelligible to a darkened understanding (Eph. 4:18); and may be but very imperfectly perceived, even by those whose understanding is enlightened (Eph. 1:18).

'With regard to controversy in general, I think it is an unprofitable, or rather a hurtful kind of reading. It is, indeed, right to search for the truth. But if one has found it, and is at all established in the faith, he has no more to gain by disputation. He may dispute, and discuss, till he has discussed away all the life and energy of the truth. For my own part, I have always found the time worse than thrown away, which I have spent in the chilling regions of controversy; and I would rather hear "five words" that would warm my love to the Saviour, or to my brother, than "ten thousand words" from the most subtle or eloquent disputant.'

About the commencement of the same year, Mr Stewart had been visited with much personal and family distress, to which he alludes in the following letter to his friend in England:

'*May* 14*th*, 1816.

'My very dear Brother,

'If drawing nearer to the eternal world, necessarily inferred our withdrawing to a greater distance from all sublunary objects, I should need no other apology for my long silence. Certainly my approaches to the confines of my present state of existence are strongly marked, in some of the mental faculties, in my bodily constitution, and in my looks. What impressive discipline did my family and myself experience six or seven months ago! and how much of the same kind may have been dealt out to you, my brother, in the same period? We were indeed brought very low with severe, lingering fever; but the Lord who smote us, spared and restored us, so that we are all escaped alive to praise his forbearance and his tender love. His mercy faileth never. But, alas! I have not rendered again according to the benefit done unto me. There never was a heart more insensible than mine to the things of God, the concerns of my people, of my family, and of my own soul. Every duty is marred, and at every step I stumble. But while I find that this is undoubtedly so, I see more clearly the great need and suitableness of many promises which I have often held forth to others, but had never heartily embraced for myself. O to have my loins girt about, and my lamp burning! But, alas! I perceive neither oil nor flame. "One word alone keeps me from sinking," "Christ is all." Forgive all this egotism.'

Not long after, to a young lady of quality in the neighbourhood, who, on hearing him preach on the subject of death, had expressed a wish to have some book recommended that might furnish her with further instruction on the momentous point, Mr Stewart wrote:

'*Dingwall*, 11*th Dec.* 1817.

'My dear Madam,

'The subject on which you express yourself with such affecting seriousness and feeling, is certainly one which ought never to be far from the thoughts of a mortal, yet immortal being. And yet how often do we find it otherwise: it is lamentable to hear young persons, when reminded of death and eternity, reply, that it is too soon to think of these things, as if one could "make an agreement with death, and a covenant with the grave." I should have thought that people must have taken pains, and exercised their ingenuity in contriving to keep the thought of death at a distance, if I did not know too well in my own case, that heedlessness and unconcern about futurity are quite natural, and that it requires the operation of a divine power to correct them. A melancholy proof this, of blindness and folly! We are already on our journey, and we know we cannot stop; we may turn our eyes aside, but we cannot arrest the progress of time; we are sure death is before us, is approaching, and inevitable; yet how seldom, how transiently, how carelessly do we think of the consequences? I dare say, my dear young lady, you have observed this to be pretty much the case with yourself, at least, during a part of your life. Now, indeed, I trust it may be otherwise. This "last enemy" has made such unsparing inroads into your family, as must have left deep, and painful, and lasting impressions. I have felt myself participate largely in your family sorrows. But natural feelings, I well know, will not suffice to awaken the conscience, or to change the heart. It is divine influence alone, that will make a person, even in the view of death, inquire with holy earnestness, "What shall I do to be saved?" And it is the same divine Spirit that can make the inquirer cordially to receive the only right answer, "Believe in the Lord Jesus Christ, and thou shalt be saved."

'Among the many pleasing and instructive anecdotes which are related of our amiable departed Princess,[1] I was particularly struck with her earnest request to a pious clergyman, to inform her what would make a deathbed easy? This was, it seems, a question which she put to several ministers. Such an anxious desire, entertained and expressed repeatedly, by a person in health, and in the bloom of youth, shows a mind accustomed to the contemplation of the important, eternal realities of the invisible world. It were easy to give a short comprehensive answer to this most interesting query, but it might require

[1] [Princess Charlotte of Wales, wife of Leopold (afterwards first King of Belgium), who died on 6 November 1817 after giving birth to a still-born son.]

a long exposition to bring the meaning fully forth, in a practical application. To the question, What can make a deathbed easy? one might answer, Trust in Christ, the only Saviour of sinners; or, A believing view of the mercy of God in the gospel; or, A firm hold and dependence on the covenant of grace,—answers of nearly the same import. They imply, however, a previous knowledge of the truth revealed in scripture, conviction of guilt, a total renunciation of dependence on ourselves, and a full approbation and acceptance of the salvation offered freely in the gospel. It might be answered farther, that to die safely, one must have an interest in Christ, Phil. 3:9; to die peacefully, one must have a persuasion of one's interest in Christ, 2 Tim. 1:12; to die triumphantly, a man must find himself victorious over the enemies of his soul, 2 Tim. 4:6-8; to die free of fear, or concern, it is enough that one be ignorant and thoughtless.

'How happy should I be, in furnishing any help to you and your dear esteemed sisters, to guide your meditations on this most important subject. I dare say you are not unacquainted with the writings of Mrs Hannah More, a lady to whose religious and charitable labours her country is under incalculable obligation. In case you may not have her works at hand, I beg leave to send a volume of hers, containing several admirable essays. Those I would particularly recommend, are the chapters on prayer, on insensibility to eternal things, and on happy deaths.

'I hope you will have the goodness to forgive me for delaying to answer your kind and interesting note, and to take in good part the freedom I have used in this hasty attempt at an answer. While you search the scriptures with attention and prayer, you will derive from them more satisfactory, and impressive, and efficacious instruction, than I or any man living can give.'

In this (1817) and the subsequent year, Mr Stewart was prosecuting his parochial labours with all the assiduity and zeal compatible with the encumbrance of a bodily frame shaken by disease, and greatly debilitated. Amid his own trials, he ever was mindful of the afflictions which others endured, as the following letters, the one written to his correspondent in Shropshire, the other to a bereaved husband, will show.

'To the Rev. Mr D.

'*Jan.* 3, 1817.

'My very dear Brother,

'It was indeed singularly kind of you to excuse my long silence, and to send me a second letter, when I had not acknowledged your former. Your two favours of July and November last, are both before me, both so full of heavenly consolation and brotherly kindness, that I am oppressed with such undeserved favour, and experience something of the same feelings with him who said, "Depart from me, for I am a sinful man."

My letters, on the contrary, are attenuated into mere bulletins, short intimations to my kind friends and brethren, that I still need their prayers in the wilderness. It excites my daily wonder and gratitude, that so many of the Lord's dear people still think of me, and take an interest in my welfare. It encourages me to hope, that poor and needy as I am, yet the Lord thinketh on me, Psalm 40:17. So you, my dear friend, have been again disciplined in the school of sickness and suffering. Well I knew that he who appointed you the trial, would take care that it should not be unprofitable to your soul. He loves his children too well to afflict them willingly, or chasten them for his own pleasure; and he is too wise to throw away his chastisement, or waste it unprofitably. You may not yet perceive what benefit has resulted from it: it is very natural for you to wish earnestly to know it, in order to be satisfied that the trial has not been wholly misimproved and lost. But this, like many other of the Lord's doings, you may not know now, but you shall know it hereafter. We must not say like Thomas, "except I shall see, and feel, I will not believe." I, your friend, should like also to see and understand how much my dear brother D—— has been refined, like gold tried in the fire. But I must be contented to know, in general, what I cannot doubt, that every branch in Christ that beareth fruit, when it is purged and pruned, it is that it may bring forth more fruit. And so it will. I remember an old, pious, very recluse minister, whom I used to meet with once a-year. He scarcely ever looked at a newspaper. When others were talking about the French revolution, he showed no concern or curiosity about it. He said he knew from the Bible how it would all end, better than the most sagacious politician,—that the Lord reigns,—that the earth will be filled with his glory,—that the gospel will be preached to all nations,—and that all subordinate events are working out these great ends. This was enough for him, and he gave himself no concern about the news or events of the day, only saying, It shall be well with the righteous.

'I do not know that ever I mentioned to you, that with regard to our time of joining in prayer, I have been long obliged to discontinue it on Fridays, as I was always exposed to interruption that day, from being obliged to go out, or to receive calls within. But I endeavour to transfer it to Saturday, when I am always at home and alone. But often in a day does my wretched heart constrain me to cry with good Mr Newton,

> I prize the privilege of prayer,
> But, O what backwardness to pray![1]

'And now, on this point of intercessory prayer, if I may be allowed to mention what I would entreat you to ask for my poor barren soul,—it is this,—more spiritual sensibility, that I may be more affected with

[1] [From *Olney Hymns*, Book 1, Hymn 130, 'The Inward Warfare,' a hymn based on the words of Galatians 5:17.]

the glories of redeeming love, with the horrid evil of sin, and with the dismal state of perishing sinners;—that I may be more watchful, and attentive, and conscientious, in performing daily ordinary duties, and in guarding against ordinary offences;—in a word, to be more alive to God, more awake to righteousness. To you, my beloved brother, I think I can unbosom my gross feelings, because I think you can and will believe me. To most of my Christian acquaintances I dare not confess my secret sins, for I feel it to be nothing else than an exhibition of myself, and a seeking of praise for my apparent humility. If I speak a word, however sincerely, condemning myself, I find I am only gratifying and feeding my pride. It is possible you may understand something of this.'

'To the Honourable Mr ——.

'*October* 23*d*, 1818

'My dear Sir,

'I was early informed by our esteemed friend Mr H——, of the heavy affliction with which it has pleased your God to visit you; an affliction with which myself and my family were affected in no ordinary degree.

'Shall we receive good at the hand of God, and shall we not receive evil? You, my dear Sir, did receive great good. The Lord gave you his own Son, and he gave you his own Spirit; and he gave you for a partner one of his own dear children, created anew after his own likeness. In these gifts were included a thousand lesser ones. The language of your grateful heart then was, "Bless the Lord, O my soul, and forget not all his benefits."

'I have an affecting remembrance at this moment, of the delight with which I witnessed your happiness for one short hour. I figured to myself what sweet fellowship you must have enjoyed in your excursion, in contemplating together the works of God, and strewing your tracts, these little winged messengers, among your poor, ignorant fellow creatures. Such was some of the "good" which you had received. But, oh how short its duration! How quickly did the "evil" follow! *Evil*, in respect of the pain it inflicted, and the good it took away; but not evil in the estimation of him who seeth the end from the beginning, and who maketh *all* things work together for *good* to them that love him.

'He had destined you for some eminent station in his employment, and therefore he put you early to school, and advanced you rapidly to one of the highest forms, and taught you one of the hardest lessons of faith and submission. Still his injunction, example, and promise, speak in most encouraging language. "Take my yoke upon you, and learn of me, for I am meek and lowly in heart, and you shall find rest to your souls."

'But why dwell only on the heavy loss sustained, the delightful enjoyment interrupted? Let us contemplate the bliss of which she is now in actual possession. When, but a few months ago, you were united on earth, you did not expect to have the honour so soon of handing your beloved partner up to heaven, nor did she expect to arrive so soon at her kingdom and her crown. But even then, the Lord's counsel was, "I know the thoughts that I think towards you, thoughts of peace, and not of evil, to give you an expected end." She is taken away from the evil to come, and if you must yet meet evil in the wilderness, you will be carried safely through. She who would have helped you is removed, yet "Fear not, saith the Lord, I am with you; lo, I am with you alway."

'You had a near view of death, but his sting was not to be seen. Nor shall the grave always boast of his victory. You know that the day is fast approaching, when this corruptible must put on incorruption, and this mortal must put on immortality, and death shall be swallowed up in victory.

'There was a time when I stood in the same predicament as you do now. While life remained, I would have given the world to have my "gourd spared"; but when she was gone, and I thought of her being made perfect in glory, I durst not so much as wish her back again.

'One special comfort (I trust you have many) yet remains to you, a sweet living memorial, which (to use Lord Strafford's[1] words) a saint in heaven has left you.

[1] [Sir Thomas Wentworth, 1st Earl of Strafford (1593–1641), cf.

What would our disconsolate Leopold,[1] what would our whole nation, not give for the like memorial? A child of many prayers, like yours, is the peculiar care of the "good Shepherd"; and one has much encouragement in devoting him early, and daily, to the God of Abraham, and of Isaac, and of Jacob. I earnestly pray, that the unfeigned faith that dwelt in his grandmother (Lois), and in his mother (Eunice), may be in him also. Forgive, my dear Sir, this incoherent attempt to impart something of my sentiments on an occasion so affecting to myself, as well as to friends whom I sincerely love. He who came to comfort those that mourn, will surely not leave you comfortless, but will send you more abundantly of his own Spirit, the real Comforter.

'I feel a warm attachment to your pious brother, Mr ——. I know him by character, and by his published Discourses. These were sent me by the kind attention of Mr H——, and have furnished me a very savoury repast. Long may his gracious Master be pleased to employ and countenance his faithful labours!'

In 1819, Mr Stewart met with a trying bereavement in the death of his unmarried sister, who had been exceedingly helpful to him at Moulin, and with whom,

---

James Robinson, *A Compleat and Impartial History of England* (London, 1739), p. 658n.].

[1] [Husband of Princess Charlotte of Wales, who died on 6 November 1817 after giving birth to a still-born son. Leopold would later be first King of Belgium.]

on her removal to Glasgow, he had maintained a very close correspondence by letters. She was a woman of extraordinary resolution, piety, and zeal, and how much he felt her loss, appeared from what he wrote to Mr D—— on the occasion.

'*October* 23*d*, 1819.

'My very dear Brother,

'Instead of replying particularly to your last welcome and refreshing letter, I proceed to announce an event which I did not look for so soon, a bereavement for which I was but ill prepared. My dear sister, Margaret, was called away from this life to a better, on the 11th instant, in her sister's house in Stirling. She had come thither on a visit about three weeks before. Her health had been declining during the summer. None of us, however, apprehended the end of her life so near. Soon after her coming to her sister's, she was confined to bed; she believed herself dying; frequently expressed her entire dependence on the righteousness and mediation of her divine Saviour, but soon fell into a lethargic state. The physician declared her case to be a rapid decay of nature, and that medicine could be of no service to her. In this state she continued, slumbering and insensible, for four or five days, and then expired, almost imperceptibly. "Blessed are the dead that die in the Lord." How different was her life from its close! She long enjoyed sound health, and was full of activity and energy in her Lord's service. In the last stage, her mind, as well as body, became torpid and inactive. But the Lord knew her frame, and remembered she was but dust. I now recollect, with satisfaction, the happy interview I had with her, during a few days in June last. I certainly did not reckon on its being our last interview. But it is not the last! No! we shall meet again, ere long, in our Father's house; and you, my brother, shall meet with us, and then we shall see each other face to face; and we shall, with open face, behold the glory of him that sitteth on the throne, and of the Lamb that was slain, but liveth and reigneth for evermore! *O preclarum diem!* [1]

'While we are yet in the wilderness, the scene often shifts. After much deliberation, and asking counsel from on high, I have come to the determination, if the Lord will, of passing a few months in Edinburgh, for the benefit of my health. My medical friends advise it,—my clerical brethren urge it, and kindly undertake to supply my pulpit in my absence. The church is under repair, which makes it necessary for me now to preach in the field. I could not do this in winter, though I were at home.'

In this letter, Mr Stewart communicates the resolution which he had taken to repair to Edinburgh, with his family, for the winter. In the spring of this year, the symptoms of his disorder had become so alarming, that

[1] ['O what a beautiful day!']

in order to procure consultation of physicians on his case, he was induced to venture on a journey to Edinburgh, which, to one who had been unable, for a considerable space, to move beyond the precincts of his own parish, was an arduous undertaking. His Lord, however, was with him by the way; and, after visiting friends at Perth, Stirling, Glasgow, and Edinburgh, he returned home, rather improved in health. The medical opinion, however, was not flattering; nor had any permanent relief been obtained by means of Dr Gregory, and his zealous advisers among the faculty, some of whom added Christian character to high professional eminence, and were assiduous in their attentions to him for his Master's sake; while the love expressed to him by many private individuals and families, made a deep impression on his grateful heart. Indeed, in the beautiful letters which he wrote Mrs Stewart during his absence, he seems quite overpowered with thankfulness to God and his people, for the providential kindnesses heaped upon him.

His return home was not attended with any encouraging circumstances; for whether he dwelt on the effects of his ministry in Dingwall, or reflected on his own declining health, there was much ground of discouragement. As to his labours at Dingwall, though not attended with those demonstrations of divine power which rendered his ministration of the gospel at Moulin so signally effectual, there is reason to believe they were not without much benefit to numbers. Indeed, the faithful exhibition of divine truth, enforced by the consistent tenor of a holy life, could hardly fail to operate beneficially on general character, though the result might be short of conversion. And that a visible reformation of open immoralities took place during his ministry was confessed even by the enemies of religion. Besides the good that directly sprung from his labours in the pulpit, he exerted himself with much zeal and perseverance to promote the religious education of the young,—having with much pains, and after many difficulties, succeeded in establishing, on a permanent foundation, a school in which children should be taught in the vernacular language.

In addition to the efforts which he made in his own immediate vicinity, he took an active part in the formation of a society in Inverness, for promoting the education of the poorer class of Highlanders on a more extensive scale; while of every Christian institution, which had for its object the circulation of the scriptures, or the extension of missionary labour among the heathen, he was the constant advocate, and zealous agent; and the sums transmitted from his little district, showed with what influence others were carried along with him in the cause of Christ.

But though many things testified his coming to Dingwall had not been in vain, with the general aspect of that field of labour he was little satisfied. Some time before his going to Edinburgh, he writes to Mrs

Calder:—'I have had no small share of trial, and no little grief, from numbers of giddy young persons being enticed by that public pest the playhouse, notwithstanding the magistrates and others did what they could to discountenance them.'—Such griefs were the more sensibly felt, because he could no more go forth to seek after the wandering, or to lead the obedient in the paths of active duty.

CHAPTER 10

EDINBURGH—AND THE END

WHILE Mr Stewart lamented the little success of his ministry in Dingwall, he saw his sphere of action becoming every day more contracted, through the pressure of his internal malady,—the nature of which was such, that for the preservation of his life, prompt medical assistance had become at times necessary, and such assistance could not be obtained in so remote a place. This made his family and friends exceedingly desirous to have him try the effects of a winter's residence in Edinburgh, where the best medical skill was always accessible; and the wish of his friends was strengthened by the advice of his physicians, who uniformly recommended the expedient proposed.

Mr Stewart at length listened to the proposal; and his church being under repair, which would have prevented his preaching during the winter months though he had been at home, and various unexpected providences concurring to promote the design, and provide for its exigencies, he left Dingwall, with his entire family, in October 1819,—little supposing he should see it no more. His voyage to Leith was attended with no difficulties; and his friends having prepared for his family suitable accommodations, he pitched his wilderness tent, for a season, on new and interesting ground.

In many respects, he found the change beneficial; for, besides the facilities of education which his numerous family enjoyed in every department of requisite knowledge, under his own superintendence, he himself soon perceived a considerable improvement in health,—to which both his relief from ministerial labours, and his ready access to medical aid, greatly contributed.

Dr Stewart,[1] however, was not like those who, for some family reasons, or the love of society, betake themselves to town, and for a season greatly divest themselves of the ministerial character. Wherever he went, the servant of Christ was manifested; and with what diversity of engagements he was exercised in Edinburgh, will appear from the following letter to Mr D——:

[1] The degree of Doctor in Divinity had been, with great propriety, conferred on Mr Stewart by Marischal College, Aberdeen.

'*January* 20*th*, 1820.

'I have too much experience of your candour to suppose, that you can be provoked to entertain the painful suspicion of my having become cold in my attachment to my dear brother D——, notwithstanding the rare recurrence of my poor communications. If my avocations in the country were many, here they are multiplied sevenfold. There is a numerous Christian society. Christian friends are extremely kind to myself and my family. This creates many claims on my gratitude and acknowledgements. My general health is considerably improved since I came to Edinburgh, so that I am able to move about; and as I have no fixed and stated duty on hand, I am considered as a kind of idler, who may answer any call that the public service of *societies*, or the wishes of individual friends, may happen to suggest. This almost constant intercourse, and extending acquaintance, with pious characters, is very pleasing for the time; but I feel already, what I apprehended from the first, that it rather distracts the mind, draws it too much from home, and gives it a turn for dissipation. I feel uneasy under the continuance of this mode of life; and I found it quite gratifying, yesterday, when the very stormy weather kept myself within, and all the world out, for almost the whole of the day. But, alas! my hard, insensible heart, profits by nothing. I have the privilege of hearing some excellent preachers, and I feel impressed by their prayers and their sermons; but how far I am really improved and edified, is a question that it humbles me much to answer.'

Thus actively was Mr Stewart employed, to the full extent of his power, and perhaps beyond what a prudential regard to health would have dictated. But it was not easy to refuse himself to those who repaired to his hospitable house, to partake of the spiritual refreshment which his conversation, expositions of the word, and devotional exercises, freely provided. At that time he was without the charge of any particular congregation in the city, otherwise public work must necessarily have abridged the extent and frequency of those private exercises; and perhaps they may sometimes be overvalued, and carried to an unprofitable excess. But though a gossiping spirit may creep into religious society, and persons without serious impressions, or solid piety, may be kept a-going in the way of profession by those means, and though unseasonable demands may be made on a minister's time and strength for out-of-season services; it is nevertheless true, that to despise them altogether argues little delight in Christian fellowship, and little love for tending the flock of Christ; for if we find any athirst for salvation, we ought not to defer rolling away the stone from the well's mouth, though the hour for the public watering of them be not yet come. And we cannot but regard it as a great improvement in the modes of social intercourse among the religious, that there is now a greater freedom of communication, and openness of fellowship, than had been practised in some years, or perhaps ages, that are past.

Dr Stewart had been only a few months in Edinburgh, when the minister of the first charge in the parish in which he resided, was taken away by one of those sudden deaths which are so much calculated to alarm the thoughtless world. Previous to this event, Dr Stewart's friends had been anxiously revolving expedients for retaining him in town, from a conviction that he could be there more useful than in Dingwall; and that, besides, the state of his health absolutely required him, if it could be accomplished, to devolve his country parish on the charge of an ordained assistant, and reside permanently in Edinburgh. Various plans were in agitation, when Providence, as in a time of similar suspense at Moulin, interposed to solve perplexities, and make the way plain. And immediately on the above-mentioned decease, the eyes of his Christian friends were turned to the vacant charge, as most suitable for Dr Stewart, and among others, the gentleman referred to at the beginning of Chapter 9 employed a most ardent and unremitted zeal to bring it about. At first, however, there was little hope of success, for the candidates were numerous, and some of them had as much interest at command, as is usually required to procure such an appointment from the servants of the Crown, with whom the nomination lay. But a distinguished nobleman, to whose lady Mrs Stewart was nearly related, having waited on the king in person, readily obtained for Dr Stewart the royal patronage, to the surprise and disappointment of not a few; but to himself and family, as well as to many others, it appeared in the light of a most admirable and propitious act of his providence, whose counsels are immutable, and to them that fear him, immutably gracious!

'Could I, with a wish,' he wrote to Mr D——, 'transport you to the house where I now dwell, and to the little study where I now sit, and place you in an elbow-chair beside me, and grasp your brotherly hand, I would tell "strange things," and would "a tale unfold," at which I cannot cease to wonder, and which I can scarcely yet believe to be true! By a train of most unexpected occurrences, marking the hand of God, and his determined purpose, overruling events, and bearing down opposition, here am I settled minister of what is called the First Charge of Canongate Parish (where seldom has *wild man* been placed before), and in the face of much opposition and influence, which was mustered against such an ominous and alarming event. It is impossible for me now to detail the circumstances which distinguish this eventful chapter of my story; but I do not think it is at all impossible, that I should have the happiness, one day, of relating these, and many other things, *viva voce*,[1] to my dear brother D——, in this very place. It is quite

[1] [Literally, 'with living voice.']

a common thing for one and another of our beloved English brethren, to make an excursion to the north, as far as this city, for the sake of health, and of Christian fellowship; and I joyfully indulge the hope, that, on some fine summer day, you may take a trip to visit your friends and brethren here, who will rejoice to see your face. We have some really sanctified pulpits too, and serious congregations, in your connection, where you will be gladly received and welcomed.

'Here I enjoy many things which are highly gratifying, and, I trust, profitable. During last winter and spring, which I found it necessary to spend in Edinburgh, to be near my medical friends, my health improved very considerably, and now continues uniformly good, though I am far from being robust; I am conjoined with an excellent colleague, Dr Buchanan, with whom I have long been intimately acquainted. I have the benefit of Christian society of the most agreeable and congenial kind, and always extending. And I have an opportunity of being useful, so far as my few and poorly improved talents go, to many of my fellow-creatures, particularly Highlanders. I figure to myself, that one principal reason of my being sent to Ross-shire, was to put me to school, that I might learn to do something afterwards in Edinburgh. So you see, my dear friend, that the Lord hath done great things for me. My living is considerably inferior to that of Dingwall, but "the Lord will provide."'

Dr Stewart was admitted to his new charge in the July following, and immediately entered upon the duties of his office, with more activity than from his previously impaired constitution could have been expected. Besides occupying the pulpit in his turn, with a conscientious regularity, which he was unwilling to interrupt by the employment of occasional helps; he entered on a course of parochial visitation, which, among the crowded population of an extensive town parish, was a work of great labour and difficulty. In a book prepared for the purpose, he not only registered name and family circumstances, but also what he observed to be the character and attainments of the individuals with whom he conversed. In his progress, he found some of his parishioners so little interested in the administration of religious ordinances, as not to have learned a new minister had been appointed. Besides his own personal exertions, he was solicitous to employ the agency of Sunday-school teachers, to the greatest possible extent.

In his highly respectable colleague, as was to be anticipated, when two men 'not seeking their own, but the things of Jesus Christ,' happen to be conjoined, he enjoyed the kindness of a friend, and the co-operation of a fellow-labourer, intent to promote the work of their common Lord. And upon a review of the way by which he had been led to Edinburgh, and the enlarged capacity to do good, of which he felt himself possessed,—in the midst of many public and many private blessings,—both himself was pleased at the change, and others, who contemplated the scene, began to hope for him a protracted space of usefulness and comfort. And as the Gaelic scriptures were still in a state of revision by Dr Stuart of Luss, and were passing through his hands for ultimate review, in their way to the press, it seemed peculiarly needful for the church to have his valuable talents long preserved.[1] But those expectations it was not the will of his heavenly Father to realize. For, early in the winter of 1820, the paroxysms of his unremoved malady

[1] Both these eminent scholars and yoke-fellows in biblical studies, fell nearly together, not many days having intervened between the death of Dr Stuart and his colleague in translation. It may be remarked, that Dr Stewart, speaking of the present version, stated to Dr Buchanan and to Dr Campbell his deliberate judgment, that the Highlanders already possessed one of the best translations, and that, though capable of minute improvements, it was essentially faithful, and amply sufficient for every Christian purpose. Indeed, the deliberate judgment of these two unrivalled Gaelic scholars, with respect to the general excellence of the present translation, will sufficiently appear, on comparing their revised version with the former; for, after the most critical examination they could bestow, no alteration seems to have been made of any real importance, or affecting the sense in any considerable degree. This is the opinion of very competent judges: and the church not affording, in every age, qualifications for the work equal to theirs, the Society for Promoting Christian Knowledge may perhaps see it expedient to discontinue the projected revision of the whole, and may prefer publishing, in quarto, the Gaelic Scriptures, including what has been done by these eminent men, with no other emendations than adjusting the orthography to a uniformity with the mode which they had adopted in the part of the work that is already executed.

returned with a violence that shook his enfeebled frame to an alarming degree. However, he so far recovered strength, as to be able to occupy his place in the pulpit during the first four months of 1821. His almost daily sufferings were, nevertheless, so intense, that it was a matter of surprise to his friends how he could continue his public appearances. But he was borne onward by a constraining desire to preach that salvation, the grace of which he felt to be so precious, and its author so worthy to be loved. Nor did his Lord, on whom he waited in the infirmity of nature, refuse to impart proportionally greater supplies of his everlasting strength. And with what earnestness, solemnity, and affection, he addressed his auditors, beseeching, entreating, praying for them in Christ's stead to be reconciled to God; they themselves were witnesses, and ought not soon to forget. While, in bringing out from the stores of his own various experience, the conflicts and the consolations of the life of faith, those hearers who had previously known the grace of the Saviour, enjoyed a rich repast, and confessed there was a savour of divine things diffused over his discourses, that was most refreshing to their souls, and mightily animated them in their way to heaven.

Dr Stewart was upheld by his Lord in the exercise of his public ministry, until the month of May 1821, on the first Sabbath of which he assisted in dispensing the Lord's supper to the congregation; and preached the evening sermon at the close. On that day his appearance was calculated to excite a tender, though painful interest, there being an air of languor and debility deeply impressed on his every feature and movement. In the evening sermon, however, at which the writer of this account was present, there was a degree of freedom, animation, and force of mind displayed, which seemed to gladden the countenances of his auditory with the hope of many such days; while there was, in the whole exercise of the evening, a serious and yet lively strain, with which, it might be thought, few could remain unaffected or unimpressed.[1]

But this was his last exertion of a public kind. Next Sabbath he accepted assistance; and his disease being evidently ripening to an extremity, he spake of his decease as at no great probable distance. Indeed, the last letter he addressed to Mr D——, shows how near to eternity he thought himself in prospect.

[1] This sermon, which was preached from Mal. 4:2. 'Unto you that fear my name shall the Sun of Righteousness arise with healing in his wings,' excited uncommon interest at the time of delivery,—an interest which did not decrease, on its being found to be the *last*. Indeed, many applications were afterwards made to obtain copies of the MS. with which it was impossible to comply, the discourse having been delivered from a few skeleton notes, filled up as utterance and enlargement were given him for the occasion. It appeared, afterwards, that several individuals had been much impressed and profited,—and thus the Lord was pleased to put honour on the closing act of the ministry of a servant, whose labours he had before often countenanced and blessed.

'*March* 23*d*, 1821.

'My very dear Friend,

'With me disease is making progress. My sand is running apace, and the time of my departure is sensibly drawing nigher. I suffer much pain, but the Lord has not forsaken me. Almost the only duty that I can perform is preaching,—that privilege is still continued with me.

'Much of the night is spent awake. I will endeavour to think on you and yours. Do you remember me, and pray that the Lord may be with me in passing Jordan. O eternity, what a weighty idea! Farewell, my dear brother, perhaps it may be the last, but we shall meet hereafter. Have we not eternity to spend together? Glory be to God, and to the Lamb that was slain, but liveth and reigneth,—and we shall reign with him!'

Thus realizing his nearness to an invisible world, having, like Israel of old, waited for the salvation of the Lord, and knowing, like Simeon, a manifested Saviour, whom he gladly embraced by faith, he began, like the one, to bless his children previous to his decease, and, like the other, to desire to be let depart. Two of his sons having laid him down one evening to rest, 'My dear boys,' said he, 'take your father's blessing, it may be the last time I will give it you.—May the God of your fathers bless you, and keep you, and make his countenance to shine upon you, and give you peace!'

On another occasion, to one of them, supporting him under a fit of pain, he said, 'You will not have it to do long.'—'All shall be well with you, my dear father,' said the affectionate youth. 'O yes,' cried he immediately, 'I have evidences which I cannot deny, that the Lord has been gracious to me. But I now live by faith, I have no sensible enjoyments.'

On these occasions of intense pain, the grace of patience had its work so perfect, that it was a common remark of his, 'David had to sing of mercy and judgment together, but it is all mercy with me.'

But, amid these conflicts, the time of victory drew on, and the last enemy fell before him, sooner indeed than his watchful family had apprehended. For, in the afternoon of Sunday, May 27, without any previous alteration sufficient to excite apprehension, he suddenly fell into a sort of deliquium,[1] in which he continued for about the space of an hour, without speech or apparent consciousness of pain, and then gently quitted the earthly tabernacle, to obtain a mansion in his Father's house, there, doubtless, to be ever present with the Lord!

Thus entered into rest, in his fifty-seventh year, a man whom all esteemed, many loved, and not a few regarded in the light of a father in Christ. Of his general character, or method of life, nothing need be added to what is set

[1] [A faint, or loss of consciousness.]

down in the preceding memoir, in which he is minutely exhibited in his public duties, and domestic manners. A few lines of the portraiture, however, have either been omitted, or faintly marked; and we have only these to retouch, in order to complete our design.

The prominent feature in his character was simplicity,—a simplicity not arising from the action of a mind that can bring but a single faculty into exercise at once; but a simplicity of combination, in which many faculties co-operate to produce unity of purpose, and evenness of tenor in the progress of life. There was no contexture of plot, artifice, or disguise in his procedure. On his professions one might always safely rely; and if he was seen moving towards an object, it could always be predicted of him with certainty, that the way of rectitude would be his path, and that, if he could not reach it in that straight, open, and unsuspected way, he would rather stop short, than move aside to courses indirect and questionable. His was the simplicity of a man who, having eternity in his eye, could say, 'This one thing I do,—I press toward the mark for the prize of the high calling of God in Christ Jesus.'

This simplicity characterized his intercourse with friends, and gave an unspeakable charm to his communications with those whom he admitted into his familiarity; for as he never professed esteem where he did not feel it, nor distinguished with the name of friend, any whom he counted not worthy of unreserved confidence;

so, towards the selected objects of his regard, he used a freedom and a frankness of disclosure, with respect to his own feelings, sentiments, and condition, which none will employ, but a man who, knowing the conscious rectitude of his own thoughts and purposes, is not afraid nor ashamed to submit them to the review of other minds. For he who has no higher object of pursuit, than to attain proper habits of thought and action, if anything is deficient or erroneous, will deem the correction of it a benefit of too great magnitude to be lost, without embracing every prudent expedient for securing it.

In submitting himself to the judgment of others, he was truly disinterested, for he neither wished to palliate his infirmities, nor to embellish his virtues. He was a man of truth, and loved truth in every form. And on this principle, he would tell what he had acquired, and what he could do, with the same candour and freedom from selfish considerations, as in pointing out what he knew not, and could not perform. He seemed to have obtained that rare victory over self, that he would neither detract from its real character, in the way of depreciation below the truth, nor give it an undue estimation, by assigning to it attributes it did not possess.

His disinterestedness in the management of secular affairs was unimpeachable. He had a large family depending on an income comparatively not large; yet the calls of charity, both for common and religious purposes, were liberally answered, and the language of his habitual conduct in his transactions with men, was, 'I seek not *yours*, but *you*.'

On his way home, in a visit he paid to Edinburgh in 1819, having at the house of a friend met with one of his earliest Moulin converts, who was in reduced circumstances, on parting with her, remembering he had just got a balance of three pounds, on settling with his bookseller, he gave one of them to this person, for the Lord's sake. 'How happy am I,' said he, in a letter to Mrs Stewart mentioning what he had done, 'in not having a worldly, covetous wife, to whom I would be afraid to tell what I gave away, and need to make twenty apologies!'

As he exercised himself in rectitude towards man, before his God, he was without guile, opening his heart to every gracious influence, and aiming to receive all God's truth, and to be altogether conformed to his will. From the yoke of no precept did he desire to withdraw his neck, nor refuse to any doctrine, plainly revealed, the ready subjection of his understanding. And no higher character of his faith and piety can be given, than that which one who knew him long and most intimately gave, in saying, 'That he believed all the Bible.' It was this unsuspecting simplicity, and unreserved extent of faith, that gave to his religious life the simplicity of tenor, and the consistency of parts, which beautified his character as a whole. In him, belief and obedience went hand in hand, or rather were dependent on each other, as cause and effect; the one furnishing motives, the other showing that the grace of faith was not received in vain.

Of his personal religion, it were idle repetition to say more than the preceding memoir discloses. His own attainments shrink back from the enlightened judgment that brought them under impartial review, and he was ready to count the least of the Lord's people superior to himself, and to act towards them accordingly. His self-abasement was profound, and would have rendered life not happy, had not the consolations of Christ opened up to his faith the fruition of 'all spiritual blessings, in heavenly places.' But this reconciled the apparent contraries,—'O wretched man that I am!' 'Thanks be to God through Jesus Christ.'—'My soul doth magnify the Lord, and my spirit hath rejoiced in God my Saviour.'

In his religious exercises, the character of his own soul was apparent. There ran through them a strain of undissembled humiliation in confessing prevailing unworthiness, and a thankful expression of the value, sufficiency, and preciousness of God's unspeakable gift, accompanied with such a sincerity of request, and such a various exercise of spiritual desire, that to join with him in acts of social or public worship, was highly interesting and profitable. It was easy to see in him, a man seeking access to God in earnest, and transacting the all-important matters of soul-concern, seriously, as a creature pleading for life and grace in the presence of the Creator; sober in expression, full in confessing sin, and, with a holy boldness, putting the Father of mercy in remembrance of the finished work of the sinner's Surety, and the promise of acceptance given us in Christ Jesus. He himself always lamented the coldness of his affections; but no friend ever found him cold. And if, in his devotion, there was no seraphic ardour, there was a desire to attain it, and humility, because his affections did not equal the height of his desire; and such a frame is doubtless the acceptable production of much grace. In those exercises, there was a spirit that warmed others,—and what communicated fervency, could not itself be cold.

As a minister of the gospel, few in our church, in latter days at least, have occupied higher ground, whether his qualifications be considered, or his success. His qualifications were eminent. With human nature, and the modifications of human character, he was well acquainted. His knowledge of the scriptures in the original tongues, was critically accurate and extensive. He had clear perceptions of divine truth, and a weighty sense of its vast importance. The truths of revealed religion he cordially embraced himself, and he could exhibit them in minute detail, or with systematic combination. His own ideas were clear and methodical; and he had the talent of placing his thoughts in the most natural arrangement, and of elucidating, by apt and familiar illustration, the doctrines which he proposed. What study could furnish, and the ingenuity of a highly cultivated mind, was at his command. But this alone had been but poor furniture for a minister of the gospel. It was the experience of a work of grace on his own soul, and the gifts of the Holy Spirit shed on him abundantly, through Jesus Christ his Lord, that made him the able minister of the new covenant, which he evidently showed himself to be. He had obtained much of that anointing which imparts an unction of refreshment to truth in the understanding, and gives a savour of divine things to spoken truths, which the most brilliant streams of eloquence cannot otherwise supply.

Viewed in the pulpit, there was nothing strongly marked in his deportment. Plain, serious, and sedate,—much impressed with his subject,—in earnest to have it understood, deeply interested to have his hearers brought to know, feel, and enjoy the salvation of Christ,—he evidently appeared. But as a rational being dealing with rational beings, he spoke the language of reason, and bore the countenance of soberness and truth. His aspect at times, indeed, portrayed every feeling of his soul, beaming with an expression of infelt gladness, or solemnized into the most affecting features of sympathy for the impenitent who would none of his counsel or reproof. But, in general, they who went to hear him in quest of what is called fine speaking, must have been disappointed; for in his manner there was nothing of display, no impassioned tones, vehement action, rapid utterance, or the fine-wrought tissue of elegant composition, or studied embellishment.

His simplicity of diction was the result of judgment early formed, and strengthened by the experience of life. In a letter to Mr Black, already inserted,[1] he observes of the discourses transmitted for his perusal, 'They are free from one blemish,—an elaborate and polished style. However sensible I am to the beauties of style, yet I cannot help considering a high degree of polish and ornament as out of place and improper in compositions for the pulpit.' And in 1814, speaking of one of the missionary sermons preached at London, he says, 'It is a piece of fine eloquence, but it is *human* eloquence. I fancy sober *scripture* eloquence goes but indifferently down with most English congregations.' His judgment further appears in what he wrote to a correspondent in 1817, concerning a volume of discourses at that time much read:—

'I know not what to say. I was carried through them like a balloon in a high wind. The author's talent is certainly an extraordinary one; but I often fear it may prove a snare both to himself and to his hearers. His eloquence has an intoxicating quality in it, not very favourable to sober thinking, nor to rational settled conviction and feeling. I would fear its effects would be

[1] [See above, p. 42.]

strong, but transient, rather than solid and permanent. Withal I have a great respect for ——. I trust he stands on firm ground, and that the Master whom he serves will direct him to such a use of his eminent gifts, as that he will "both save himself, and them that hear him."'

It was not the character of Dr Stewart's mind, to excite the affections before convincing the judgment, and it was repugnant to his sense of pulpit propriety, to run fast, or soar into the regions of lofty declamation, in going over the field of his discourse. He delighted and he excelled in the exhibition of clear statement, accurate discrimination, and demonstrative certainty, in his conclusions; and with these views, a style loaded with ornament, or spread into diffuseness, was incompatible. This unassuming simplicity of pulpit address, however, was by some great admirers of exhibited talent, interpreted into an incapacity to rise high in the regions of intellectual exertion; but none acquainted with the character of his mind could have fallen into so great a mistake. And we have seen, that this very simplicity was adopted on full conviction of its superior excellence. Whether Dr Stewart was right in his judgment on this point, we need not formally decide. That the plain style has least to flatter pride, accords best with the practice of St Paul, and seems to put most honour on revealed truths, by holding them forth in plain testimony, and leaving the result to God, will appear evident to some;

while others will deem all the persuasion of oratory necessary, and well employed, to arrest the attention of the careless, and captivate the ear of refinement to give audience to the gospel report. As to the point of impressing the attention, let oratory do its utmost; but in guiding enlightened souls in the way to eternity, we delight to hear the simple accents of the Good Shepherd's voice. 'No spectacle,' says Johnson, 'is nobler than a blaze'; but for doing work, who does not prefer the more limited light of a candle?

Perhaps the union of the plain and the impassioned would be the most useful style of address, and a capacity to employ both at will, would constitute a most desirable gift; for then might deep-toned, and high-wrought feeling, 'cry aloud, and spare not,' while 'the still small voice' spoke the counsel of peace. But the divine Spirit *divides* his gifts, and more commonly employs a number of moderately endowed individuals, than combines manifold gifts in one; this alike cuts off occasion for glorying, and for finding fault,—seeing it is grace that regulates the proportions.

If success in the ministry be received as an evidence of a man's qualifications for it, then there are few in our times, or in our church, who can pretend to rank higher than Dr Stewart. Survey him at Moulin, in the midst of a large company converted under his ministry,—the fruits of his labours,—the blessed seals attached to his commission,—and go round about our Zion, and see in what street of the city of our God, a similar company shall be found. We may, in the search, find some ministers preaching with more force of eloquence, and adorned with accomplishments ostensibly superior to his; but inquire into the number of decided converts, and genuine Christians, formed under their ministry, and, we apprehend, few will equal the success of Dr Stewart. We do not say this to enhance the value of his labours, by a disparaging reference to those of his brethren less successful in their work. No; while we rejoice in his success, we grieve that it is greatly singular; and we know, that though 'Apollos plant, and Paul water, it is only God that giveth the increase.' And we are sure, many would wish to equal him in usefulness, from whom the Lord withholds the pouring out of the Spirit in an equal degree. Faithfulness is our part, the rest belongs to a sovereign God. Various gifts and qualifications, too, are employed by him; and perhaps there is only one thing, besides the general grace of Christian character, essentially the same in those by whom the Lord works in the church, and that is, humility, or the mortification of self-seeking, with the reigning desire, that the Lord may be all in all,—that sinners may have the benefit of salvation, and he the undivided glory. Other gifts are not common, but humility is common to all whom God makes useful in his church.

It was Dr Stewart's opinion, 'that we had many able divines, sound, orthodox, and laborious; but not many truly humble ministers of the meek and lowly Saviour.' With respect to his own humility, though himself saw it to be exceedingly small, to others who had access to know his worth, it always appeared the master-grace in his character, and truly admirable in its influence.

If we wish to be successful in the work of Christ, we see, in Dr Stewart, what is the CHARACTER of those whom the Lord delighteth to honour. They must be first converted, obtain like precious faith, and an experimental knowledge of divine things. The Lord manifested himself to Paul, before he sent him to open the eyes of others; and so it was in the case of Dr Stewart.

The subject and manner of his preaching at Moulin, affords an example of DOCTRINE which the Lord will own and bless; and similar earnestness, faith, and zeal for converting sinners, are seldom altogether in vain. But his ministry at Dingwall admonishes us how ineffectual MEANS in themselves are. For though the same doctrines were taught, with equal diligence, by the same man, and he matured in experience, the day of small things continued to the end of his ministry in that place.

On his published works we need offer no judgment. They were not numerous, indeed; and to estimate the usefulness of his labours, by the number of treatises a minister shall publish, were to set up a fallacious standard. In fact, a man without extraordinary endowments, who gives himself in earnest to the work of the ministry, will neither be a reading man, nor a writing man, to a great extent, beyond the department of knowledge and study that lie within the compass of official qualification. And many who have been eminently useful in the church, have often left few literary productions behind them. Indeed, he who sits down to write a book, or to read a book, not bearing on present duty, might, unless for needful relaxation, in general better employ himself in doing a good work among the living objects around him.

We do not mean, by this remark, to insinuate that literature is not necessary, and not ornamental, in the pastoral character; for it will be found, that those most useful in the church at present, are, in general, men of solid and various learning; nor has it been otherwise, we apprehend, in times past. And to disjoin literature from theology, would be to throw aside an instrument of great moral power, which, if not wielded by the friends of religion, will soon be employed for annoyance in the hands of its enemies.

But when we state the incompatibility of going far into literary pursuits and ministerial duties, in the same person, instead of representing theology and literature as at variance, our view furnishes an argument for an extensive course of study, and for the propriety of having a large provision of general knowledge laid in, previously to the assumption of the pastoral office; for it is then too late to have habits of acquisition to form, when a man ought to be able to spend. Neither is our remark, as to the incompatibility of authorship with pastoral duty, intended to apply, except to men of ordinary endowments, who ought not, we conceive, to divert into extra-ministerial channels their limited modicum, which, from its smallness, can yield refreshment only to few. He who can pour forth streams, ought not to keep the fountain closed up; and it may be inferred from Dr Stewart's talents and grace, that, had his life been spent in places where literature was in greater estimation, and where excitements to write and publish had been more pressing, his works had been more numerous and diversified. As it was, while the Gaelic exists as a spoken tongue, future generations will owe to him important obligations. His Grammar displays a mind profoundly versed in the philosophy of language, as well as minutely acquainted with the particular tongue, the principles of which it lays down;[1] and no Highlander, who draws instruction or comfort from his Bible, or opens his Psalm-book to praise his Lord, is unindebted to his industry and skill.

[1] Not to mention other testimonies for the excellence of that performance, we shall only repeat what a most accomplished scholar said of it, 'that though he did not understand Gaelic, he would read Dr Stewart's Grammar for the illustrations it contained of the philosophy of language.'

BANNER *of* TRUTH

The Banner of Truth Trust originated in 1957 in London. The founders believed that much of the best literature of historic Christianity had been allowed to fall into oblivion and that, under God, its recovery could well lead not only to a strengthening of the church, but to true revival.

Interdenominational in vision, this publishing work is now international, and our lists include a number of contemporary authors, together with classics from the past. The translation of these books into many languages is encouraged.

A monthly magazine, *The Banner of Truth*, is also published, and further information about this, and all our other publications, may be found on our website, banneroftruth.org, or by contacting the offices below:

Head Office:
3 Murrayfield Road
Edinburgh
EH12 6EL
United Kingdom
Email: info@banneroftruth.co.uk

North America Office:
610 Alexander Spring Road
Carlisle, PA 17015
United States of America
Email: info@banneroftruth.org